Melissa Doyle & Jo Scard

the
working
mother's
survival
guide

Your complete guide to managing life and work with a new baby

First published in 2007

Allen & Unwin
83 Alexander Street
Crows Nest NSW 2065
Australia
Phone: (61 2) 8425 0100
Fax: (61 2) 9906 2218
Email: info@allenandunwin.com
Web: www.allenandunwin.com

National Library of Australia
Cataloguing-in-Publication entry:

Doyle, Melissa. Scard, Jo.
   The working mother's survival guide.

   ISBN 978 1 74175 034 8 (pbk.).

   1. Working mothers – Life skills guides. 2. Working
   mothers. 3. Work and family. I. Scard, Jo. II. Title.

646.700852

Set in 11/17pt SyndorITC Book by Midland Typesetters
Text design by Kirby Stalgis
Printed and bound in Australia by Griffin Press

10 9 8 7 6 5 4 3 2

the
working
mother's
survival
guide

For all of us mums out there, in paid or unpaid work,
juggling a family and trying to smile through it all.

Visit our website www.workingmotherssurvivalguide.com

contents

Returning to work and adapting to the changes • Going
back to a changed workplace • Managing colleagues
• How to get out the door on time • Resources list •
Returning to work—handy hints

preface

It's true—once you have kids you'll wonder what you used to do with your time. But while life is about to get a whole lot busier, it will never be better. Welcome to the Mums' Club.

Enjoy it, enjoy your baby, enjoy doing all those things you haven't done since you were a child.

Don't waste time looking over your shoulder at the next mum who appears to have it all. She is just as fallible as the rest of us. In fact, we think the words 'Supermum' and 'guilt' should be banned! A supermum doesn't exist and guilt shouldn't.

Life is about choices and compromises and challenges, and once you have children those factors are even greater.

A supermum would be one who handles all these perfectly. We all *think* we've met her—either at mothers' group or sitting behind the boss's desk. But trust us, she's an illusion. Every mum struggles, every mum has moments when she questions what on earth she's doing and why—why the house is a wreck or the kids are screaming or your sex life is but a distant memory.

Then throw into the mix the demands of a job and the logistics of childcare and you find your time stretched ever further.

We're so worried about what other people think, particularly other mums, that we forget the only opinion that counts is our own child's.

And we can be our own worst enemies. We all want to do everything perfectly, but sometimes we just can't. We are way too harsh on ourselves. We feel guilt no matter what we do—guilty because we work too hard, guilty because we don't work, guilty because we don't have enough time. AHHHH!

Let's take a breath, give ourselves a break and remember the choices we make are the best ones for *our* circumstances.

Our dear friend and mother of four, Sharine, sums it up beautifully—'We all have the same journey, feel the same emotions, the same fears and the same inadequacies. Some of us just take a different path to get there.'

Nor are you alone on that trek. We all have meltdowns, days we can't manage, moments we question it all and times when we want to pack it all in and run away. That's when we need each other. Look at the next mum as your ally in this whole convoluted journey. Nurture your true friends. They are on your team and you'll appreciate them even more on those days that go completely to the dogs.

We're all juggling and struggling and laughing and crying. And there's nothing wrong with admitting it. Forget trying to impress, let's just be honest.

Time is precious, so love every moment with your gorgeous new baby, and nurture every second with your growing family, because it will get easier. You may have to make a few changes like relaxing on the housework and cutting back on those three-course meals you were once famous for—but it will be okay.

Promise us this, you won't forget to stop and enjoy the fairy floss once in a while—the laundry can always wait.

introduction

Working mothers hear a lot about 'work–life balance'. Politicians tell us how they'll solve it and academics lecture to us. None of them have provided practical solutions as far as we can see—no tips and few real-life suggestions. No one has written a guide—so here it is.

The Working Mother's Survival Guide isn't the total solution—and reading this book won't solve everything. But we've written down the things that have helped us survive—we've talked to lots of friends, working mothers and experts—and we've assembled a book that we hope will help you to sort some of the 'work–life balance' stuff out.

The Working Mother's Survival Guide isn't attempting to provide answers to the big questions about how we might need to change the attitudes of our governments, workplaces and schools. But what *The Working Mother's Survival Guide* will do is:

- Provide some very practical, very real, and very accessible solutions to how you can plan to take the anxiety out of being a working mother.

- Plot the course of many of the dilemmas you'll face—from before conception, through pregnancy to finding daycare or a nanny, to negotiating your return to work, understanding your legal rights and planning for your financial future.

- Each chapter sets out a compendium of useful information, websites and resources to keep as a handy reference guide as you embark on your own journey as a working mother. And some useful 'how-to' checklists to keep on hand.

We've spoken to dozens of working mothers. From cleaners to CEOs, stay-at-home mums to mothers with full-time paid work, mothers who live and work on farms to those who live in regional Australia. Their insights, their lives and how they've coped with their individual circumstances, have provided some practical tips for how we can all manage.

The book is written for working mothers—and working mothers to be—whether part-time, full-time, occasional workers, workers in the family business, single mums or women working for a charity. Being a mother and working isn't new. We all head off to work thinking—have we made the right choices? Will our children be well taken care of? Should we be working less, more, differently, or perhaps not at all? Are we good mothers? And if we want to be mothers and have a career too, how do we manage it?

It's a dilemma faced daily by women who want to be involved mothers, but who also want to work, or need to work, to support their families. Only fourteen per cent of families in Australia with children have a father at work and mother full-time at home. For the other eighty-six per cent it is a constant juggle to care for the kids, please your employer, pay the bills and have a life.

The pressure on performing as a parent, as a mother, starts early. Natural birth or caesarian? A three- or four-wheel pram? How long should you breastfeed? And what is the right age to put them in to childcare? When should you return to work? What if you don't want to go back to work? And along with all these questions comes guilt. Guilt that you couldn't breastfeed for long enough, guilt that you've got a babysitter so you can get an hour to yourself.

And then comes the anxiety. Anxiety because you've stopped work and can't contribute to the mortgage. About staying away from work too long. Because you've gone back to work and can't spend as much time with your kids. When you sit down and think about it—when you get the time—all this guilt and anxiety seems so unnecessary.

There are women out there who do cope. Whether it's because they have a husband or partner who stays at home, works part-time or shares childcare responsibilities equally, or because they put in place their own personal strategies to survive.

So what could we do about it, we thought? We armed ourselves with lists. We got organized. Found out what free services were out there. Investigated online nappy stores that offered free delivery and we ordered in bulk. We still had meltdowns, but at least we had a cupboard full of nappies.

Being organized and informed about what we could change helped us deal with the other chaotic parts of life that couldn't be changed. Being prepared about lots of things helps quell the sense that everything is hurtling out of control. It helps us have more time to think—even if the washing pile rivals Mount Everest.

We had no idea before we got pregnant how hard this balancing act could be. How you have to take a half-day of precious leave to queue up for swimming classes and book Wiggles tickets seven months ahead.

We don't profess to be experts, just two mums like you who manage day by day. But we hope what we've collected here are some really helpful ideas to help you manage everything from how to nab that spot at the daycare centre to negotiating your maternity leave and return to work.

But while being organized helps, don't forget to take time out to lie on the floor next to your gorgeous new baby and just look at each other. It's true, they are only little for such a tiny moment.

chapter 1
preconception

In this chapter:

- What to do if you're trying to conceive. How to de-stress, improve your chances, and organize all your medical stuff.

- Some simple advice from GPs, gynaecologists and obstetricians to help you along the way.

- Embarking on the IVF journey. The costs, the risks and the emotional roller-coaster.

As working mums with lots of friends who have done the hard yards of years of conception attempts—some via IVF—we know this preconception time of your life can be really hard. There's a lot to be said about being as chilled out as you can, being informed, getting the best advice you can find, and treating your body well. But ultimately go with whatever works for you. Your body is amazing, so trust it and, hopefully, it will inevitably work it all out.

Pregnancy is completely different for every single woman. For me, it was rather predictable, I was the pregnant woman they use in the text books. When the book told me things would happen, they did. Pregnant the regular way—off the pill, lots of sex (remember those days?), then bingo—excited and blossoming. We bought a bigger car, renovated the bathroom and bought everything in white to cover both contingencies. I was blessed with two happy, healthy, smooth pregnancies, calm natural deliveries and two healthy babies.

I tell you this not because I was special, because there were days when I felt like crap, times I was so tired I could fall over (in fact during pregnancy number two I did, and broke my arm), times I stressed, times when weight piled on. I tell you this because pregnancy doesn't always have to be scary for everyone. Some people struggle to get pregnant, others don't. Some get sick, others don't. Some hate pregnancy, others like me love it. I embraced every single moment, and every little hurdle—which is probably easy to say. But trust me, I give thanks every day as I genuinely know how lucky I am. – **Mel**

I was thirty-seven when I attempted to conceive my first child. Even my boss Brian, a father of three himself, had begun to lecture me on how I should be 'getting on with it'. Having spent my most fertile years studying, travelling or working I felt that I may (just may) have left it too late. I started to worry—and a level of panic set in. My game plan had always been: 'I can have it all' (the career and the kids).

But really I knew the statistics were against me. I panicked some more. So I started to research. I treated the event a bit like training for the 'Conception Olympics'—

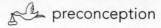

and I'm not talking marathon sex sessions, I mean the big 'D-E-T-O-X'. I turned to preconception 'gurus'. No alcohol. No coffee for eighteen months. Only the occasional, very occasional, cup of tea. I took folate for months longer than I actually needed. I went to an acupuncturist specializing in conception who gave me a 'chakra cleanse' and prescribed the use of a 'Moxa' stick (a cigar-sized incense stick which you can get from any Chinese herbalist) that I was to ignite and wave in a clockwise direction over my uterus (which I did). I started doing more exercise. Yoga. Swimming. Eating the right foods. Vitamins. 'Detoxing'.

My partner, now husband, tolerated all this. In the end it took only three months and unknowingly I conceived. To even out all the 'chakra balancing', I spent a weekend in Portugal followed by a week travelling for work in Europe drinking a reasonable quantity of good red wine when I was just pregnant but didn't know it. My son Marlow is now almost six and happy and healthy. My second child, Frida, was conceived in one month—in an environment with a reasonable amount of toxins, a fair amount of coffee, some wine and not that much exercise.

This time I was forty, but more relaxed about my body's ability to deal with pregnancy. She was an experiment in sex-selection—the idea being that you attempt to have a girl by conceiving four days before you ovulate. (To have a boy you try to conceive on the day you ovulate—the logic being that boy sperm swims fast but dies quickly and girl sperm swims slowly and lives longer!). We were successful and I now proudly tell anyone who cares to listen about this old wives' tale method. – **Jo**

66 **Abbi Stove, nurse, 34**

When I turned thirty my husband and I started to try for a baby, went off the pill for twelve months, carefully documented my daily temperature and period cycle.

Due to a history of irregularity I went and saw a gynaecologist. The first thing he said was 'forget the temperature, you're just stressing yourselves out'. We walked out of his office, with me booked in for surgery and Andrew booked in for some sperm tests.

I had the clean out, holes drilled in the ovaries, endometriosis removed, and my tubes cleared. Andrew did his duty and produced the tests. So we went back to the doctor and discovered Andrew had a low sperm count and due to my polycystic ovaries our best chance of conception would be to try some fertility drugs and a process called Intrauterine Insemination (IUI), commonly know as artificial insemination. I started taking the required tablets and began to experience hot flushes.

It was then time for the trigger injection that would cause the follicles to release their eggs within twenty-four hours and then back in the doctor's office having Andrew's sperm introduced into my uterus. We attempted this twice with no success, our next step was In Vitro Fertilization (IVF)—Intracytoplasmic Sperm Injection (ICSI). This is the process that you often see on television where they show a sperm being injected into an egg. This was rather scary so we started to Google like crazy and read up on everything we could. We talked to friends and found out they were doing the same thing, but were keeping it close to their chest (fear of failure is a huge issue). It was amazing how many people around us were doing IVF (we have since been informed that approximately forty-five per cent of couples will have trouble conceiving).

We took four weeks off the program over Christmas and started again in January. First I started on the tablets to bring on a period then a nasal spray to shut down my irregular cycle, then the morning needle in the belly to stimulate egg production, (an injection in the bum to prepare the eggs for release, an injection in the arm to put me to sleep, and finally a huge needle to harvest the eggs). Anyway, we ended up being pregnant first go. This was amazing. We had done it. Nine weeks later our world came crashing down when the pregnancy came to an abrupt end. We now understood the emotional roller-coaster that people warned us about—from total happiness to despair in less than fifteen minutes.

We took a break for a few months to rebuild emotionally and financially and then started on yet more fertilization drugs in preparation for some of the embryos that we had frozen after the first IVF collection cycle. Pumped up and ready for the next phase, knowing that success was only a matter of time, we arrived at the hospital on the morning of the embryo transfer. Once again we crashed; none of our embryos had survived the thawing process.

Again we waited a few more months. It was Christmas again. Things were progressing well. Except for the odd side effect like raging hormones, no sense of smell, and a painful sensation that I can only describe as like carrying ten million golf balls on each of my ovaries. Unfortunately this one didn't take, but our doctor was positive and started us straightaway on different drugs for a frozen transfer. We were also given a sheet of paper with the next round of costs highlighted for us. I could tell Andrew was near breaking point. The emotional strain of seeing me go through all of this was too much and he finally snapped.

We stopped the program and went and sought counselling; this IVF roller-coaster had physically and emotionally almost destroyed us and we didn't want it to destroy our marriage. I'm glad that Andrew finally said 'stop'—I hadn't realized the effect it was having on us both and our marriage. We stopped IVF for two years. This helped me work through the feelings of why us, why me? Eventually we didn't shy away from couples who were having kids, it took some time but we eventually got there.

We were almost accepting of our fate that we would be D.I.N.Ks for the rest of our lives. I had convinced Andrew that we should buy a boat and he was trying to convince me that we needed a sports car to tow it. I started my new career as a graduate nurse and Andrew started a new job that would hopefully let us live a comfortable lifestyle.

Time went by and my period had not shown up after forty-five days. I became a bit suspicious, but wasn't too excited as forty-five days wasn't too unusual for me. I had picked up a vomiting bug at work and the doctors said I wouldn't feel right for about three weeks. Three weeks passed and I was still feeling nauseated and tired. I went out for my birthday dinner, drank margaritas and beer, then the following weekend a girlfriend and I went to a Korean bath house for a day of hot and cold spas, saunas and full body massage. That week I found myself standing in the supermarket debating about getting a pregnancy test or sanitary pads. I got home and did the test—the positive came up before the control. It's a weird feeling being happy and scared at the same time. I phoned Andrew and he just about cried, passed out and jumped for joy all at the same time.

I had a beautiful healthy baby boy, Oscar, by caesarean. Now its time to stop and smell the roses and enjoy our miracle.

What had changed? Is there something about stopping, accepting reality and moving on, that makes the body do what it's supposed to do? Or does life just like to keep you on your toes when you start to get too comfortable? It was an incredibly hard decision to stop IVF. When you're doing IVF, one of the most annoying things you will hear from family, friends and acquaintances is 'Maybe it will happen naturally if you just stop thinking about it'. Every person who has ever said this to us has never had to go through an IVF cycle—and really needs to think more before opening their mouth. But wait, what about us. We gave up, we planned for a new life, we stopped thinking about it.

My boat and Andrew's sports car have turned into a nursery and a need for more storage space under the house. But who really needs all that stuff anyway!

Is it all over? (your career that is)

Apart from the huge decision to have children, one of the big concerns for working women planning to start a family is: what impact will having a baby have on my career or work prospects? Years ago women couldn't even be married and remain in some parts of the workforce and for others when they had a baby it was just assumed they'd stop work. Well not anymore. Women have choices. Not as many as men, it's fair to say, but a lot more than we used to.

Having a baby *shouldn't* affect your career or work prospects. There are legal safeguards to ensure your employment rights are protected, and you can read more about them in Chapter 9. If you can handle a slightly different pace for a while, slow down and take a step sideways rather than up the ladder—then you'll cope with it. It boils down to one fairly 'simple' conundrum: what's more important right now, having a baby or your job or career? Only you can know the answer to that. But one word of advice: don't let worry about your career or future job prospects or questions of timing eat you up, slow you down or hinder your preconception attempts. There often is no perfect time to have a baby and as we age our bodies will often play havoc with our plans anyway. What follows is advice to help you get over the line.

Preconception medical care

Visiting the doctor used to be something you did after you'd found out that you were pregnant. These days many doctors and health providers recommend you schedule an appointment *before* you conceive.

As soon as you are thinking about having a baby organize a visit to your doctor. The appointment is to discuss your general health, any problems you may have conceiving because of your medical history, prescription (or non-prescription) drugs you may be taking and how they may affect the baby—and importantly, how to take care of yourself in the weeks when you may be pregnant, but don't know for sure.

Your doctor will also talk with you about what prenatal vitamins you may need to take and about which medical and alternative therapies are safe during the preconception time. They'll recommend that you begin taking folate, a vitamin that will reduce the likelihood of your baby having spina bifida. They will probably also do a blood test to check if your immunizations are up-to-date and if they're not, they'll recommend you get vaccinated before you conceive. In particular, rubella during pregnancy can cause miscarriage, stillbirth or birth defects. All this is best done a few months before you conceive.

The doctor may suggest you consult a genetic counsellor if

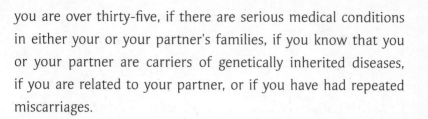

you are over thirty-five, if there are serious medical conditions in either your or your partner's families, if you know that you or your partner are carriers of genetically inherited diseases, if you are related to your partner, or if you have had repeated miscarriages.

Questions to ask your doctor

- What prescription, over-the-counter or herbal medications are safe to take when I'm trying to conceive?

- What changes to my and my partner's diet should we consider?

- Do I need to think about making changes to my work practices—such as exposure to chemicals or cutting back on my hours?

- Are there any activities that I should curtail while trying to conceive (eg. non-prescription drugs or extreme sports)?

- How will any pre-existing medical conditions affect my chances of conceiving?

- How do I know when I'm most fertile, when I'm ovulating and when I have the best chance of conception?

- How might hereditary diseases affect our baby? And should we consider seeing a genetic counsellor?

- Will having a sexually transmitted disease (STD) affect my ability to conceive or have a vaginal delivery?

Your pre-pregnancy checklist

Dr Ronald McCoy, Royal Australian College of General Practitioners, provides guidelines for your pre-pregnancy health:

- *Take simple health measures before you become pregnant.* This can help prevent some serious health problems for you and your baby. This is especially important for women who are older or who may have medical conditions requiring specific advice and management, such as diabetes, hypertension, and epilepsy.

- *Visit your GP before becoming pregnant.* They can offer advice and check on immunizations.

- *Take a folic acid supplement*, which will help reduce the risk of serious diseases of the spinal cord, such as spina bifida. Folic acid is available over the counter or from your doctor. This should be taken at least one or two months *before* you conceive. (Note that most preconception multivitamins have the correct amount of folate included in them.)

- *You may want to see a genetic counsellor* if there are genetic conditions in your family. Your general practitioner can arrange a referral. There is screening available for a range of genetically inherited conditions in addition to Down syndrome.

- *Prevent infectious diseases.* You should have a blood test to screen for immunity to rubella (German measles) to avoid serious birth defects in your baby. Your doctor will check for a past history of chicken pox or related conditions. If there has been no evidence of past infection, you'll be offered a vaccination for measles, mumps and rubella at least one month before you plan to conceive.

- *Live a healthy lifestyle.* The use of tobacco, alcohol and other drugs by pregnant women can cause adverse health outcomes for your baby. Tobacco affects the

growth of the foetus and women need to stop smoking during if not before pregnancy. Alcohol and other drug use is dangerous for the developing foetus and women should stop using drugs, and limit, or preferably stop, drinking alcohol during pregnancy.

- *Avoid listeria.* Listeria is an illness caused by eating dairy and processed meats contaminated by bacteria and can cause miscarriage, stillbirth, and premature birth. The risk is very low—one in every fifteen thousand women contract listeria in pregnancy across Australia. You can *avoid listeria by following sensible and hygienic food preparation and storage rules.*

Health, diet and exercise

There is a wealth of information out there about what you should—or could—be doing in order to conceive. We'd advise doing what seems right for you. If you're a three-long blacks before lunch and a few glasses of chardonnay after work-sort of girl then it's unlikely that detoxification, endless vitamin and mineral supplements and acupuncture—or standing on your head in a yoga class—will appeal to you. What you *do* need to ascertain is whether your lifestyle and diet is in any way preventing you from falling pregnant—or whether it might harm your baby when you do conceive.

It's important to be as healthy as you can to help your conception. There are lots of books you can read which we've detailed at the end of this chapter. You can make changes to your diet and lifestyle. You can consider alternative therapies or just rely on your doctor's advice. A lot of medical evidence points to stress as a factor that may prevent a woman falling pregnant. Often some exercise is all you need to help you de-stress.

If, after getting good medical advice and doing your own research you feel there is a case to change your lifestyle and diet then you should seriously consider doing it. Apart from anything else it will make you feel more energised *and* more virtuous.

Dr Christine Tippett, gynaecologist/obstetrician and President of the Royal Australian and New Zealand College of Obstetricians and Gynaecologists, offers some tips:

- Busy—and working—women often try to plan conception like they plan their working lives. *It's very important not to plan your pregnancy out of existence.* In lots of women ovulation can take place anytime from day 8 to day 19 of your menstrual cycle so having sex two or three times each week during this time is the best way to assist conception. Overplanning or constant use of ovulation kits may not help your stress levels—which in turn may make your cycle irregular.

- Most women *won't* require advice from a gynaecologist to conceive. They are healthy and well-informed, get the necessary immunizations and pap smears, and take folate a few months before they start.

- Women who do extreme sports such as scuba-diving or abseiling will need to give them up for the duration of the pregnancy, and until they feel up to resuming them again after the birth.

- Women who need to seek advice from a gynaecologist to manage their conception and pregnancy include those with diabetes or other illnesses, and those taking medications.

- Women who are very overweight, or underweight, may need to get specialist advice on what they may need to do to conceive. Being severely overweight will have an adverse impact on your fertility and also on your pregnancy.

- Women can be very vulnerable when trying to fall pregnant. Getting lots of advice during this time is the best course of action for peace of mind.

- It's easy to feel guilty about what you should or shouldn't have done if you miscarry. Bear in mind that at least one in six pregnancies end up miscarrying. Over the age of forty-four, the figure increases to one in two.

Preconception tools

Getting pregnant can sometimes be harder than you imagine. There are a variety of products available from chemists that are designed to help you keep track of your ovulation so you know when your most fertile time is each month. You'll need to research these methods thoroughly before you set out. But be warned, don't overplan it, and don't rely on them—using all this stuff may very well just make you stressed out. Remember that having more sex is the best thing to get you pregnant.

The tools available include:

- ovulation kits that work by detecting a hormone increase in your urine twenty-four to thirty-six hours before you ovulate

- thermometers, which are used to plot your temperature and detect when you are ovulating

- microscopes, to detect subtle differences in the structure of cervical mucous in the few days before ovulation.

If you are planning to conceive you'll want to find out when you fall pregnant. There are a variety of brands of home pregnancy tests available at the chemist. It's cheaper to buy a two-test kit and remember that your doctor will usually want to confirm your pregnancy with a urine test.

> I suspected I might be pregnant with my first child and bought two pregnancy tests from a Parisian pharmacy as I was working in Europe at the time. The first test had a very faint blue line and the second tested negative (both done on a train) so I assumed I wasn't. I travelled for a week through various cities happily attending late night dinners in local bistros, followed by a long weekend in Lisbon— enjoying the local vino. It wasn't until I returned to London where I was living at the time that I thought I should test again—this time it was positive and I was in a state of shock, but luckily about to have dinner with a good girlfriend who helped me process the news. I ran out, bought a second test and, yep, it was positive again—the journey had begun! [She drank the champagne (and later became my first child's godmother).] – **Jo**

What you can and can't eat and drink

This can be one of the most confusing areas. The best tip is when in doubt, leave it out. One considerable danger is contracting food poisoning or listeria, a bacteria that can harm your unborn baby. If there's a chance it could make you sick when you are not expecting, such as a dodgy oyster, then its best avoided when you are.

Foods and chemicals to avoid

- **Unpasteurized dairy products.** Most Australian cheeses including the soft types (apart from in South Australia) are pasteurized so eating them is generally quite safe.
- **Salad bars**
- **Pre-cut cold meat.** It might not be fresh.
- **Raw fish and smoked seafood**
- **Rare or raw meat**
- **Fish.** The main concern is about mercury levels in some types. A good rule of thumb is the higher up the food chain the fish is, the higher the mercury levels. So try to avoid shark (also known as flake).
- **Smoking.** Smoking reduces the amount of oxygen available to your baby through the umbilical cord and limits the flow of blood in the placenta, which in turn reduces the amount of nutrients that reach the foetus. Smokers have a greater risk of having a premature baby, an ectopic pregnancy or complications during the birth, and the risk of miscarriage is four times greater. Nicotine replacement therapy is less harmful as the mother and the baby receive less nicotine and no exposure to carbon monoxide and other toxic substances.
- **Alcohol.** Regularly drinking alcohol during pregnancy can cause problems for the mother and the baby. Drinking a lot can lead to losing the baby before it is born or the baby being born with foetal alcohol syndrome (slow growth before and after birth, and mental disabilities). Doctors recommend that pregnant women or women trying to get pregnant should not drink alcohol at all.
- **Caffeine.** Doctors recommend that you limit caffeine during pregnancy and breastfeeding because it is passed on to your baby and increases heartrate.

- **Hair dye**. Colouring your hair will not affect your baby. Your scalp may become more sensitive though.

For more information about food and chemicals to avoid during pregnancy ask your doctor or see the Royal Hospital for Women's website www.rhw.org.au

"" *Each time I did a Google search in preparation to conceive both my children it put the fear of God in me and made me more resolute in about equal proportions. Google searches told me not to drink coffee. To drink coffee the day before I ovulated if I wanted to conceive a boy. To drink decaffeinated coffee. Not to drink decaffeinated coffee because the decafeination process produced strychnine as a by-product, which itself was a poison. To drink tea, instead of coffee. That tea had more caffeine than coffee. Not to drink even one drop of alcohol. That one glass of alcohol a week was okay. That more than one to two glasses per week would cause foetal alcohol syndrome. That you should increase your exercise. That increasing exercise could dramatically impede conception. That weight loss would assist conception. Too much weight loss might hinder it. I was informed but I went mad. I'm glad I did all the reading, but after a while, it can make you into a fanatic. Our advice—take from it what you want, what you feel comfortable with. Get a second—a third—opinion. Talk to your doctor. Read some books. Avoid getting to the stage that you are so stressed about what you should or shouldn't be doing that life's not much fun—and that the stress is not working against you. Trusting your common sense usually wins out in the end. – Jo*

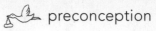

Your medical options

When having a baby you will need to decide what sort of medical care you want or can afford: whether that is public or private, an obstetrician or midwife. Before you become pregnant you should consider what choice you want to make. Speak to friends to get some idea of what they think, what worked for them and what they were happy with.

> **When I became pregnant** with my first child I thought that's it, I'm having a private obstetrician and hang the expense. I was thirty-eight and needed a private obstetrician, or so I thought. I chose an alternative breed of obstetrician that came with a ponytail and an interest in indigenous art and adventure travel (something for my husband to talk about on our regular visits).
>
> The funny thing was we spent most of our regular consultations discussing our mutual interests and when my husband came along we'd talk about his trips to war zones as a newspaper photographer. I luckily had a trouble-free pregnancy and so the intelligent chat was much more pleasant than talking about how big my girth was becoming each time!
>
> However, four thousand dollars poorer at the end of the pregnancy I found that the obstetrician was usually too tired on most of my visits to remember when I needed a scan or some other procedure (I of course reminded him, being dutifully anal). He was a great guy and at the birth he was a laugh and in the end was the sole reason I didn't have a caesarean but I wasn't convinced I needed it the next time.
>
> So for my second pregnancy, which began when I was forty, I decided to go public. I was more confident about how I'd cope and how I'd manage. This time I saw

an obstetrician once for precisely fifteen minutes during the ten months, had a two-hour labour, no drugs and was seven thousand dollars better off this time because I saved by not having an obstetrician and received the federal government's baby bonus. Talk to friends who've been through it but, ultimately, it's your decision, so go with what you feel comfortable with, and can afford. Read more about your different options in the Chapter 2. – **Jo**

Before you become pregnant check what your health insurance will cover and if you'll need to alter it.

Are you covered?

It's important to know that many health insurers will only cover you as a private patient if you've been paying for maternity care for twelve months or more.

It's imperative at this stage to call your health insurer and find out what sort of cover you have as this may be an important factor in planning on whether to go public or private.

Medical costs include prenatal visits, the labour and delivery and often post-partum care and you'll find more about these costs in following chapters. Health insurance will not usually cover all of the payments for private services. You need to check what your obstetrician charges and how much you will be out of pocket—this can often add up to be quite a sizeable amount.

Also, if you use a private hospital you may be charged for some extras.

Your medical costs

Even if you are a public patient you may still be up for some outlays through your pregnancy. These may include GP visits if

you are in a 'co-share' arrangement for your prenatal care with your hospital. You will have to pay for some medical procedures such as scans or tests which are done at an early stage in the pregnancy and determine whether the baby is healthy or if it may have Down syndrome (these include nuchal translucency, amniocentesis or CVS tests). Read more about these in Chapter 3. Because of the pressure on public hospital resources not all patients will be offered these scans free of charge.

It's worth checking what these costs are and what the policy of your chosen public hospital is about offering these services during pregnancy so you can assess how much you will need to outlay, and if you want to have them in the first place.

At a glance—how much will it cost?

- GPs are free if they bulk-bill, but if not you'll need to pay the gap between what your GP charges and the federal government will pay for.
- Specialist medical care may come with an additional charge if the specialist doesn't bulk-bill. This will vary a lot so best to check before you go so you can plan how you'll pay for it.
- IVF is more costly—between $1000 to $2500 at least—so get a handle on the costs early. You may need two to four cycles, so you'll need to plan how this will be paid for.
- Check with your private health insurance fund to see what they cover.
- Ovulation and pregnancy test kits are pricey.

Considering your options at work

Even though you're not yet pregnant it may be worth considering how your work will fit in with your pregnancy, what your maternity leave options are and how you will return to work.

You should give some thought to how supportive your place of work is toward women having children; what the implications may be on you getting a promotion—although legally it should have none; and what sort of options might you have for returning to work, in terms of flexibility, part-time or job-share arrangements?

Even at this early stage you might want to *discreetly* talk to other women at your workplace who have had children to see how the company or organization responded, what difficulties they encountered and how they managed it.

There is more information on thinking about how to tell work in Chapter 2, managing your maternity leave in Chapter 4 and your return to work in Chapter 8.

Being asked about your baby plans at an interview

66 *I was at a job interview in my mid thirties when I was hit with a veiled statement: 'We just want two good years from you and then you can get on with whatever you want to do next'. It took me a moment to realize that I was, indirectly, being asked if I was planning on having a baby real soon. I wasn't but as I was in a long-term relationship it wasn't off the cards. I was a bit taken aback and nodded attentively as you do but later realized I was entitled to fall pregnant when I wanted to. – Jo*

Remember that it is against the law to ask a potential employee at an interview if they are planning on having a baby. It's discrimination and they can't do it—so don't tell them even if you're asked. We have a lot more detail about your legal rights and organizations you can approach if this happens to you in Chapter 9.

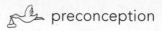

Coping with infertility

If you find you are having trouble falling pregnant there are a wide range of treatments available to help. Most doctors will suggest fertility tests if you have not been able to conceive within a certain timeframe (see the infertility information on the next page). Once you have a handle on what the problem might be you can discuss the treatments available with your GP or fertility specialist.

There are both traditional and alternative infertility treatments available to consider. Research them both thoroughly and make a choice about which is best for you at the time.

When do you consider seeking specialist fertility advice?

Dr Devora Lieberman, fertility specialist, provides some guidelines.

Who should seek advice?

- A couple who knows that they have a problem—such as a woman who has irregular cycles or endometriosis, or a man with a low sperm count.

- If you haven't conceived after a year of unprotected intercourse—for women under thirty-five—or after six months—for women over thirty-five.

Who do you contact?

- Your GP will be the best first port of call. They can then refer you to a fertility specialist or to a fertility clinic.

What are your options?

- There is a range of options that you and your doctor can consider depending on what is best for you. These include

assisting ovulation with medication to stimulate egg
production or intera-uterine insemination (depositing
sperm into the uterus).

- After discussion with your fertility specialist sometimes
IVF will be the best and first option that is suggested—
but this depends on your medical history.

Who's eligible?

- If you are a single parent or lesbian wishing to use IVF to
conceive you will be able to use the service but you may
not be eligible for the rebate after the procedure as you
need to demonstrate infertility following unsuccessful
intercourse prior to starting any treatment.

The cost?

- Out-of-pocket costs—what you pay after the Medicare
rebate per cycle is between $1000 and $2500 per IVF
treatment including egg extraction and implantation.
- Some clinics will charge for additional specialist treatment.
- Medicare pays most of these if you encounter fertility
problems and need to seek specialist care. Currently
Medicare pays an eighty per cent rebate once you
and your family's medical costs exceed one thousand
dollars each financial year.

What happens during IVF treatment—
what will I feel?

- Hormone stimulant medication, used to encourage
egg production, is dispensed by a 'pen'—a relatively
painless instrument similar to that used to dispense
insulin to people with diabetes.

- Blood and urine tests to monitor your hormone levels are done early in the morning so you can then go off to work straight afterwards.

- There have been huge improvements in IVF treatment over the last decade so that now when your eggs are extracted you will experience something ranging between no discomfort at all to at worst bad menstrual cramps.

- On average, a woman will go through two to three cycles. IVF specialists believe that if you haven't conceived after three cycles then your situation may pose greater challenges.

- Fertility specialists won't encourage people to persist against the odds but there is no limit to how many cycles someone can try if they are willing to pay.

Can I use an egg donor?

- Egg donors are allowed under Australian law but they can't be paid.

What about sperm donors?

- IVF clinics provide access to sperm donors but recent legislative change now means that sperm donor children are able to contact the sperm donor if they decide they want to.

Coping with IVF?

- Dr Lieberman says, 'All women go through an emotional roller-coaster each month with their normal cycles— these peaks and troughs are exaggerated when you're on IVF because a woman's expectations are higher. One of our primary roles as doctors is managing expectations and encouraging the women we treat to be as realistic as possible.'

- A counsellor is available through the fertility clinic free of charge with each cycle and this service is actively encouraged.

More information?

- Get in touch with ACCESS at www.access.org.au— Australia's national infertility network that provides infertility information, support and advocacy.

- Pick up a copy of *Getting Pregnant* by Professor Robert Jansen from the Sydney IVF Clinic.

Psychologist Jo Lamble offers advice for handling difficult situations:

When you are going through a very difficult time personally, colleagues will often notice that something is going on for you, but they don't know how to react. Maybe you've suffered a miscarriage either before anyone knew you were pregnant or after if had been announced. Perhaps you are enduring the roller-coaster ride that is IVF. Then there are the cases where a woman has had to make the very difficult decision to terminate a pregnancy as a result of diagnostic tests and scans.

How do you let your colleagues and friends know? The best idea is to firstly tell someone with whom you are close or your immediate boss. Then ask that trusted person to spread the word in a compassionate way. It might sound cold, but having an email sent around that lets everybody know why you might be suffering with mood swings or why you might be taking time off work is far better than having a lot of people ask you directly what's wrong. If you have had a termination, you can avoid the possibility of being judged by telling people that you've had a miscarriage.

It's also important to let everyone know *how* you want them to react. Your friend can encourage people to acknowledge your situation with a simple 'I'm thinking of you. Let me know if I can do anything'. In this way, you don't have to endure the awkward looks and silences that can follow the spreading of personal news.

Resources list

Books and magazines

- *Fertility and Conception* and *Natural Pregnancy* by Zita West. These British books are excellent guides to how to optimize the chances of having a healthy pregnancy, understand fertility treatments and what you should be doing and eating before, during and after pregnancy. Available in good bookstores or on the Internet.

- For an Australian perspective, *Up The Duff* by Kaz Cooke is a slightly irreverent, but very useful week-by-week guide to your pregnancy.

- For magazines, try Australian titles *Pregnancy & Birth*, *Practical Parenting* or *Mother & Baby* or from the United States, *Fit Pregnancy*—they all include information about preconception as well pregnancy and post-partum care.

Websites

- The Family Planning Association or FPA Health (formerly Family Planning NSW) provides reproductive and sexual health services in New South Wales and is an independent, not-for-profit organization. www.fpahealth.org.au or phone 1300 658 886.

- The Royal Australian and New Zealand College of Obstetricians and Gynaecologists has an excellent website that leads to a host of online information and information lines about conception, pregnancy and women's health. www.ranzcog.edu.au

- Each state government or state health centres provide an Internet portal as a gateway to a range of services and information about having a baby. Do an Internet search to find yours. The sites contain a whole stack of information you'll need about preconception, through pregnancy, to the birth of your baby, postnatal care and childcare options.

- **Ovulation calendar.** There are lots of these on the Internet. They allow you to enter the dates of your menstrual cycle and calculate the best time in your cycle to try to conceive. Some of them will even tell you what days of the month to try for a girl or a boy. Just do a search to find one you like. A word of warning—gynaecologists are sceptical about relying on this inexact science.

- The Queensland government runs a free preconception and pregnancy support advice line that anyone in Australia can call on 1800 777 690. If you live outside Queensland you can be referred to services closer to home after you've received advice over the phone.

- **Medications.** There is a lot of information on the Internet about what is safe to take before and during pregnancy; have a good look, do a lot of reading and make sure to ask your doctor.

- **Herbal remedies.** There is also a huge amount of information, some reliable and some not, about what

herbal remedies are safe or useful during preconception. We suggest that it's imperative you get a second opinion before going it alone on this stuff, as some remedies *can* be dangerous—or just useless and costly.

- For information on foods to avoid www.foodstandards.gov.au/foodmatters/ pregnancyandfood.cfm or www.rhw.org.au (the Royal Hospital for Women)
- Information on the safety of medications www.motherisk.org/index.jsp
- Information on genetic risk factors www.genetics.com.au/
- www.access.org.au—Australia's national infertility network.
- **IVF blogs.** There are a number of blogs out there aimed at supporting women going through IVF. If that's you then take a look and see whether you think joining in the discussion—or even just reading the entries from others—may help.
- The Waiting Womb www.waitingwomb.blogspot. com
- A Little Pregnant www.alittlepregnant.com
- Life in the Stirrups http://layout-lady.livejournal. com/

✳ Preconception—handy hints

- Make a preconception appointment with your doctor.
- Consider changing your diet and increasing your exercise.
- Check with doctors about all prescription and non-prescription drugs you may be taking.
- Talk to friends about how they balanced their own work and family pressures.
- Decide if you need to see a genetic counsellor.
- Check what coverage you have with your health insurer.
- Purchase a few pregnancy testers.
- Get some ovulation kits if you think you need them.
- Have a think about what medical care you may want—read more about that in Chapter 2.

chapter 2
so, you're pregnant

In this chapter:

- Now you're pregnant, when do you need to tell work and what are your legal rights?

- Your medical choices. Where to have your baby—public or private?

- How to find an obstetrician or a midwife.

> **Sometimes you feel like** nothing is working in your favour, other times it all happens at once. I got the career break of a lifetime when Stan Grant vacated the hosting chair of Today Tonight in Sydney back in mid-2000. I also found out the very same week I was pregnant with my first child. The former came after ten years of hard work as a journalist, the latter came a lot easier!
>
> I was thirty years old and ecstatic—with both pieces of news! September was a busy month. I was struggling

through my first trimester having told no one other than my husband John, and working on the Olympics, hosting the program live from Homebush each night. I tried to keep up appearances and help the crew carry the gear, marching around the games site each day in high heels with a smile on my face. I was exhausted and would get home each night about 7.45 p.m. and be asleep in bed by 8.00 p.m. I thank my lucky stars I wasn't sick because that would have made it impossible.

The athletes weren't the only ones a little nervous at Sydney Olympic Park. I worked until three weeks before my due date—the camera shot just kept getting tighter each night as I strained to do up my jackets. Eventually I could only fasten the top button, so by week thirty-six we had a rather extreme close-up! Nicholas was born in April 2001 and I took six months' leave and loved every moment.

The birth of Talia in December 2003 was even more public with Kochie flashing my ultrasound pictures on Sunrise as soon as we'd told our families. But this time I didn't have the liberty of closer shots, instead I proceeded to fill out the co-host chair as the months went by.

There is something special about sharing such joy with so many people. Other mums-to-be would write and let me know how they were doing, viewers started knitting, others suggested names or would stop me in the street for an update. I returned to work when Talia was three months old, and have been sharing with our viewers just about every moment of her life since. – **Mel**

Who to tell and when

Between the last chapter and this one, magic has happened. Congratulations! You are probably dying to shout it from the roof tops, buy a pile of baby clothes, rethink the size of the car and renovate the bathroom. All telltale signs probably best kept under wraps until you're ready to announce your news. It probably won't be obvious you are pregnant for at least the first four months—as long as you're not sick. Muscles may hold your growing belly in a little longer with a first pregnancy, just don't count on it as much for subsequent ones. Just watch for those little giveaways like protectively rubbing your tummy!

Many women wait until they are past the twelve-week mark before they announce their pregnancy as most miscarriages occur in the first trimester. Usually at this three-month mark a doctor will conduct an ultrasound to check the baby's heartbeat, size and just how many might be in there. But then again, you may not be able to keep such news hidden for a single moment. Some doctors now have their own ultrasound unit in their consulting room and can scan the baby as early as eight weeks, leaving some mums confident to announce their news right away.

You may also choose to confide in a trusted friend or work colleague. This way, should you need to rush off in an emergency, they can diplomatically cover for you. The same could apply if you have morning sickness that requires frequent trips to the bathroom.

One of the first things women notice is when one of their girlfriends, who would previously enjoy a glass of wine or two with dinner, no longer does. So began my lengthy spell as 'designated driver'. Friends who knew us well would pour me a glass of red wine and my husband John a beer. He would drink his and when no one was looking reach over and take a swig out of mine. Not a drop would pass my lips, but he had to be all but carried home! – **Mel**

How to deal with work

Legally you are not required to tell your boss until you are ten weeks from your due date—but the practicalities are that you're unlikely to be able to hide it for that long.

How and when you tell your boss will depend on the sort of relationship you have and the reception previous working mothers in the office have had. It will also depend on the type of work you do—digging ditches or standing at a cash register is a lot tougher on the body than sitting behind a desk. Before you break the news, give some serious thought to how long you want to have off, the job you want to return to, and how you and the company can make the situation work for you both.

> ❝ **Mandi Wicks, general manager, Sydney radio station, mother of two**
>
> When I fell pregnant with Georgie, I had just started at DMG and we were launching Nova 969 in Sydney. I had stopped the fertility drugs and decided to keep focussing on my career because there were no guarantees we would get pregnant and launching Nova was a once-in-a-lifetime opportunity. I was shocked when I became pregnant and was anxious about telling my bosses. I didn't need to worry, the two guys jumped out of their chairs and gave me a huge hug and said having kids would be the very best thing I could ever do and they were thrilled for me. I couldn't believe my luck!
>
> We built the radio station and my maternity leave was fine. I took about five months off. My second child, Henry, was born eleven weeks early . . . and that was a huge shock. I left on a Friday and didn't return. Again, work was incredible. I was very sick but I remember calling my boss on the night

Henry was born and apologizing profusely for leaving them in the lurch. My first thought was that because Henry would be in hospital for ten weeks, perhaps I could go back to work in the meantime? My boss knew that within a few days I would realize the huge journey ahead and that the stress of having a baby in intensive care would completely swamp my world, which it did.

Going on maternity leave is a strange feeling—you are leaving, but then you are not saying goodbye. It is hard to let go, especially when you enjoy what you do. At the same time, you cherish every minute with your new baby.

It is a moment in time to fill up on family time and just 'be'. I took nine and a half months off for Henry, which is a long time these days. I needed to feel happy that he was on track—he was healthy, albeit extremely small. He was just 2.2 lbs or 1020 grams when he was born so I was obsessed with getting him to put on weight. Henry couldn't take the bottle, he was too small and weak to suck so I expressed for nine and a half months. Every three to four hours, I had to make a bee line for the pump and I was even setting the alarm overnight to ensure I kept the supply going! When I went back to work, Henry was taking expressed milk and formula and I had frozen plenty of milk to keep him going!

It's only when you look back you realize how crazy and tired you were during the first twelve months of each baby. At the time though it's your reality and you just get on with it. I am also extremely lucky to have a husband who is a true partner.

The big question

66 **Anne Hollonds, from counselling service, Relationships Australia**

The big question every boss wants answered is will you come back, so engage them in your plans. Let them know when you intend to return. Be honest and admit the baby will no doubt take over your life, particularly in the early days, but you will emerge.

Spell it out as clearly as possible. Don't let them make assumptions. Reaffirm your commitment to the job and you are more likely to be seen as a reliable employee. Assume it's a safe conversation to have with your boss as they would appreciate knowing what you want to do. Tell them what childcare you have arranged and what support you have. Make clear how you intend to handle it all.

But remember it's not all about you. They have a business to run and plans to make.

Thinking about leave

66 **Sharan Burrow, president, Australian Council of Trade Unions**

You will want some certainty about your future and so will your employer, so it is important to know your options and be upfront about what you want.

Before you go on leave, you should have sought advice about your rights and requested information as to how your workplace has accommodated other colleagues who have returned to work. If possible it is helpful to have a preliminary discussion about your future role before you take time off.

Whether you work full-time or part-time as a permanent or casual worker you are entitled to maternity leave. You must have been employed by your employer for twelve months before you intend to start maternity leave. You are entitled to a period of unpaid maternity leave of up to one year which you may share with your partner. Many employees will be entitled to request up to two years of unpaid leave and expect that the employer will not unreasonably refuse. Those same workers are entitled to request part-time work on return to work for the period before your child is of school age. Again, an employer cannot unreasonably refuse you part-time work.

Many employers provide maternity leave to workers with less than twelve months' service. Having a baby should not be the end of your job. Even if you do not have an entitlement to leave, employers cannot discriminate against you because you are pregnant, or have caring responsibilities.

While you are away

Most awards and many agreements require your employer to let you know if there are significant changes at the workplace that might affect your return to work, and you are also obliged to tell the boss if you have had changed circumstances that will require you to change your plans.

Show the boss you are keen

While you are still on leave, retain an attachment to the workplace if you can. Ask to be sent regular emails about projects or restructuring, and attend or show interest in planning days. Maintain your skills if possible and ask to be advised of any opportunities for training or professional development. Occasional phone contact about your return date will also keep you in the loop.

Some state governments provide grants for skills training or maintenance before returning to work.

Remember if you are returning from an extended period of leave, you might want to work part-time or in a particular role. Your local member of parliament can assist with such information.

Be confident in your request, marshal the arguments supporting your case and know that you can take along a representative to help support your position.

If the boss turns you down

If the boss turns you down, ask if he or she will think about your request and set a time to discuss the matter again. If they flatly refuse to discuss your request, it is worth asking again, perhaps after a short cooling off period. You may consider a more formal approach at this time with a letter of request which sets out your legal rights before a final approach is made.

When negotiations come to a complete impasse, there are legal options to consider. The refusal may be a breach of your award, or it may amount to illegal sex discrimination. Call 1300 362 223 to seek union support, or call the equal opportunity tribunal in your state or the Human Rights and Equal Opportunity Commission.

Depending on your employment circumstances, the industrial relations commission may have the power to help you resolve the matter, particularly if you are covered by an enterprise agreement or an award in the retail, hospitality, health and community sector industries.

You'll find more information on maternity leave in Chapter 4. And Chapter 8 explores your work choices, be they full- or part-time.

In many industries there is no doubt that having a baby will have an impact on your career. Time is no longer all yours, you'll need to share it around. All those hours you could spend at meetings, staying late at the office, socializing with work colleagues on a Friday night, on email at home, reading for work—well some of that will need to give. And bear in mind there are a lot of career women who underestimate how much having a baby will impact on their desire to remain so focussed on their career. Whatever your hopes and plans regarding work, it's likely that you'll need to remain flexible and allow for things to evolve as you adjust to your new life.

If you can, ask other working mothers in your office how they have managed, what strategies are working for them and most importantly how your company dealt with their time off.

Find out what your company's maternity leave policy is. Do they have any provisions above and beyond their legal requirements? It's also worth finding out how much holiday leave you have accrued. This can be another way to support your maternity leave, particularly if you work for a company that doesn't offer any or only limited paid leave.

Some of these questions can be addressed once you are pregnant, but thought can certainly be given to the future before you even conceive. You may be able to work your way into a role that offers flexible hours or can be partly done from home.

Don't forget to take into account that the time required to fall pregnant is such as unknown quantity. For example if you have been offered a promotion, but are hoping to have a baby in the next twelve months, conception could take one month or it could take years. Legally you can't be held back from a promotion because you are pregnant. Our suggestion would be to do what feels right at the time for you.

Your legal rights at work

- Under the federal government's *Workplace Relations Act* you are entitled to fifty-two weeks of unpaid parental leave. This can be taken by one parent or shared by both parents as long as you have both been with your employer for at least a year.

- Special maternity leave can also be taken for a pregnancy-related illness, or to recover from a miscarriage that occurs up to twenty-eight weeks before the expected date of birth or in the event of a stillbirth.

- Dads are entitled to one week of unpaid leave when the baby is born, and up to fifty-two weeks if he is to be the primary caregiver.

- During her pregnancy, a woman can be transferred to a safer job if she provides a medical certificate that states she is unable to continue in her role. If this is not reasonably practical in the employer's opinion, she is entitled to paid leave.

- A medical certificate must be provided to your employer at least ten weeks before your due date, and to return to work, you are required to give at least four weeks' written notice.

- You are also entitled to return to the usual position you held before the start of your maternity leave, and if that no longer exists, then the position nearest in status and remuneration to the former position.

- A parent is also entitled to fifty-two weeks' leave when adopting a child under the age of five, as long as it is not the child or step child of either parent.

- Of course, employers and employees can negotiate different provisions under their own workplace agreements. Check with your Human Resources department or your union if you have one as to what particular guidelines are in place at your workplace.

We have more advice on how to negotiate with your boss and manage your return to the workforce in Chapter 8.

Where and how to have your baby

Once your pregnancy is confirmed, either by a home pregnancy kit or your GP, you will need to organize a few key things, such as where you want to have your baby and how you want it delivered. These are decisions best made as soon as possible, particularly if demand for the type of service you want is high.

You have a number of options:

- Public patient in a public hospital
- Private patient in a public hospital
- Private hospital
- Group midwifery practice
- Home birth

Services differ between states so we have given you as general an overview as possible.

Public hospital

The public hospital system offers mothers a few different options.

Midwife clinic

A midwife is a registered nurse with special training who provides prenatal care, attends the birth and then provides post-partum care to the mother and her baby.

A midwife-led maternity unit is where a woman can choose to have her pregnancy and labour managed by midwives, although it may not necessarily be the same person at each visit. This option is for women with a low-risk pregnancy.

Obstetricians are available if complications arise for either the mother or baby, or where a medical procedure is required, such as an epidural or caesarean.

Some hospitals also offer a Shared Antenatal Care Program. This means you visit your local GP for regular check-ups, but also have a number of scheduled visits to the hospital antenatal clinic during the pregnancy. That GP can then look after your new baby immediately after the birth and beyond, essentially becoming your family doctor. They must be registered with this program to take part. If you already have a family doctor, it's worth asking if they are part of this program.

Doctors clinic

This clinic is essentially run by midwives and doctors, and mothers will quite frequently have an assessment with a doctor. Again, it may not be the same one each time, but will be a member of a medical team. This type of clinic is good for women who want contact with an obstetrician throughout their pregnancy, who may have a slightly more complex obstetrics history or extra risk factors, such as high blood pressure or abnormal position of the baby.

High risk obstetrics clinic

This type of clinic is run by doctors who specialize in riskier pregnancies.

These may be issues that were known from the beginning or that may have developed during the course of the pregnancy and which may affect the mother or baby. These issues could include medical conditions, such as diabetes or high blood pressure, or even multiple pregnancies. These clinics are available in some hospitals only.

You can also enter a public hospital as a private patient and have the obstetrician of your choice. When contracting your doctor you just need to make sure that they are accredited with the hospital in order to deliver there. You will visit your obstetrician in his or her own medical suites throughout your pregnancy and they will then deliver your baby at the hospital.

A new mother can leave as early as four hours after the birth if she and her baby are well enough. If she does leave within 48 hours, a community midwife will visit mum and baby at home as part of the early discharge program. Most women will stay two to three days after a vaginal birth and five nights or more following a caesarean.

As far as costs go if you are a public patient your bills are covered by Medicare. If you are a private patient in a public hospital you will be billed by your obstetrician and any other specialists required, such as an anaesthetist or a paediatrician.

If you have private health insurance it's also worth checking if it covers your baby. If it's needed, a neonatal intensive care unit in a private hospital can be very expensive if you aren't insured. Usually the costs of a private patient will be covered by the parents' insurance. If it's not covered, the hospital will usually meet the bill.

> **When I first got pregnant** at thirty-eight I decided I needed a private obstetrician. I wanted it to go well. I wanted personal service. I didn't want to leave things up to pot luck. So I spoke to my GP who gave me names of four or five obstetricians locally—and a good briefing on their world outlook.
>
> He was dutiful and professional and in the end was the only reason why I wasn't whipped in for a caesarean after a long labour. And the positive experience gave me the confidence to go public for the birth of my second child. – **Jo**

Private hospital

This is the most expensive option, depending on your level of private health cover. Here you are essentially choosing the venue, which in many cases can be similar to a hotel.

Private hospitals are sometimes co-located with public hospitals. Major public hospitals usually have the highest levels of facilities and skills, such as neonatal intensive care units. If there is a major complication with either mother or baby, they are usually taken to the largest nearby teaching hospital. Again, make sure your obstetrician is able to practice at both the public and private hospital so they can be with you the whole time. Similar to a public hospital, at a private hospital a woman will stay up to four nights following a vaginal delivery and five nights after a caesarean.

One in three of all deliveries are now via caesarean—either as an emergency or by choice, and this number is steadily increasing. The rate is higher among older women, and for those admitted to private hospitals.

Costs in a private hospital are higher. You will pay for accommodation, tests, an anaesthetist, if required, and your obstetrician. Some obstetricians require payment up front, others are happy with staggered payments.

Most obstetricians charge anywhere between three and eight thousand dollars. Your final bill will depend on your level of private health care. Eighty per cent of all non-hospital costs such as your antenatal care will be covered by Medicare once you and your family are above the safety net.

Check with the private hospital to see what extra services are available such as physiotherapists or lactation consultants. These may come at an extra cost.

Both public and private hospitals usually conduct tours so you can see the facilities before making up your mind. Often they are on the weekend, but check with the hospital for days and times.

Most hospitals also run classes for new parents—both before and after the baby is born—covering essentials such as sleep, feeding and post-partum health. It's worth asking just what is available and when you need to book in. These classes can also be a fun way to meet other new parents.

In places where demand is high, you will need to get in quickly if you want a private hospital bed and obstetrician—it's usually best to book in as soon as you find out you are pregnant. Incredibly, at some private hospitals this needs to be as early as the five- to six-week mark. Many obstetricians limit the number of new patients they take on each month.

> It's a very personal choice to spend the money, whether to go private or public, but it was one of those areas I didn't want to skimp on. – *Sue Vercoe, CEO, Market and social research company, mother of two*

Choosing an obstetrician

Obstetricians are physicians who specialize in pregnancy, labour and delivery. Most are also gynaecologists.

When choosing an obstetrician, your GP is a good place to start and they can refer you to an obstetrician in your area. Your local hospital can also provide you with a list of accredited obstetricians. They need to be accredited with the hospital in order to work there. Or ask a friend who has recently had a baby for a recommendation.

Ask your obstetrician when you first visit them at which hospital/s they deliver as some choose to deliver in specified hospitals only and you might have your heart set on delivery at a particular hospital.

If you want a private obstetrician, find one before you become pregnant and book in for a Pap smear. This way you will get to know them, and immediately become an existing patient.

Questions to ask your obstetrician:

- *Birth plan and flexibility.* Are they open to your views on how you would like the labour to progress? This could include issues such as pain relief and surgical intervention.
- *Attendance.* Will they be at the birth? Do they work every weekend? Are they planning holidays when you are due? If so, you have the option now to find another doctor.
- *Payment.* Some require payment up front. Others will charge you at regular intervals over the course of your pregnancy.

66 *I had already consulted a gynaecologist a number of years earlier after having an irregular Pap smear. So when it came time to have my baby I already had a doctor I felt comfortable with and had confidence in. And after paying private health insurance for so long, I decided the time had come to get some of my money back, so I booked into a private hospital. We made the dash at 2.30 a.m. and Nicholas was born just as my husband finished his breakfast and Tiger Woods won the 2001 US Masters. Talia was born at the same hospital two years and eight months later, helped out by one of the same midwives and my same doctor. The sense of familiarity certainly helped my nerves. And little did Talia know, but Charlie Crowe was born in the next room two days later. – Mel*

Midwife-only birthing centres

Also known as group midwifery practices, such centres are slowly growing in numbers but still less than five per cent of babies are born here.

These centres are for women with healthy, low-risk pregnancies who want minimal intervention but more one-on-one contact than the clinics within the hospital system can provide. The mother-to-be has one midwife who looks after her throughout the duration of her pregnancy and birth. The midwife gets to know her patient, her complete medical history and builds a rapport with her family and any other children she may already have.

This midwife conducts the basic physical checks such as blood tests, blood pressure and routine antenatal screening and can arrange for extra tests such as an ultrasound if required. The same midwife will then deliver the baby and offer postnatal care for up to two months. There is usually no in-house stay, so mothers go home around four to six hours after the birth.

Women who choose this type of birth experience must meet very strict criteria. They must be in good health with no complications in the pregnancy. They cannot have any complicated obstetrics history or have had a previous caesarean. Natural pain management strategies are favoured, although in some centres nitrous oxide (gas) is available. Epidurals are not available.

If at any time during pregnancy there are concerns, another midwife, a doctor or an obstetrician is consulted. If the woman experiences any number of changes such as a rise in blood pressure, development of gestational diabetes or a problem with the baby such as an abnormal position or delayed growth, she is usually taken off the program and referred to another service. Some centres are now more effectively linked with hospitals, so should a woman need a higher level of obstetric care, rather than remove her from the program, the midwife may be included in the consultations and work in with the doctor.

If during labour complications arise, the woman will be immediately transferred to a hospital. If this is not possible, a medical emergency team will be brought to her.

The main role of such centres is to provide a service for those women who want minimal intervention in their child's birth. They work with the midwife to have the type of labour they want, be it a water birth, on a birthing stool or even a ball. But if you want this type of care you also need to be flexible because you will be moved to another care area if either your health or that of your baby is in jeopardy.

State governments are now starting to address the growing demand for such centres and regulate them accordingly. The cost of using these centres is covered by Medicare. They are usually located within your local public hospital, so call them for more information. They offer information sessions.

Home birth

A very small number of women choose to have their babies at home.

There are two ways to have your baby this way. Most capital cities now have at least one major hospital offering a Home Birth Service. In this service the hospital will provide a free midwife for women with a low-risk pregnancy. The midwife will meet with her patient throughout the pregnancy and be present at the birth. The pregnant woman will also meet a backup midwife as in some states two are required to be present at the birth. The woman can then choose where to give birth, either at home or in a birth centre.

Demand for this type of service is slowly growing and some state health departments are now directing their area health services to look into the provision of home birth services.

The other way to organize a home birth is to employ your own midwife. There are now only a limited number practising in Australia because of insurance issues (around two-thirds fewer than in 2001 when the insurance industry went through a major upheaval). Because private midwives can no longer get insurance, many will ask their patients to sign a waiver.

A private midwife will work one-on-one with her patient throughout the pregnancy, the birth and up to six weeks after the baby is born, usually forming a very personal relationship. Sometimes a GP will work in tandem with a midwife in your home.

A private midwife will cost you between fifteen hundred and five thousand dollars.

It is advised that you organize a backup plan involving a hospital should the birth not go as anticipated. Some midwives recommend that their patient arrange a meeting with the hospital and supply their medical history in case a transfer is required. The midwife will in many cases accompany the woman to this visit.

The Australian College of Midwives publishes the 'National Midwifery Guidelines for Consultation and Referral'. This is a list of all the specific factors that would recommend a woman be transferred to a GP or a specialist obstetrician, either at the initial introductory meeting, during pregnancy, labour, birth or the post-partum period. You can access this guide from the Australian College of Midwives in Canberra, or via their website, www.acmi.org.au.

Some important things to ask your private midwife

- *Resume.* How much experience has she had?
- *Previous clients.* It might help to speak to other mums who have used her services. This will also give you more information about home birthing, particularly if it's your first.
- *Intervention.* At what point will a doctor be called or a hospital transfer arranged? And who makes this decision?
- *How many clients does she manage?* What happens if two women are in labour at the same time?
- How much does it *cost*?

You will find a number of private midwives listed on the Internet or in the phone book, or try calling your nearest birthing centre, as a number of these midwives also work in private practice. Some states also have their own Home Birth Association. You can also get more information from the Australian College of Midwives or www.homebirthaustralia.org.

The key thing to remember as with all births is to remain flexible. The health of the mother and the baby is paramount and in order to maintain this, sometimes the best laid plans must be abandoned, or at least amended.

Susie Cameron gave birth in the loungeroom of her Mosman apartment, watching the storm clouds roll out over Sydney's Balmoral beach and listening to the wind chimes on her balcony. Her husband David lit the candles and cradled baby Oliver's head as he was born. Then the three of them spent that first night cuddled together in their own bed in their own home.

It was Susie's deepest desire to have a home birth, and she did exactly as she had planned.

'So many people are so removed from the process of birth itself, they don't want to feel any pain. I wanted to know what my body could do and I wanted that rite of passage. I knew that after I birthed Oliver, I could do anything.'

Susie employed Maggie, a private midwife, and discussed at length at what point she would change her plans and go to hospital if it was required.

'I had faith in Maggie, I had faith in me.'

It was the experience Susie and David wanted, but she says so many people were sceptical, including family and friends. After being abused by strangers, even a work colleague over the phone, Susie stopped telling people.

The birth was so idyllic that second time around Susie says she felt 'ripped off' when her labour went wrong. She started contractions at home, but started haemorrhaging and was rushed to hospital for an emergency caesarean. Both she and her baby Phoenix were safe, and naturally that was her priority, but it didn't compare to the tranquillity of her first.

Doula

Another form of support you may come across is a doula. 'Doula' is an old Greek term that refers to a woman who personally serves another woman. She is essentially a non-medical assistant in pre- and postnatal care. The doula may care for you in the lead up to birth, and also during labour, with massage and aromatherapy for example. Some will also support the mother after the birth with feeding advice and help your emotional and physical recovery from the birth, and even with light duties around the home.

Renee Adair, Director of the Australian Doula College explains about doulas:

- A doula provides emotional support and encouragement and a continuity of care, especially in a system where many women will not know the hospital staff on the day they go in to give birth. She can build a relationship with the mother and establish what her birthing needs are, whether they be in hospital, a birthing centre or even at home. She can also step in and support the father or partner in what will also be a new and daunting experience for them.

- Doulas will generally conduct about three meetings in the lead up to the birth, be there during labour, and visit the mother a couple of times post-birth. Fees range from four hundred and fifty to twelve hundred dollars depending on her level of experience and more visits can be arranged if required, paid for on an hourly basis.

- When hiring a doula, always ask for her qualifications. The Australian Doula College also runs a background check and insists their doulas are trained in CPR.

- Although significant in the United States and Canada, the industry is still relatively small in Australia, but is growing.

There are doula agencies in most states. You can also search on the Internet, or refer to this site: www.birthcentral.com.au

However or wherever you decide to give birth, just remember to keep an open mind. Many first-time mothers are unaware of the sheer force of childbirth. What you'd hoped would be a carefully structured event, may not go according to plan and can quickly become a free for all. Remain flexible and don't be disappointed if your baby or your body completely dictates the birth. A healthy baby and a healthy mum is all that matters.

Resources list

- Look at your state's Department of Health website such as in NSW www.mhcs.health.nsw.gov.au or in Victoria www.health.vic.gov.au.

- *My Child* magazine is worth taking a look at: www.mychildmagazine.com.au.

- Relationships Australia website: www.relationships. com.au.

- Australian College of Midwives in Canberra: www.acmi.org.au

- Doula information:www.birthcentral.com.au.

- Australian Council of Trade Unions website: www.actu.asn.au.

* So, you're pregnant—handy hints

- Decide where and with what type of medical professional you want to have your baby.

- Book your doctor, midwife or hospital bed, particularly if your choice is in high demand.

- Chat to, or at least observe, other working mothers in your workplace. See how they manage, and find out how your company reacted.

- Start giving some thought to how long you want to take off work and what you want to do when you return. Just remember, the best intentions can go right out the window when you're holding that little baby.

- Make your plans now, but be prepared to change your mind or have it changed for you when the situation demands it.

chapter 3

pregnancy and preparing for your baby

In this chapter:

- How to balance the demands of pregnancy with work.

- What maternity gear you really need.

- What baby gear you really need.

- What to pack in your hospital bag.

> ❝❝ **Catriona Dixon, journalist, mother of two**
>
> The first thing I did was buy a bucket.
>
> And while a green plastic bucket isn't normally high on the shopping list for expectant women, after two pregnancies I've come to terms with the fact I'm not entirely normal.

Nope, I didn't blossom like Katie Holmes, nor radiate like Angelina Jolie with either of my pregnancies. I spent my entire forty weeks—make that eighty, and never again—with my head in my bucket throwing up. Yep, from the moment the Goddess of Fertility waved her magic wand, my life was a whirl of nausea. I puked morning, noon and night, *every* day of my pregnancy. In the car, elevator, at the shops, office, restaurants, exercising—you name it, I did it. I even threw up on my husband! It was exhausting, it was demoralizing, embarrassing and down-right disgusting. Worse still was the fact that life didn't stop. I spent my first pregnancy covering the Olympic swimming for News Limited's newspapers at the Sydney 2000 Games. By the end of the competition I'd seen more porcelain in the ladies room than I did Aussie gold medals. I was so sick, I ended up in Sydney's Mater Hospital on a drip, between the Olympic and Paralympic Games.

And for the second, well, with only eighteen months between my girls and still working for the *Daily Telegraph* part-time, there was no stopping anyway. The fact I suffered from severe carpal tunnel, and have since had surgery on both hands, only added to my discomfort.

It seems some people are made for pregnancy and others, like me, are not. Gone is my dream of a large family. Gone are the two teeth I lost from my eighty-week puke-a-thon and gone is my green bucket. I adore my two beautiful healthy girls Molly and Sophie, but I never want to be pregnant again!

Let the fun begin. Once you've told the world your news, decided on your birth plan and bought your first pregnancy books you can really kick back and get into the full swing of this whole pregnancy thing.

How it will affect you will be entirely different from anyone else's experience. You may feel as sick as a dog, you may be lucky enough to never feel a moment of nausea. You could be so exhausted you struggle to put one foot in front of the other, let alone turn up at a meeting and contribute in an intelligent way. The jokes about 'baby brain' may fit you to a tee. On the other hand, you may have that unmistakable glow and feel better than ever.

How you feel is one thing, how others treat you is another. Be prepared for the inevitable jokes to come your way, either about sickness or 'baby brain', and get yourself a couple of snappy come-back lines. You may work in a male-dominated industry where the jokes are coming thick and fast, or you could find your pregnancy becoming public property with everyone having a view, from the male boss with four grown-up kids to the tea lady with six grandchildren.

" **Everybody had an opinion** on everything, from how I sat—crossing my legs would give me varicose veins—to what I wore—waistbands would constrict the baby—to how I hung out the washing—reaching up to the line could strangle the baby. (I was happy to believe the third tale and relinquish that job, but at the end of the day it just wasn't practical.) Well-meaning viewers had theories on what I should be eating to how much I should be working, how to avoid stretch marks and what to call my child.

Lucky for me I loved being pregnant. I wasn't sick, I had no complications, I simply packed on the weight and grew before everyone's eyes. I did have a problem lasting three hours on air without a few dashes to the loo, and missed my return cue a few times, the wardrobe department struggled towards the end to keep me dressed fashionably as well *as comfortably, and the high heels were ditched pretty early on. Oh and I did stop crossing my legs—but I still got varicose veins.*

I got stopped in the chicken shop once by a proud grandfather showing me his photos, and Jill at my supermarket always knew exactly what week I was up to. Even the postman would stop for a chat to see how I was going. You can fight it or go with it. Pregnancy and motherhood is almost one of the last areas to remain untouched by political correctness. Everyone has an opinion and strangers will touch your tummy, but if you think you are public property now, just wait till the baby is born! **– Mel**

Managing at work

Managing at work when you are sick is very different to when you have a comfortable pregnancy. Confide in a couple of trusted colleagues. Their support will be vital for those moments or days when you can't drag yourself out of the bathroom. The good news is that for most, the nausea passes after the first three months.

66 **Both pregnancies I needed** *to drink cold drinks—and eat lots of ice. I found that early on flat ginger ale worked well. The difficult part was disguising swigging litres of the stuff from others in the office—and one colleague did guess my plight. I found that regular, smaller snacks helped keep the nausea at bay during my daylight (working) hours, luckily.* **– Jo**

66 Natalie Barr, newsreader, mother of two

Working with morning sickness was exhausting and depressing. It kicked in at five weeks, stayed until the morning after I gave birth and made it incredibly difficult for me to like much about my pregnancies at all. The first pregnancy, before I'd told anyone, I'd haul myself in to the office to read the late news, often pulling over to throw up in the gutter of a side street on the way. Then I'd sit on the set, with a packet of biscuits and some potato chips, telling everyone I was just a little hungry at 11 p.m. I'd read an introduction to a news story, then stuff a biscuit in my mouth and finish it in the 1-minute–30-seconds it took to complete the journalist's pre-recorded story. I'd pray I wouldn't throw up live on national TV—but many times I came so very close. Stodgy food stemmed the nausea sometimes, but many nights I ran from the studio to the toilet in the dressing room to throw up as soon as I'd said goodnight!

Nat's top tips—Dealing with nausea

- *Lemonade and Gatorade.* Water didn't absorb quickly enough before it came up again.

- *Stodgy food.* Biscuits, bread and pasta seemed to stay down longer. I'd get up, throw up, then try to eat breakfast, because nothing would stop that early morning vomit.

- *Medication.* I took Avomine, which worked some days. But it should only be taken under medical supervision, so don't take anything without talking to your doctor.

If you're nauseous find what works for you and keep a giant stash at your desk. It may be salty crackers, or sweets, it may be medication advised by your doctor. If mornings are your worst time of the day maybe you can arrange to start and finish a little later.

One of the most important factors when you are pregnant is to listen to your body. It's doing some pretty amazing work in there and knows what it wants or needs. You may experience cravings. That can be your body telling you it wants something. And you will probably be very tired, particularly in the first and third trimester. So don't try to achieve the impossible. If your doctor advises you to slow down, then slow down. It may seem forever now, but you really are pregnant for such a short amount of time.

Is it really worth being more gung-ho to make a point to your colleagues that pregnancy will not slow you down, when in fact you feel like death warmed up and your body is screaming out for a rest? Or do you just accept it and take it easy?

66 **Emma Angel, scientist, mother of one**

Emma's brain was telling her to slow down—but she was too busy to listen. That's when her body stepped in and made the decision for her.

Emma had morning and night sickness—but kept pushing herself to complete her PhD in the physiology of sheep infections.

'I was pushing myself to work, but felt so sick I couldn't, but I kept going until my body finally said no—enough is enough.'

At about twenty weeks, Emma's blood pressure skyrocketed. Her doctor told her to stop work immediately so she suspended her PhD and had some time out. Within two weeks her blood pressure had returned to normal.

While Emma knew she was doing the right thing for her baby, her boss wasn't as sure she was doing the right thing for her job.

'He was a little annoyed. I think he felt this pregnancy was getting in the way of my research. I was made to feel work should be my priority. He would say to my colleagues "don't do what Emma did and get pregnant". He thought I'd never come back and finish my research—I think he was disappointed he'd lost me and my work.'

Emma gave birth to a healthy baby girl, Hannah, and returned full-time when she was about five months old.

'I got back into it when I felt the time was right and he was happy once I was back on track.'

If pregnancy is getting the better of you, it can be pretty hard to maintain the status quo at work particularly when no one knows you are expecting. Pregnancy number two saw me hit the 8 month mark just as the sporting calendar of 2003 reached a crescendo. We were broadcasting from Melbourne for a week for the racing carnival about six weeks from my due date. I was enormous and tired and struggled to sit comfortably on the stools we were using on set. They were shiny and slippery at the best of times, let alone when you're carrying an extra sixteen kilograms. Kochie still laughs about what he calls my swan dive almost into his lap during one interview. If only I had been as elegant as a swan!

Then a few weeks after that we hosted a show at Homebush for the Rugby World Cup. Getting my huge tummy into a XXL wallaby jersey was one thing, trying not to go into premature labour when we lost to England was quite another.

I knew I was pushing myself too hard, but sometimes it's unavoidable. If you can cut back, try to, because soon enough you will need all the strength and energy you can muster—both to give birth, then to manage with little sleep for the next few months. Don't wear yourself out before you even start. – Mel

Medical check-ups and tests

The other thing you will have to take into account will be making time for your medical check-ups and tests. For the first twenty-eight weeks you will need to visit your doctors or midwife monthly, then fortnightly, then in the last four weeks of pregnancy, weekly.

Depending on your age it may also be recommended you undergo a number of tests. This could begin with the nuchal translucency scan at the twelve-week mark to check for birth defects such as Down syndrome. Depending on the outcome of the tests you may then be offered further testing such as a CVS (Chorionic villus sampling) immediately between nine and eleven weeks or an amniocentesis at the fourteen to fifteen-week mark.

The next regular scan is around eighteen to twenty weeks to check the placement of the placenta, and examine different parts of the baby, such as the four chambers of the heart, the spine, the kidneys and the brain.

If your baby appears to be underweight or the placenta is low and could impede a natural delivery, your medical practitioner might then advise another scan at around thirty-two to thirty-four weeks.

Time for all these appointments needs to be factored in although many clinics are open on Saturdays. Just book well ahead as those spots are in high demand among working women.

66 *I fell pregnant with my second child at age forty, which meant there was a one in thirty-five chance of having a Down syndrome baby. I decided to have a CVS—a Chorionic villus sample—to give me some peace of mind through the pregnancy. I always say to people that they can't test if you're going to have a child who is naughty*

or doesn't eat its veggies, but at least they could give me some comfort on the issue of Down's and some other major chromosomal problems. I worked myself up in to a bit of a state before the procedure, which involves having a needle inserted into the uterus through your tummy so a small sample of placental tissue can be tested. The doctor performed the test using ultrasound technology, isolating the location of the baby before inserting the needle into the wall of the placenta—showing just how small the baby was at that stage . . . I didn't look but my husband did! It was quite quick—about fifteen to twenty minutes all up.

*On the pain stakes I shouldn't have been concerned. It was a little bit uncomfortable, but the local anaesthetic helped to numb what little pain there was. The doctor doing my procedure was great and we ended up comparing notes on dance clubs and drinking venues in London. It certainly helped having someone there to hold my hand, and my husband performed that role admirably. The exciting thing was that I was able to find out the sex of the baby and after I found out I was having a girl (my first child had been a boy) I had an excuse to start buying new clothes for her! – **Jo***

Ah, buying clothes!

We girls never really need a reason to shop, but pregnancy gives us one anyway. Whether it be for us, or that little bundle growing inside.

Maternity gear

There are two key points to consider before you hit the shops— where you work and how much you want to spend.

You'll probably be in maternity clothes for about four to five months of your pregnancy and for a while after your baby is born.

Those who wear their regular jeans out of hospital are few and far between. If it's your first pregnancy, you may last in regular clothes for about the first four months. After this you'll start to feel uncomfortable with anything tight around your tummy. You will probably also need to refit your bra—but more on that in a moment.

What you will need for work largely depends on your job and the type of environment you are in. It's amazing what you can adapt from your own wardrobe and what you can purchase from regular stores. If you are one of those women lucky enough to be a small size to start with you can simply buy the next size up. Never underestimate how much give a drawstring or bit of elastic has.

You can also purchase a range of clever products that allow you to adapt your regular clothes. For example the 'Belly Belt' is a small panel of fabric that attaches to your regular trousers to give you a bit more room. We both found it very useful. Just search on the Internet and you'll find stockists.

In many offices how you dress affects how you are perceived. So if you wear suits to work you might invest in a couple of maternity suits that you can mix and match, particularly given you can use them again if you want more children.

If your dress code is slightly more relaxed, you might find that buying a couple of pairs of decent maternity pants and a skirt will get you through, and a pair of casual pants for the weekend. Those ones with the big stretchy panel may be ugly, but they are practical and very comfy towards the end. Stretchy tops are good too and remember your regular jackets can always be left undone.

Check out the chain stores. 'Babydoll' styles are fashionable and perfect for round tummies. And jersey is a growing woman's best friend. Wrap dresses and dresses with plenty of stretch are all handy, comfy and can also be worn after your baby is born, particularly when those elasticised maternity pants may be too big, but your regular clothes are still a bit snug.

> **I pretty much survived** pregnancy number one with a cheap pair of black jersey elastic-waisted pants and a skirt two sizes bigger than usual. Having worn them every day for six months, once my baby was born I never wanted to see them again and promptly donated them to St Vincent de Paul. I then totally regretted my haste during pregnancy number two when I couldn't find anything so handy and had to pay twice the price at a maternity shop.
>
> I also bought a couple of jersey dresses and a wrap dress from a regular chain store—once again just a few sizes bigger. They were a little short at the front by the time my stomach stretched them to the limit, but for the short time required they did the job. – **Mel**

For more casual attire, you could try a pair of yoga pants from a sports store. You can roll them under your tummy, and still get some use out of them after the baby comes. A couple of big singlets under an open shirt also work. Borrow from your girlfriends if they have kept their maternity gear, or pinch shirts from your partner.

> **When I got pregnant** with my first child I was very excited. An excuse to buy some new clothes, I thought. Look pretty and pregnant—have those tight maternity tops that hug your tummy and scream to be noticed. I sourced my clothes in about equal proportions via the Internet or from local maternity wear shops. The Internet was usually cheaper and very reliable. There are a whole lot of sites you can find online, depending on what you're after. And I got a few things from friends.

I was careful about what I got—mainly concentrating on work wear as I knew I could wear tracksuit pants, or drawstring pants and T-shirts and jumpers on the weekends. I found that three pairs of washable pants, and five or six tops and one jacket was enough to survive. In summer I wore little Capri pants that were able to be worn at work and on the weekend.

Because I was size twelve (then!) I found I had to rely on maternity wear, rather than normal clothes a few sizes up, to get something to fit after about the third or fourth month. Women who are more petite can often just wear normal clothes a size or two bigger through their entire pregnancy.

The other thing that grew, along with my belly, was my feet. I had to get a few new pairs of shoes to fit and found that slip-ons and casual sandals were the best thing as no matter how big my feet got they'd fit.

A lot of maternity items claim to be able to be worn after you have the baby. Take it from me that once that baby is out and you no longer resemble a beached whale you'll want to be free of anything that reminds you of only being able to wear stretchy or smocked things! But keep them in case you have another baby or for friends that may need things.

Maternity wear is so expensive I actually sold some items in good quality second-hand clothes shops, recouping only a fraction of what I'd outlaid but it made me feel better!
– Jo

Online maternity wear

There are loads of great Internet sites where you can order maternity wear online and often make great savings. We'd advise visiting a maternity shop before you go crazy to work out what your size might be.

Get some recommendations from girlfriends about what sites they used. Look at Australian maternity sites—you'll find dozens of outlets. Dedicate a night or two and have a browse, and then decide what you like and order a few items. Some of the sites we used include Belly Basics, Frou Frou and Pumpkin Patch—but there are literally dozens more out there. Some, like Belly Basics, produce a few standard items that will provide the basis of your maternity wardrobe. It depends on your budget, work and casual needs, and personal style preferences.

Also check out *The Nappy Bag Book*—a great resource handbook for parents of young children which lists dozens of reputable sites. You can get the book at most newsagents, baby stores, book stores or online.

Bras

You will need to invest in a few decent maternity bras—and for a lot of women this could be sooner than you think. Many mums-to-be get bigger breasts before their tummy even starts to show. Once you start noticing the changes—or your appreciative partner does—go and get properly fitted. You need to be comfortable as you will continue to wear maternity bras after your baby is born and for as long as you breastfeed. And, unlike maternity clothes, you probably won't mind using these again for the next pregnancy.

The Australian Breastfeeding Association recommends you avoid underwire bras while you are pregnant or breastfeeding. This is because the breasts can change in size during the day and the wire may put pressure on the breast when it is fuller. This could lead to blocked milk ducts or mastitis. You can buy maternity bras on the Internet but it's preferable to have them professionally fitted.

Shoes

You may be a high-heel girl through and through—and choose to wear them right through your pregnancy. Half your luck. But if you struggle to lug the extra weight around, get puffy ankles and feel a little unbalanced on your feet, go for flats.

66 *I've never been much of a stilleto girl. At 176 centimetres I hardly need help in the height area, but never have flat shoes been more sensible than when I was pregnant. I can be a little clumsy at the best of times—but both pregnancies threw me completely off balance. I took a relatively harmless tumble down the back steps with pregnancy number one. I say harmless because in no way did I fall hard enough to jeopardise my unborn baby. Instead I just bruised my knees and my pride.*

Pregnancy number two was a little worse. At the six-month mark I took a fall in the rain, slipping on the wet road and landing heavily on my bottom and arm. A snazzy little red car did slow down—long enough for its driver to ask if I was okay. Well of course I said I was, as I lay crumpled, wet and humiliated in the gutter. Still dressed from work (wearing sensible flat boots I might add) the woman at least told me I looked nice before driving off. I made it back to the car, soaked and in tears where I sat for nearly an hour hoping the pain in my arm would ease. When it didn't, I called my husband to come and collect me from the car park.

Later that night, after spending hours in emergency, the doctor found I had a broken arm. The X-rays had me most concerned. I was wrapped in two lead vests to protect my baby.

For six weeks I wore a full plaster, fingers to armpit.
I couldn't write or drive a car and had to change my son's
nappy on the floor as I couldn't lift him.
Very unglamorous and very inconvenient. – Mel

You'll also want a couple of pairs of decent pyjamas, particularly for hospital. Buy something that unbuttons at the front as they will be easier if you breastfeed your baby. They'll also be handy for once you return home—especially if you're still schlepping around in your PJs at 10.00 a.m. when someone decides to stop by. Don't laugh—you will surprise yourself by how often you are still in your slippers at this time. When you have a newborn, there are some mornings when showering and dressing just don't happen no matter how hard you try!

And maybe consider a warm dressing gown or blanket if you are up feeding in the middle of the night.

Feathering the nest

All the things you'll need for your baby can be purchased at either specialty baby stores, department stores or via dozens of Internet sites that cater for baby necessities. We both *love* the convenience of Internet shopping—Mel buys her groceries online from time to time and Jo buys anything she can get her hands on. It's particularly handy during maternity leave when you might be housebound, or too exhausted to get dressed and out of the house. You can get anything and everything on the Internet—from clothes to nappies, food and toys.

Bassinet or cradle. They might look pretty, but they are not a necessity. Most babies are out of them by about three months. They are handy if you want your baby sleeping in your room in the early days as they are much smaller than a cot. This can be a good item to borrow from a friend or relative. You may even be able to hire one from your hospital. If it's on a stand make sure its stable and a comfortable height for you to lean over your baby. The alternative to save on the cost of buying a bassinet is to move the cot into your room for the first month or two, then move it back into the baby's room when the baby is more settled into a routine.

Cot. This needs to be safe and sturdy. Check that the bars are close enough together so your baby can't get its head stuck, that the sides are high enough and that the drop-side catch is secure.

There are plenty of varieties. Some have adjustable mattress height positions which make it easier to reach your baby, others will even convert into a junior bed when your little one is ready for that next step. Have a good look at what's available before you buy as this is one of your most expensive and important purchases. Cots can be expensive, but as tempting as it is to use a second-hand one, be aware of the dangers. Safety standards have changed a lot in recent years. There's more on second-hand equipment further in this chapter.

SIDS and safety

The Sudden Infant Death Association recommends you avoid pillows, bumpers and too much clutter in the cot. For more information check out www.sidsandkids.org.

Linen. A fitted bottom sheet and regular top sheet is the handiest combo. Have at least two or three sets as babies can be pretty messy. You may also consider having flannelette sheets for winter and lighter cotton sheets for summer. A waterproof mattress protector is also a good idea.

You will also need a blanket or sleeping bag for the colder months. A 'baby sleeping bag', when your baby is over six months or so, is handy as it stops them getting cold—and waking up as a consequence. There are lots of them on the market and online.

Handy hint—save on washing cot sheets

If you baby tends to vomit try a soft towel or cloth nappy under your baby's head in the cot as it's much easier to replace that when they chuck their milk than a whole sheet.

Prams and strollers. This is almost as complicated as buying a car. Ask friends what they have. Look at other parents in shopping centres and ask them if they're happy with their pram.

Your decision will depend on how you will be using the pram or stroller.

Choosing a pram: key questions

- Do you walk a lot? You may choose big chunky tyres that make it easier to handle bumpy footpaths and grass. If you jog, you'll be after something lightweight and manoeuvrable.
- Can it fit in the boot of your car?
- Can you lift it and fold it up (sometimes with only one hand)?
- Is it the right height for you and comfortable to push? Or can the height be adjusted?
- Will you be having another baby before the first one is out of the pram? If so, you might consider one to which a toddler seat can be attached.
- Is it easy to clean?
- Is a storage basket underneath important to you?

Those big old fashioned prams with removable bassinets are gorgeous and comfy for your baby, but the baby won't be in it for long. They are handy for walking and shopping, but can be difficult to manoeuvre and put in the car.

Three-in-ones start out as a pram with a fully reclining bassinet, but also convert into a stroller as your baby grows and wants to be in the upright position. They are the most versatile, but can also be rather big and heavy—and also expensive.

Strollers are usually lighter and easier to carry. They don't have a removable bassinet, but most will allow your baby to lie right back. And you might want to check how flat it lies if you plan to put a very small baby in it. They have swivel wheels for manoeuvring and fold up easily to fit in the car.

The three wheeler, or jogger, is popular now. You can choose big chunky tyres for walking, or thin bicycle-type wheels for running.

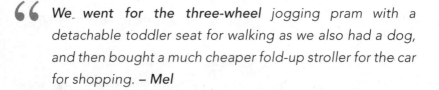

> *We went for the three-wheel jogging pram with a detachable toddler seat for walking as we also had a dog, and then bought a much cheaper fold-up stroller for the car for shopping. – Mel*

> *We bought an expensive stroller for our first baby and a lightweight one for travelling. Then when my daughter arrived and my son was only three, we discovered soon enough we needed a stroller that catered for both of them, so they'd both be safe. What we should have done first up was buy one that could have a toddler seat or platform attached later. A costly mistake first time around. – Jo*

Prams and strollers can be pretty expensive so keep an eye out for a good second-hand one. Ask friends, look on the Internet or at a pre-loved baby equipment shop.

> ## Safety tips
>
> Check that the pram or stroller meets Australian standards, *always* strap your baby in and never hang too much on the back so it topples over.

Baby pouches and slings. A baby pouch where you can carry your baby on your front can be handy as it frees up your hands. Just make sure it's strong and easy to put on and off while you hold your baby and support its head. Some are far too fiddly. The backpack-style is designed for older babies who can hold their own heads up.

There are lots of varieties of baby slings available in shops and particularly online. Get a recommendation or see one used before you buy as they can look easier to use in a photo than they actually are.

> **Nicholas wasn't overly keen**, but Talia all but lived in the pouch for about the first six months. I even managed household chores while she slept in it when she wouldn't settle any other way. It also gave me the freedom to hang on to a speedy toddler. – **Mel**

> **For Marlow I relied heavily** on the front pack and would take him everywhere in it. Because Frida was my second there wasn't as much time for fussing and I actually found a sling I really loved which we still use now she is a toddler—just varying the positioning from lying to sitting up, it's been great. – **Jo**

Car seat. It is a legal requirement that your child travels in a suitable restraint. Your baby's safety is paramount. Don't skimp here. Although all seats for sale in Australia meet safety standards, some are better than others.

You need to start with a capsule. This is a rearward-facing restraint for babies up to nine kilograms, or approximately until they are six months old. Many cities have capsules available for hire. Ask at your hospital or local clinic for capsule hire services near you.

The biggest advantage is being able to take the actual capsule out of its shell and out of the car without waking or taking your baby out of its seat.

When your baby can sit up, weighs more than nine kilos and can easily hold its head upright, you can move into a forward-facing seat. If your child is too tall for the capsule, but not yet nine kilos then you will need to place the seat facing rearwards for a while. This seat can be used until your child is about five years old, or when they outgrow the seat, and you can then use a booster seat. Booster seats are for toddlers, once they weigh over approximately fourteen kilograms.

You can buy convertible restraints that are used for children from birth to four years. These are probably the best value for money. They lie almost flat and back to front in your car until it's time to turn it around when your baby is old enough.

The handiest place for your baby's seat is behind the passenger seat. This makes it easier and safer to access from the kerb. The most important factor is ensuring the restraint is fitted correctly. Seek expert help if in doubt. There are authorized fitting stations, often where the restraints are sold.

You can also get extra information from your state motoring body, such as the NRMA or RACV, in the form of a 'buyer's guide' in which they rate the different brands.

And don't forget, you'll need to have the seat fitted *before* you can take your baby home from the hospital—best to get this done a week or so before your due date so it's done.

Baby clothes. As hard as it will be—hold yourself back a little here! Newborns don't really need a lot of clothes. Start with a few little body suits and add layers depending on the time of year, such as singlets and socks. At least three suits in white is a good starting point—one on baby, one in the wash and one spare. Just remember they grow very quickly. Besides, if your baby's sex is a surprise you will probably want to rush out and buy something pink or blue anyway.

And never underestimate how much washing you will be doing.

> ## Nat's top tip—keep on top of the washing
>
> I would get up and put a load of washing on before breakfast. It was a good way for me to get a routine going and keep on top of the enormous amount of washing motherhood brings.

Keep clothing items simple. They need to be easy to undo to change a nappy and not be too fiddly when it comes time to undress.

This is another area to make the most of hand-me-downs. Maybe not so much for the everyday basics like singlets and jumpsuits as they can get pretty stained and worn, but less used items like coats, beanies, and pretty dresses that are often only worn a few times before they become too small.

As your baby grows you'll get to know what they need and what you tend to use the most. And don't forget, baby clothes make good gifts so you could be lucky and receive some lovely things.

You can never have enough bibs, and the bigger the better. If your baby likes to be wrapped you'll need a few large flannelette or muslin wraps depending on the weather.

Handy hint—on sale!

We both stock up on children's clothes during end-of-season clothes sales. You can usually predict pretty accurately what size your child will be a year out, and it's a good opportunity to get some of the more expensive items at half price or even more.

A word of warning though, this approach isn't good with shoes which really need to be bought as you need them because shoe sizes are unpredictable and fast moving in babies and toddlers.

Nappies. Whatever you choose to use, stock up before baby arrives.

If you want disposables, grab a few boxes of the newborn size when you see them on sale at the supermarket. Disposable are also available in bulk via online outlets or from some baby stores—a good way to stock up and always have a ready supply.

If you want to be kind to the environment, there are also biodegradable nappies on the market such as Baby Love Eco-Bots endorsed by Planet Ark—many of these are available online, or at health food stores and work very well and are not much more expensive than the garden variety nappy.

Handy hint—cloth nappies are handy

Buy yourself a pack of cloth nappies even if you intend to use disposables. They are the handiest things for cleaning up mess and throwing over your shoulder so baby burps on that rather than your clothes. Carry extra in your nappy bag, leave some in your car, even at the grandparents' house. They are so useful.

If you decide to use cloth nappies you'll want at least two or three dozen, a box of liners and some fasteners. Pilchers or some sort of pull-on overpants in either plastic or heavy cotton will help prevent leakage or dampness. When buying a nappy bucket make sure the lid is very secure for safety reasons. Toddlers have drowned in them.

You can also look into using a nappy service—they take the soiled nappies away and do all the hard work for you, replacing them with a pile of fresh clean ones. You'll pay about twenty to forty dollars a week for enough nappies for a newborn.

There are a huge range of alternatives to disposables available—including organic cotton, and a range of different washable nappy systems. You can also get washable nappies that clip on like disposables, or another style where you wash the outer pants, but throw the soiled liners away. They can be a little more time consuming and fiddly though. If you want to research alternatives to disposables we suggest that you start on the Internet—do a search for 'washable nappies' in Australia and then go from there as there are whole sites dedicated to disposable nappy alternatives. Some of these systems are also available at baby stores or health food stores. You can always choose to use a mixture of nappies and use cloth or washable at home and disposable when you're out. Doing your sums, it is usually the case that exclusive use of cloth or washable nappies will save you a considerable amount of money in the long run—but this is also balanced with convenience, increased washing and how you want to live your life.

If all this leaves you confused you can always test run a few different styles, see which one/s you like best and go from there—good luck!

Nappy bag. This can be cheap and cheerful or purpose built, but buy one you like because you will be taking this everywhere you go for the next few years of your life! You'll need to pack nappies, wipes, a change of clothes, the handy cloth nappy for cleaning up, a few bags for wet clothes or dirty nappies, bottles and dummies if your baby uses them, a toy as an urgent distraction and food when they are older.

There are so many styles to choose from—a backpack, an over-the-shoulder bag, or one you carry in your hand. Check it can fit in your pram or hang on the back. And make sure it's easy to clean. Some are even lined with plastic which can be handy if a bottle leaks. There will be a time when you no longer need a nappy bag, but the day you decide not to bring one after toilet training your toddler will be the day disaster strikes. There are top-of-the-range designer numbers from the likes of Louis Vuitton or Oroton, or just your run-of-the-mill yet entirely practical travel bags that come with lots of pockets. Don't get too obsessed with this purchase, because you can. It is useful to have a bag with loads of inside and outside pockets, but take it from us, you'll probably end up using a range of different bags to suit different uses.

But one handy hint, always take one out with you even if it's just out the door for a 10-minute stroll, because you'll end up needing it. You might also keep one permanently stocked in the boot of your car for those times when you and your partner look at each other and say 'But I thought *you* brought the nappy bag'.

Change table. These are optional depending on your space and budget. There are a number of styles—the chest of drawers with a mat on top, the trolley sort or the foldaway type. Whatever your choice, make sure it's stable, safe and the right height for you when you bend over. You'll also want to have everything within easy reach such as nappies, wipes and creams. A cheap alternative is to have a change mat on your bed or on the floor next to the cot, but bear in mind that this means you'll need to crouch down to change nappies.

And never leave your baby unattended on the table or bed—you don't want their first roll over to be when you are not watching.

Breast pumps, bottles and sterilizers. If you want to continue breastfeeding after you return to work you will need some equipment. If you are lucky enough to have on-site childcare you can simply join your baby at feed times. But if you are away from them during the day, you will need a breast pump if you want to express your milk to avoid introducing formula. You can either buy a manual pump, or buy or hire an electric one.

A small manual hand pump will set you back around one hundred to one hundred and fifty dollars. You can also buy an electric single breast pump for around one hundred and fifty dollars or a double electric for around two hundred and fifty dollars. These are best for women who will use it occasionally when they are not with their baby for a feed.

You can also hire a larger, stronger electric pump that does most of the work for you. This is suitable for women who will be using it regularly as their primary method of feeding, for example if their baby is premature and can only drink from a bottle. You will need to pay a deposit of between four and eight hundred dollars depending on the brand and then a monthly rental of eighty to one hundred and twenty dollars.

This is one of those items best left until you know what you intend to do or need—how your baby will feed and how long you intend to breastfeed for. Your midwife or lactation consultant will be of assistance, and the chemist within your hospital is a good place to start. The Australian Breastfeeding Association can also offer information and advice.

You will also need breast pads, either washable or disposable, to prevent any leaks onto your clothes, and you may also require a nipple shield if you have trouble feeding and your nipples become sore and cracked. Your baby health clinic nurse will help you here if this is the case.

If you are bottle feeding your baby it's handy to have enough bottles to get you through a whole day and then one spare. You can either buy a sterilizer or boil the bottles in a saucepan. You can also buy self-sterilizing bottles that clean themselves in the microwave.

Check out your local baby shop or chemist—the choice is endless, but if you go for a well-known brand you will find it easier to get new teats and adaptations as your baby grows. A small container that carries a predetermined amount of formula is handy for when you go out.

If you are bottle feeding or combining breast and bottle it is a good idea to choose one bottle system and stick with it, as the pieces mix and match.

Handy hint—getting used to a bottle

Even if you intend to continue breastfeeding, it's a good idea to get your baby used to a bottle early using your milk. Express some extra milk at the end of a feed and store it in the freezer. This makes life so much easier for when you go out, start to wean or want to give Dad a turn at feeding to let you have the odd full night's sleep. Some babies struggle to adapt to a bottle after being breastfed. And if your maternity leave is coming to an end, this is one extra stress you don't need.

Read more about breastfeeding and returning to work in Chapter 8.

Dummies. We all vow before our baby is born we won't use one, but sometimes it's the only thing that will settle a screaming baby in the middle of the night. Some babies love them, others just spit them out. Choose a good quality brand that meets Australian safety standards. And never dip it in honey or anything else.

Baby monitor. This is entirely up to you. If you have a huge house and sleep in the west wing while your baby snoozes in the east wing, then go for it. But trust us, you will hear your baby cry if it needs you—no matter how heavily you may have slept in the past. We can't guarantee the same for your husband though! It can be handy for a two-storey house, or when you are doing chores during the day, such as hanging out washing or gardening. You can always buy one down the track if you feel you need it.

Highchair. Make sure it's stable, has a secure harness, is easy to clean and easy to move out of the way. There is no hurry here, though, you won't need one until your baby is at least four or six months old. You may even want to consider a portable highchair if you do a lot of travelling.

Baby bath and lotions. A baby bath can be handy if you have a big bath as they are quicker to fill. But they are not a necessity. Babies grow out of them pretty quickly and they can be hard on your back. Don't spend a fortune here. The bathroom basin or laundry tub can be just as good!

What type of lotion or soap you use is entirely up to you— there are dozens to choose from—organic, hypoallergenic, fragrance free or supermarket varieties. Again these are available on many online sites.

Bouncinette. We all remember the old fashioned crochet and wire frame ones. Nowadays you can buy so many different types— ones that rock, play music, or have handles so you can carry them around. They can be very handy. You can pop your baby in it and move them around the house, garden or home office with you. Ensure that whatever you buy meets Australian standards and, for your baby's safety, never place it on a table. The baby can 'bounce' themselves off.

Playpen. These are used once your baby starts crawling and you want to keep them in one spot, or keep other children or animals away from your baby. If this is something that appeals to you or you think you'll need then ensure it meets Australian standards.

Second hand

Good quality second-hand baby items can save you a lot of money, either bought or handed down. You just need to be sure they are safe, in good working order and that you know their history.

If you use a pre-loved cot, be extra vigilant in making sure its safe and those catches are in good working order. If the paint is old, it may contain lead so you will need to strip it back and repaint. Babies chew anything! You should also consider a new mattress, but make sure it fits properly and you use the size recommended by the manufacturer. You should find this information stamped on the base of the cot. If it's not there the cot may also be missing other vital safety information, or will have been made prior to the introduction of safety standards so is best avoided.

Be very wary if you decide to use a second-hand car seat. Only use one if you know its history as they are designed to only ever survive one crash. Do not use one with worn straps, bent or worn buckles, or any cracking in the shell. If in doubt don't use it.

Safety standards are reviewed every four years so any restraint older than this is unlikely to pass current safety requirements.

If using an old highchair, make sure it is stable and the safety harness still works. Older style chairs often have big gaps that your baby can slip through.

If you are buying off the Internet or out of the paper, be extra careful and make sure you physically see the product. You want something that's been well looked after, has either a warranty or its assembly instructions and all its spare parts.

Ten children die and more than six thousand under the age of three are injured every year in nursery equipment accidents. Ninety-four per cent of accidents are caused by the products not being used correctly, rather than the products themselves. That means those accidents are avoidable.

Baby equipment guidelines

The Infant and Nursery Products Association of Australia Executive Director, Tim Wain, offers a few tips:

- Only ever buy a second-hand product if it comes with the instructions and all the parts are in good working order.
- Always buy a new car seat. Never buy second hand unless you can guarantee its history, and never buy one out of the paper or off the Internet.
- Avoid second-hand cots and never use one for sentimental reasons or because it's a family heirloom. They can be unsafe and difficult to find a mattress that fits properly. Just because no previous baby has been injured doesn't make it safe.
- Avoid second-hand porta-cots. They are designed only as a temporary sleeping arrangement. Often

older and heavier siblings climb in and out, leading to bends in the side and weakening of the safety locks. Never use a porta-cot that doesn't have a dual locking mechanism.

- If buying a second-hand pram or stroller, make sure it's in good working order, checking in particular, the harness, brakes and a head barrier if the pram has a reclining base.
- Same for a highchair. Check that it's stable and that the harness works properly.
- The key is not so much the age of a product, but the way it's been treated. Make sure it has all parts in good working order and it complies with current safety standards.
- The most important point with any product, new or old, is to use it properly and not to make modifications to the original design.

For more information on safety guidelines check out some of the websites listed below:

www.babysafety.com.au (This is the site of the Infant and Nursery Products Association. They have clear safety guidelines and also the latest safety warnings on products.)

www.kidsafe.com.au (Kidsafe is run by the Child Accident Prevention Foundation of Australia which has branches in each state. They list tips on choosing furniture and keeping your home safe.)

www.choice.com.au (This is run by the Australian Consumers Association. They do a lot of research on baby products. You will also find a list of what not to buy.)

Packing the hospital bag

Your hospital bag can be partly packed as the day approaches, but obviously some things will need to be thrown in at the last minute.

Leave a list by your bag for what else has to be included so your partner can toss those last minute items in, as you may be a little distracted.

Things to include are:

- Your medical records and antenatal card

- Any medication you require

- Toiletries, including maternity sanitary pads and breast pads

- Nightwear

- Clothes. It will make you feel good to get out of PJs and get dressed. Don't think of yourself as a hospital patient. Shower and dress and think of yourself as a new mum. Pack something comfy though; unless you are Victoria Beckham, you are unlikely to walk out of there in your pre-pregnancy jeans.

- Maternity bras and extra knickers

- Address book or mobile phone so you can spread the good news

- Camera and/or video camera

- Music or anything else to make you feel comfortable in the delivery suite. You could be in there for some time.

- Clothes for your baby to wear home

>   " *I **began packing*** a month out before the birth of my
>   first child, Marlow. It was like a military operation. I had
>   a box of aromatherapy oils to deal with whatever mood
>   I may be in during labour—and ditto homeopathic
>   remedies, at least ten to cover any type of dilemma from
>   nausea to hyperventilating to panic or anger. An electric
>   aromatherapy burner, my acupuncture pressure point
>   instructions and at least half a dozen CDs depending
>   on what might take my fancy. Well, this was the stuff of
>   dreams. I had a twenty-one-hour labour, aromatherapy
>   made me feel nauseous for the most part and all I wanted
>   was for my husband to massage my back for about eight
>   hours straight! – **Jo***

A thought about childcare

If you intend to return to work, now is the time to start putting
some plans into place regarding your baby's care. Many childcare
centres have waiting lists of a year or longer, and finding the
perfect nanny could take some time and is costly. Many women
go on a number of local waiting lists almost as soon as they
find out that they are pregnant to ensure they have some care
arranged when they choose to go back to work. Believe us, this is
not too soon.

Childcare options are detailed in Chapter 7 to help you
decide. But start thinking about it now—don't wait until you
are packing your briefcase. You may also want to start looking
at budgets as this could determine the decision for you. There is
more information about budgeting in Chapter 11.

Resources list

There are some wonderful resource books out there that will come in handy when you are trying to find suppliers, shops or online resources. Try these for starters:

- *The Nappy Bag Book* is a great Australia-wide resource guide for parents with children between birth and five years—a ready reference which contains details of how to locate the resource, service, book or retailer.

- *The CHOICE Guide to Baby Products* is produced by CHOICE magazine and available through their website www.choice.com.au.

- The *Sydney's Child* monthly magazine is available in city-specific versions in Adelaide, Brisbane, Canberra, Melbourne and Perth. Pick up a free copy at your baby health clinic or childcare centre—it offers a vast directory of products and services specifically geared towards children and families, and very helpful articles on parenting topics.

- The Global Shopper is an online resource to find the best online buys around the world—they also produce a printed resource guide available through their website: www.theglobalshopper.com.au.

- Some other sites we love are:

  www.breastfeeding.asn.au

  www.butterflykiss.com.au for cute sleepwear

  www.lillylolly.com.au for bedding

  www.baybeecino.com.au

  www.pumpkinpatch.com.au

www.kidscentral.com.au

And to get some inspiration from overseas . . .

www.babygap.com

✳ Pregnancy and preparation—handy hints

- Book as many of your medical appointments in advance so you can get the times that suit your schedule.

- Assess what clothes can double as maternity gear and what you need to buy.

- Start researching what baby products you need and want and shop around for good prices.

- Start thinking about childcare, particularly if you need to book in to a centre.

chapter 4
maternity leave

In this chapter:

- Your legal rights and balancing career—how long should you take off?

- Staying sane—changing roles and how to find time for yourself.

- How to find out about the resources available to you—and how to access them.

- Surviving and thriving as part of a mothers' group.

Thinking about your maternity leave

While you are busily eating the right food to help your baby's development in utero, your attention will inevitably divert to thinking about your maternity leave itself. What will you do for those three, six or twelve months (apart from endure no sleep, breastfeed like a cow and change nappies!)? What will it be like? Will you go mad?

For many working women with busy jobs the change of pace to maternity leave can be both a blessing and a curse. Most women these days have children after they've been in the workforce a few years. So just the change of pace from being at work every day with other human beings to being with a little baby that doesn't talk much will have its challenges.

If you have a busy job, manage a hectic work schedule or have a very stimulating or responsible job, then you're definitely in for a bit of a surprise when you go on maternity leave. Any woman who enjoys what they do at work can find it a challenge. Aunties and grandmas won't know what you're talking about when you say that you're bored during the day.

Maternity leave is certainly a change of pace. For some this can be a wonderful thing—where every moment is relished. They accept the change of pace, realize it won't be forever and adapt.

For others the sudden removal of work stimulus—particularly for mothers that have worked for a long time and are busy at work—can be suffocating. Long days on your own, with a small (and of course beautiful!) gurgling baby, but with little adult interaction can drive the most sane to utter madness.

It's a very, very special and precious time. And despite your exhaustion you'll look back at this time whimsically and wish it could have gone on for longer. It's so nice not to have to go to work, not to have to meet endless deadlines—to slob around as you like, with no makeup or in ugg boots (if they take your fancy), and not get out of your pyjamas until lunchtime if you feel like it. It's your time to be with your baby—take it as it comes, as every day will differ, and each day you'll learn something more about your beautiful baby.

Here are some ideas to help you plan your maternity leave and cope with the months off.

> **When Marlow was born** I was in my late thirties. It was the third night at hospital and my ever-dutiful husband had gone home early (8.00 p.m.), leaving me to fend for myself. Up to then Andrew had changed every nappy (and if not him a midwife had helped out). I detected the need for a nappy and, never having changed a nappy by the age of thirty-eight, buzzed the nurse. She came in, looked a little down her nose at me and my three-day-old son as I exclaimed 'I've never changed a nappy before so can you show me what to do please?'. She obliged and at that very moment I began my reluctant grip on this motherhood thing.
>
> A day or so later and back at home I logged on to get an email fix and check who'd sent their good wishes. A promise I'd be just fifteen minutes, which lapsed in to fifty, was confronted by my husband standing in front of me, cradling our son in his arms, saying: 'I think he needs to be fed, could you possibly do your emails later?' – **Jo**

How much time should I take?

When planning for your maternity leave you need to give yourself plenty of space to take as much leave as you feel you'll need. Plenty of women have intended to be back at three months, only to find that they love being at home with their baby and extend their time to six or twelve months.

Often you won't know this until you're in the middle of things, you've established that you can cope with the pace and are happy to give up the additional income and time away from your job for that extra time with your baby.

You might have the sort of job that means you'll need to consider taking a fixed time off—or a fairly short time. This may be the case if you run your own business.

Give all this a fair amount of thought early on in your pregnancy. It may not be your decision alone if there is a business partner to consider or a team of people who rely on you. And money might be a real issue. Talk with your husband/partner—work out what you think might work. Our advice is, if you can, remain flexible and don't lock yourself in and plan for more than you need.

Your legal rights on maternity leave

There are a whole lot of laws that govern your legal rights while on maternity leave and these are spelt out in detail in Chapter 9. Here's a snapshot:

- Know your rights—make sure you understand what you are legally entitled to, and what your employer can and can't do.

- Make sure you comply with the notice requirements, and give your employer a doctor's certificate ten weeks before your due date, formally apply for maternity leave at least four weeks before you intend to start the leave, and notify your employer of your start date four weeks before you intend to return to work.

- Discuss your return to work plans early and get any agreement with your employer in writing.

- You can extend parental leave only once within the fifty-two-week period, provided fourteen days' written notice is given to your employer. Any further extension within or after the fifty-two-week period is at your employer's discretion.

- You can only shorten parental leave with your employer's agreement, and you need to give at least four weeks' notice.

- Be prepared to put forward the business case for why any flexible working arrangement will work.

- If you and your employer can't agree to arrangements for your return, consider making a complaint to an anti-discrimination body—although these can take some time to resolve. If you have to go back to work full-time and you don't want to, make sure your employer knows you are unhappy about it and are challenging the decision.

Don't overcommit

When planning your maternity leave, be aware of not over-committing yourself too much in your enthusiasm to maintain your links with work—like agreeing to read reports from home, or doing the occasional freelance contract for instance. Keep it open and flexible. You don't know what sort of baby you'll have. If your child sleeps for hours at a time, freeing you up to spend a decent amount of time doing some work most days then committing to do some work may well work for you. If they aren't good sleepers then you may have your hands full.

How will the money work?

Very early on in your pregnancy, if you're planning on taking a big chunk of maternity leave, you need to negotiate with your partner about how you'll organize the money when you're off work. It's important to talk about these issues and resolve them upfront, as they can lead to tension in a relationship and you won't want to be adding that to sleep deprivation and caring for your new baby.

If you're used to having ready access to funds then often the hardest thing is to get used to not spending as much as you once did. And do you want your partner to give you a certain amount each week for shopping and entertainment or will you have access to a joint account? See more about financial planning in Chapter 11.

One way of not feeling so deprived during your maternity leave is to dedicate a certain amount each week to a little luxury, budget permitting—a visit to a café, a quick manicure, a magazine—whatever it is that'll keep you happy and entertained. It only needs to be a small amount, as little as five or ten dollars. But earmark it and spend it—it'll be your little indulgence.

Housework

Now you are home full-time for a while you may find your roles changing a little. This role adjustment may be easy, it may be a struggle. Your partner may have done the shopping or all the cooking before, but now you have days at home you'll probably be pleased just to get out of the house and stare at supermarket shelves—we know we were!

That said, just because you are not doing paid work it does not follow that you should do *all* the housework—it's a big job coping with a baby 24/7. We suggest that you talk openly with your partner before the baby is born and regularly afterwards. Talk to your partner about how they think this can work. How often will the vacuuming be done, who will wash the clothes, the dishes, or do the washing, the washing up or stack the dishwasher? If your partner isn't a very keen domestic god you'll need to negotiate this in advance and agree on some rules. It's a good time to renegotiate a few key tasks in your relationship. Make a few changes and talk about who will do what so the whole situation doesn't create extra tension.

You're a team now, a new family, so it's imperative that you talk to each other about how domestic duties should be divvied up so you don't feel lumbered with the 'domestic goddess' role unhappily. You could also consider getting some domestic help if you can afford it, even fortnightly. An extra set of hands will ease your workload and let you spend more time with your new baby, will remove a lot of tension and prevent you from thinking that you've become a 'housewife'.

It is absolutely critical to have this discussion before the baby is born, otherwise it slips past you in a sleep-deprived, hormonal blur, and every time you try to raise it with your partner, it either disintegrates into tears (yours) or you get interrupted by crying (the baby's). Stand your ground and negotiate an arrangement that you are happy with—otherwise it will build up into resentment while you're at home on maternity leave.

> For the first few months of maternity leave I'd tidy up rather than sleep or take some time out when my baby was sleeping. The result was I ended up comatose and then in bed by 8.00 p.m. every night. I remember my husband returning from work one day and saying he'd rather come home to a happy wife than a tidy house.
> – *Sue Vercoe*

A great book to help you through this time or even read before your baby arrives is the *Post Baby Conversation* by Alison Osbourne. It's a great book to help you navigate through the relationship issues that most couples experience after the arrival of their baby.

A time to adjust

The reality of stepping out of the workforce—emotionally, financially and personally—can be *really* hard. It is one of the most difficult things to adjust to in your new working-mother role. Suddenly your whole world changes from one where you are in charge, you have relevance—people want to talk to you every day—to one where the baby takes centre stage. Some days there are often very few people to talk to other than the woman in the corner store or the man in the newsagent, and they talk to the baby, not you.

Don't underestimate the impact all this can have. Not working is a blow to your bank balance, your ego, your relationship, and your self esteem.

Unfortunately, maternity leave is not all rose-coloured glasses or pina coladas by the pool while the baby is asleep. Getting used to the new reality takes a bit of work. As a woman used to a working life outside the home you have to try to adjust. You're used to structure, routine and socialization—so the change of pace may be a challenge. On maternity leave, you're often home alone all day. It is disorganized, messy, and often nothing gets done or achieved. The baby won't sleep when you want it to, it might cry a lot, the washing won't be done—you sometimes (often) can't be bothered to even cook dinner you're so tired. Turn to your partner or close friends to talk this 'relevancy deprivation' through—or 'brainstorm' with the other mothers in your mothers' group.

As a working woman, you're also often used to a fairly high amount of acknowledgement, praise and thanks. This just doesn't happen when raising your baby. No one praises you for getting the baby to sleep three, four or five times a day and the baby certainly doesn't acknowledge your efforts to purchase and puree organic fruit for their first solids. Even when your partner/husband does congratulate you it sometimes just doesn't feel heartfelt—somehow, from your perspective they just *can't understand* how you feel being at home *all day*. How can they? Sadly this is something you have to get used to.

Routine

You'll often hear experienced mothers tell you 'get the baby into a routine and you'll be right'. No truer words have ever been spoken—but what exactly do you need to do?

We are not baby experts and we certainly aren't medical experts. There are a whole stack of books out there such as *Baby Love* by Robin Barker which will guide you.

But what we will say is that in our experience as working mothers, getting your baby into a feeding and sleeping routine is the best way of helping you get back to work. There is more about this in Chapter 8. And being able to structure your day a little more will restore a sense of control and order.

You will have such a sense of achievement once you do sort it out—you'll be *so* proud of yourself!

Take each day as it comes—and stay sane

Enjoy each day as it comes. Some will be better than others. Some will be disastrous and you'll have no sleep—and some will be idyllic, wandering down to the park, the baby sleeping on cue and leaving you with enough time to send some emails or wash your hair.

It's so important to try to stay sane on maternity leave. Here are some ways to avoid going mad.

Get out of the house every day. Even if that's just popping to the shops. The regular human interaction will help you prove to yourself that you can still converse. Have a daily plan, and make it part of your routine, for example go out for a walk before your baby's morning nap, or after lunch and before their afternoon nap.

Fresh air is good for you both—and babies that won't settle just might sleep in the pram. Give it a go.

New mothers often battle either inertia (sheer exhaustion) or nerves. Nerves because it's really daunting being responsible for this new person who is there every day when you wake up. And it can be near impossible getting the baby out of the house by yourself for those first few weeks. It's vital that you try to wrestle with this as best you can in the early months. If you can conquer the feelings of inadequacy, inertia or nervousness about being with your baby all day then that is a big part of the battle of coping with being a new mother.

Develop new networks. You've entered a whole new world so why not approach it as you might a normal 'networking' opportunity. Other local mothers, your mothers' group or playgroups all present an opportunity to learn about different techniques, new products, good online stores or about child development.

Make use of occasional care babysitters, family or friends. Sometimes you will need someone else to lend a hand, either because your partner is away for work, you have an appointment during the day or you just really need a break or to go to the gym. Word of mouth recommendations or the local paper or even the notice board at your local baby health care clinic are good places to get details of potential babysitters. Some mothers' groups organize babysitting clubs where you accrue points and no money changes hands. You might even consider starting one yourself.

Do stuff. One of *the best* ways of staying sane is to keep busy, get out of the house and just do stuff with your baby. You will probably find that they will sleep well when you are out and

about and they are really portable when they are very little in the first month or two, so pack a nappy bag, put on some sunscreen and put the stroller to good use. Movies (such as Babes in Arms sessions)—some cinemas even have a 'crying room'—or coffee or lunch with a girlfriend or other new mothers or a family member, museums and art galleries are all possibilities.

Have a look at the 'What's On' section of your newspaper and plan a few trips. As your baby gets more mobile and more vocal then play dates at local parks, other mother's homes or at cafes that accommodate and welcome mothers' groups are all good options to explore.

Start a *mother's pram walking group*, or join one. Have a look or advertise in your local paper or baby health clinic.

Use the early months to *go out to early evening movies or evening dinners*. Often the baby will sleep straight though in their baby capsule under your table.

Draw up a weekly calendar or daily list of what you intend to do. If you're like us then writing things down helps insure that they might get done—and in your sleep deprived state it will help you remember that you wanted to do them in the first place.

Consider getting Internet access if you don't have it at home. It's a good way to keep in touch with friends who work and it's great for shopping.

And try to spend some time just enjoying your baby. Lie on the floor with them and play. Gaze at them lovingly. Just lie on the bed and stare at one another. It is true, they grow so quickly, so savour these moments and just enjoy this little time before you head back to work and begin the busy juggle.

Keeping in touch with work

Whether you need to keep in touch with work will depend to a large extent on what you do. If you run your own company or small business, for example, then it's obvious that you'll be in touch, probably quite regularly. You may still be involved in guiding the business from home and will need to pop in for regular meetings—with or without the baby—or direct things via email or Blackberry from home.

But for most people, employees in some capacity, staying in touch really regularly isn't expected, nor is it something you'll have the energy to do very often—particularly in the first few weeks and months.

Keeping in touch with work is probably more about our own expectations than anything else. Ask most of your colleagues and we bet they'll tell you that they don't expect it and won't demand it. Putting in place someone to deal with your projects or responsibilities while you are off will help you feel better about the period of forced 'hibernation'.

> **Quick tip**
>
> **Anne Hollonds, from Relationships Australia counsels:**
>
> 'While you are away from work, it's easy to fear you will lose touch with the workforce and your job. You may be worrying you will never regain your credibility at work. Those fears can erode the pleasure you have with your new baby. They are young for such a short time. Enjoy your little one while you can.'

If you are very keen on not having a baby slow down your career—*and* you have a baby who sleeps occasionally—then you can use some of your time to keep up with what's happening in your industry or career. This might include reading industry journals or using email and Internet to keep in touch with developments in your field. You can consider the occasional lunch, or visit to the office, either with or without baby, depending on where you work.

❝❝ **Nicole Sheffield, group publisher, mother of four**

It's always a good idea to stay in touch with your workplace, even if it's to show off the baby—remember, out of sight, out of mind!

But don't ring every day, you need time to get into baby mode too. I made a big mistake after my first child and was speaking at conferences two weeks after giving birth and then in and out of the office from three weeks— I ended up exhausting myself. This was all because I had started a new role and was nervous of letting go. In the end that isn't good for you, the baby or the business.

If you can do part-time try to, at least in the beginning. Once you're back full-time it's near impossible to pull back to part-time and people will assume you are not coping. It's much easier to build your days up. I also found starting with shorter hours helpful, so the first three months I returned 10.00 to 4.00 p.m. so I could get the home life sorted.

Mothers' and parents' groups

Mothers' groups are great sanity savers during maternity leave and beyond. We all need some form of support during this time —someone who's happy to talk endlessly about sore breasts, cracked nipples and the colour of baby poo. It's useful to start planning your support network before your baby is even born.

There are lots of opportunities to join groups of new parents; here are a few suggestions:

One of the first places you can start is at your antenatal or birth classes—often groups of mums-to-be will keep in touch after their births and meet weekly at local cafés or each others homes. Get a list of each others names, contact numbers and email addresses which can be photocopied and circulated before the classes finish. That way you can get in touch after your birth and make arrangements to get together.

New mothers' groups are usually established by your local child health nurse. Ask your child health nurse or baby health clinic when a new one will be created and when and where they will meet—usually weekly. Your local baby health clinic will encourage you to join one of these to ensure that you are meeting with other mothers—they know this is an important way of helping you stay sane!

Meetings of your local Australian Breastfeeding Association welcome all mothers (breastfeeding or not), fathers and grand-parents, to their regular get togethers. Look on the Internet for details in your area.

Groups for parents and babies—you could join an existing group or start your own informal playgroup with parents who were in hospital with you. Check in with your local baby health clinic, local council or community centre to see if any new groups are starting up.

Meeting parents at swimming classes, baby gym, your local park or at a local playgroup are all great ways of making contact with new parents of children a similar age. You'll find yourself talking to complete strangers with children as you share something—being a parent.

You are not alone

Know that other people feel the same as you. You are not an island. You are part of the sisterhood and we all need help sometimes.

Wherever you end up meeting, whether it is in a group or just two of you, it may need someone to take the initiative to get the ball rolling. It may be as simple as making arrangements to meet somewhere for coffee and sending out an email to one or two mothers or as complicated as finding a regular meeting time for a larger group of mothers/parents to meet. Either way it'll pay off for all of you.

Mothers' groups often use the weekly meeting as an opportunity to get experts in baby sleep, speech development, massage or another field to come and speak to them.

Depending on what sort of pre-existing social network you may have with other parents of young babies, mothers' groups can often be a blessing in those first few lonely weeks at home after your partner has returned to work and you are left staring at four walls. This is especially the case if you are the first among your friends to have a baby.

And yes, throwing together a group of women who have never met before and may come from very different social, cultural and political backgrounds can be challenging. The best thing is to take the group for what it offers you at the time—an opportunity for social interaction for both you and your baby, and an opportunity to exchange information and learn from each other. Don't be immediately judgemental of individuals who don't share your world view, or don't understand what you do at work. There will be plenty of areas of mutual interest that you will be able to have over the weeks and months ahead—even if that just revolves around the inevitable poo, vomit and sleep discussions.

Women in mothers' groups often form long and strong bonds that survive for years, stretching way beyond their babies' first years, as they watch their children move on to primary and secondary schools. A sense of belonging to your community is a wonderful thing—and you can often witness important, enduring friendships develop among your children.

Kerrie Goodwin is a clinical nurse specialist in Child and Family Health, at the Hornsby Ku-ring-gai Health Service. She says that mothers' group is a wonderful way to meet other parents, learn some vital skills, ask some questions and find a bit of reassurance.

Groups at the clinic run for between four to twelve weeks, allowing those organized and those not so organized to join in at their convenience. They can be a place to ask questions, gain information or just sit and listen. After that it's up to you to swap numbers and stay in touch.

You can always come back to your local clinic nurse if you are concerned in any way. It's a place for reassurance and comfort, a place to ask questions and find answers. Baby health clinic nurses are here to support parenting, not tell you what to do.

Kerrie's top tips for making mothers' group work:

- Come along.
- Give it time—you might warm to the whole idea.
- Allow yourself to get to know the other women in the safe environment of the centre.
- Don't be frightened of speaking and asking questions. The only silly question is the one not asked.
- What you have to say may be exactly what someone else needs to hear. What you ask may be exactly what someone else wants answered.
- Even if you have lots of friends with babies, mothers' group offers a real venue to network within your local community. It can be the start of some lifelong friendships.
- For the children, it offers the chance to make friends and socialize with their peers.

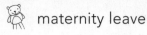

- Don't compare children, especially their development. They all move at different speeds.
- It's about not always having to be right. Mums fear being told they are not doing the right thing. Keep an open mind about other mums and the way they do things.

What about sex?

When you have just managed to get your baby to sleep after a particularly gruelling day, you're often in the mood for a bath and an opportunity for an early night. Sex can feel like a thing of the distant past. It won't last forever and the first few months are particularly tough.

A word about sex

66 **Anne Hollonds, from counselling service, Relationships Australia:**

One of the things—apart from sleep deprivation—that you will need to think about on maternity leave is sex. For some it may be the last thing on your mind while you are juggling breastfeeding and all the craziness a new baby brings.

Having a baby changes a lot of things—for both women and men. New dads are just as overwhelmed by the whole experience and they often feel pushed to the periphery of the family as they are no longer the centre of their partner/wife's attention.

It's at this time that they seek intimacy and for men that usually means sex. This happens pretty much at exactly the same time you don't want to go there. Both of you have emotional and physical needs, but they are so different. He wants you, but you might not feel you have enough to share around. My message to young men and first-time dads is just don't panic when the sex is turned off. It is just a natural stage.

How you get through this phase is what is important and preparation is the key. Before the baby arrives, you need to talk about the 'what ifs?' A baby is often the first big test of a relationship and there are a lot of changes happening, from the arrival of your child to your emotional and physical needs, even the loss of one income. Anticipate that this will be a crisis for you both. Don't think 'it won't happen to us' because it will. You need to work as a team. How will you manage? How will you negotiate your different needs?

Some women can't bear to be touched for a while. Your feeding baby is touching you, doctors and nurses have been poking and prodding. Your body hardly feels like yours anymore, so it can be tough to feel sexy.

It is usually only a short term thing, so you need to talk. Talk about what you can do to keep connected, both emotionally and physically. Set aside some time together— a space for the two of you that is apart from the baby.

You can work through it, as long as it's negotiated together. The danger is when one partner thinks the baby comes first and the other thinks 'what about me?' If you change the way you relate to each other, make sure you both know what's going on.

It's important to remember that sexual intimacy is about connecting and having fun with each other. So if sexual intercourse is on the back-burner for a while, you do need to find other creative ways to reconnect and have fun with each other. This is particularly important when we feel burdened by our new weighty responsibilities (caring for the infant, managing our financial responsibilities, and so on).

Both parents need to have times they can relax and be playful, preferably with each other. Playing in turn helps us

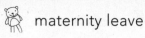

to deal better with the stresses, so it's a win/win situation. The more relaxed we can be, and able to be playful and affectionate with each other, the more likely it is that, when both feel ready, there will be a desire for sexual intimacy again.

Massages, sleep, warm baths, moonlight walks on the beach—there are lots of things you can do to look after yourself and the relationship. You don't need to stress about the sex.

Resources list

Maternity leave rights

- See Chapter 9 for a list of government and non-government organizations that can help advise you on your maternity rights.

Mothers' and parents' groups

- Do an Internet search for mothers' and parents' groups in your area, call your local baby health clinic or try:

  www.mothersgroup.com.au/

Books

- *How to Stay Sane in your Baby's First Year* by Tresillian
- *Baby Love* by Robin Barker, Pan Macmillan

✳ Maternity leave—handy hints

- *Think ahead about your maternity leave* as much as you can. Ensure you are aware of your legal rights and have put in all the relevant leave applications, and discuss your return to work and your options with your employer before you take leave.

- *Don't overcommit yourself to work* before you have the baby. You may be able to be involved in some events, meetings or projects from home, but wait until after you have your baby to decide how much you really want to do.

- Talk about how the *money* will work with your husband or partner before your leave starts—what's your budget, how much will you have to spend each week on yourself and groceries. It will help to set some ground rules and avoid the stress later on.

- Likewise on *housework*. Talk it through during your pregnancy and allocate some basic responsibilities for each of you to do after the baby is born. If you can afford it, consider getting some domestic help for a few weeks or months just after the baby is born. If workmates ask what you want for a baby gift, ask for a 'cleaning' gift voucher.

- *Maternity leave is a big adjustment* for working women. It's a day by day proposition. Take it slowly, enjoy it for what it is and relish the time getting to know your new baby.

- *Keep busy and active.* It'll help you stay sane, so don't lock yourself inside staring at four walls. Pack up the stroller and get walking, catch a ferry, bus or train or drive somewhere new. It can be a challenge initially, but once you get the hang of organizing yourself and a baby it will get easier—and be a lot of fun in the process.

- *Let work go for a while.* You and they will cope and you're exhausted enough as it is.

- *Join a mothers' or parents' group.* One of the best sanity savers around during maternity leave.

chapter 5
how to cope

In this chapter:

- Some simple strategies to avoid a meltdown and help you cope with juggling a family and work.

- Being a working mother comes with guilt and anxiety. Who can help and who to talk to when you're anxious or depressed.

- How to involve your partner, family and friends to help you stay sane.

- Staying healthy and planning your 'mummy time'.

Mummy anxiety

There's a lot of truth in the suggestion that we're a lot more anxious about our choices now we have more options as working mothers. Feminism has given us more choice, but sometimes it's hard to know what to do with that choice without going completely mad. Before us, a couple of generations back, women largely knew what their lives would be like—work for a bit, have children, stop work, look after the kids. For us there is no exact formula but instead a range of ways we can choose to live life. Once we've had children we can choose to be stay-at-home mothers and that's okay. We can choose to work either part- or full-time and that's okay too. All these choices bring anxiety with them. Whatever your decision you need to be 'at peace' with your own life choices, otherwise you'll constantly be in a state of anxiety.

> 66 Don't beat yourself up if you decide to go back to work.
> – *Sue Vercoe, mother of two*

> 66 And don't if you plan not to return.
> – *Catriona Dixon, mother of two*

We're always anxious. Anxious about our careers. Anxious about not being at work. Anxious about spending enough time with our children. Worried about what people at work will think when we have to leave early to look after a sick child. Worried about what our family and stay-at-home mum friends will think about us putting our children into childcare.

There's no perfect way. There's just your life, your series of choices. They are all valid. Just make your choice as good and as productive as you can. Enjoy the moment, enjoy your time at work and your time with your child—be that at an important meeting or playing dress-ups. Enjoy time with work friends and your achievements at work. But learn to be in the now. Be proud of the fact that you're setting a good example to your own children that it *is* possible for *both* their parents to enjoy productive work and family time. Hopefully you'll bring up kids that will share the responsibilities of work and family in their own homes when they grow up and have a family.

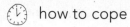

> **Balancing your time** can be the hardest thing—particularly once you return to work. There is your baby, your family, friends, your paid job in the office, your unpaid job at home, and last but not least yourself.
>
> You want be the best mum, the perfect wife, you need to prove to those at work that you can manage it all, and sometimes you also find yourself wanting to prove to those that may raise an eyebrow about your decision to return to work that you can handle it all. No one wants to expose a chink in their armour.
>
> The sooner you realize we are all human the better. Wonder woman only exists in Hollywood—with all the hard bits edited out.
>
> If you can afford it, now may be the time to find a cleaner. Even if it's just for the short term. Who cares who scrubs the bath—not least of all your baby. I remember my mother-in-law used to come and stay and bring her Gumption. At first I was horrified, offended and embarrassed. Now I love it! Besides, she scrubs it much better than I do!
>
> Or maybe you only wash the floor half as often as you used to. If ever you can let things slip a little, now is the time. It won't be like this forever. One day, in the future, you will get enough sleep, you will feel in control—we promise. But in the meantime let's just concentrate on surviving.
> – Mel

So much to do—so little time—so out of control

It's really easy to see how, as a working mum, you can so easily descend into a cycle of stress.

Picture this: you've been in control of yourself, your life and work for years, even decades. Lingering sleep-ins, weekend coffees, nights at the pub, hangovers. An enjoyable job, regular money, challenging work and great colleagues.

Suddenly the miracle of pregnancy happens and takes over—and it's all finished. Instead of planning that next round of meetings or your next career move you're planning the colour of your baby room or what brand of nappies to buy. You focus on the pregnancy, then the birth—then the baby. And any hope of being able to do everything you did before, *exactly* the way you used to do it, just goes out the window—fast.

And, when you're ready to go back to work, there is a sense that you'll never be able to do everything you want to do—ever again—properly. Disorder. If you're anything like us, piles of things gather around the house, waiting to be put away. Washing sits in baskets, and the pantry cupboards are not organized like they used to be. There's a loss of control—even a sense of hopelessness sometimes. Things have changed and life's not going to be the same as it was pre-baby. That's not bad, it's just a different world that you now inhabit.

This chapter details some ways to help all this so instead of getting you down, you get help, get organized, make time for you—live in the moment—rather than constantly thinking of *what needs to be done*.

Be in the moment

By this we mean live for the now, stop thinking about what has to happen tomorrow all the time, or how ordered things used to be, because it will stress you out. Being 'in the moment' is a really simple thing and, once you can do it, will bring you instant stress relief.

Stress is often made worse because of the enormity of what confronts us, what lies ahead, what we can't control. Life burdens us—and as working mothers juggling work and a family

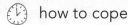

there is often a lot to do. You can't live or be in the moment all the time. You do need to plan, to write shopping lists, to think about what has to happen tomorrow, next weekend. But when you are together as a family take some time out to stop all that organizing, that list-making, that tidying up and sit, quietly with your children—or with yourself—and just be. Relax. Try to do this every day and it will become a part of your life.

Constantly being on your mobile or sitting on your computer while engaging with your children is bad for work and bad for your kids. Stop photographing and filming your children as often—and just observe them. Laugh with them, sing with them, dance with them, play with them.

66 **Nicole Sheffield, mother of four**

It often gets hard and you make decisions on the fly, but I do think managing motherhood and career has made me far more organized and strangely less emotional. You just have to get on with it. The first few months are the hardest but once I have an established routine and everyone is comfortable then I feel like 'I can do this'. I do often find working easier than running around after the kids but I love the balance. Many times I will complain to my husband that 'I'm not doing either properly' and he'll remind me of something I have achieved like Zac's improvement in reading or a good sale we had at work and I think yeah. It's best not to think of what I'm not doing but rather what I am achieving.

I rely heavily on my mother and mother-in-law to help me with looking after the kids when I work as they come to me and have to start early and I often feel guilty as I know how tired they get. I am really lucky my kids have grandparents who love looking after them. As I'm so reliant on them for work I try not to bother them with other things like night functions—so often my husband and I will rotate the caring at night so we can work late or do functions— this means that we can go through periods where we don't see a lot of each other—which isn't fun. I have found that I only go to the bare minimum for work as I want to spend every last second with the family but sometimes it can't be helped!

> Nothing prepares you for the constantness.
> *– Sharine Ruppert, full-time mum, mother of four*

> I was overwhelmed by the drudgery, the monotony.
> *– Sue Vercoe, mother of two*

I'm not coping

This is your life: you're managing a baby, working three days a week, studying part-time and trying to occasionally smile at your partner. Your house is chaotic, you haven't had a haircut in over four months, you badly need your legs waxed and you feel unkempt, frumpy and desperately in need of some exercise. Then your son suddenly starts throwing up one morning and you have to stay at home because he can't go to childcare. You burst into tears, sit in a crumpled heap and have problems breathing.

> *I'm the first to admit that I have 'Mummy Meltdowns'. At times quite often. I don't cope very well when my husband, who works at a newspaper, has to go away on one of his many trips taking him interstate or overseas. In fact I dread it when he goes away. I can't pretend to be a wonder woman when I'm simply not. I get cranky with him, I get cranky with*

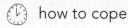

my kids and I just manage to keep my head above water and the house ticking over. Extras don't get done and it's difficult. That's just our reality. I'm still working out ways to cope better with all the juggling—and, I'm certain I'm not alone. I've gone to see counsellors, I've taken up yoga and I've learnt meditation. And none of it provides the perfect solution—I guess there just isn't one.

And I don't know a single working mother who doesn't find working, balancing children's needs alongside the interests of her and her partner's careers really, really hard. The thing for me has been to acknowledge my faults and to try to change them. Acknowledge that my life has changed—it's different now. Seek help when I need it. Learn some techniques to relax. Try to slow down when I can. Be in the now, the moment. Value the present with my children because that time can never be recaptured. Be realistic about what can be achieved every day. Schedule some 'me' time every week. And as my children get older and, hopefully, more rational, it may, just may, get a little easier (I hope). – Jo

66 Meltdowns—is this a pattern or a one off? What can I or my partner do to change this? Who can I call on to help me? Can I break this pattern?
 – *Feyi Akindoyeni, research director, mother of one*

We all have days like this (or at least we do). It's not a nervous breakdown exactly, but you have to get on top of it, otherwise you could descend further into the abyss. 'Losing it' is something we all do occasionally, but when it starts to get really bad we need to go into damage control—and seek help.

Here are a few of the things you might experience in your journey as a mum, and some thoughts on how to manage them.

Baby blues and postnatal depression

You may well have dealt with the baby blues just after you had your baby. A few days when, for no apparent or rational reason, you may have suddenly descended into floods of tears. This often coincides with when your milk 'comes in'. It feels different for everyone and affects between fifty to seventy per cent of new mothers. You can read more about this in Chapter 6 which covers your and your baby's health issues.

Postnatal depression is a whole different ball game. It affects around ten to fifteen per cent of new mothers in the first year of the baby's life and can be very serious. It can even happen beyond that first year. It may start with a woman's stress at trying to balance motherhood with work pressures, or from the lack of support from a partner. If you feel more than just a little down for more than a few days, it's important to seek the advice of a health professional, usually your GP as a first stop. Read more about it in Chapter 6.

Depression

Being a working mother will bring guilt and anxiety. Sometimes it's impossible to feel you're doing anything right or bringing anyone happiness—including yourself. Sometimes that anxiety will become a bigger demon that needs to be dealt with. Depression is not associated with bereavement or the result of taking drugs, that's different altogether.

If you are depressed, you may experience some or all of these symptoms:

- An inability to function normally

South East Essex College
of Arts & Technology
Luker Road, Southend-on-Sea Essex SS1 1ND
Tel:(01702) 220400 Fax:(01702) 432320 Minicom: (01702) 220642

how to cope   119

- Exhaustion

- Trouble sleeping or wanting to sleep all the time

- Overwhelming feelings of anxiety, depression or panic, irritation or apathy

- Suicidal or self-harming thoughts or plans

- Feeling frightened of social contact

- Feeling hopeless or helpless, guilt or a sense of failure

Whether it's 'postnatal' or just depression—badge it however you like—depression is very serious and you will need help to overcome it. Depression might not happen in the few months after you've had your baby—it can strike at any time. If you are concerned about depression, seek help. Talk to your doctor and reach out to your friends who've been there before you. You might be surprised how many women have experienced this disease. With support, therapy and at times medication, anxiety and depression can be treated effectively.

Being a new parent

> 66 **Anne Hollonds, from the counselling service at Relationships Australia, offers some advice for dealing with the wonderful, but often overwhelming, feelings of being a new parent.**
>
> Having a new baby is one of the hardest things you will do. And you have no way of knowing how you will feel because you've never done this before. So it's best to be open about it. Tell people you have no roadmap and you are finding your way.
>
> You may find people will offer their opinions anyway. Having a baby tends to make you public property and lots of people will have an opinion on your baby and your mothering skills.

It's helpful to have someone to talk to, but you need to find someone safe, someone you feel comfortable with and who you know won't judge you. That could be a friend or family member or it may be someone one step removed from you, such as your local clinic nurse or even a counsellor. It's important to find someone who will listen and not take over.

Just remember, if you're feeling overwhelmed by it all, chances are you are not the only one. Most women feel exactly what you are feeling.

Asking for help

Never be too proud to ask for help. You will probably have plenty of offers, so take them up! It's about developing a partnership with the people who want to lend a hand, be that your mum, mother-in-law or friends. The first step will probably have to come from you, but invite them over and give them a job. They will feel useful, you will be engaging their support and most importantly, getting the help you need.

Also by getting the jobs done in half the time, you will be able to goo and gaa over your baby as much as everyone else does!

Friends without kids

Like with any change preparation is the key. Tell your friends when you are pregnant that this new baby *is* going to take over your life. Tell them you value their friendship and that you don't want to lose them, and although the baby will be important for a while you will eventually emerge.

Be as direct as possible because if you leave things unsaid they will fill in the gaps with their own fantasies and probably expect the worst.

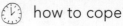

You might also want to tell them not to assume you only want to talk about the baby. Sometimes our friends can provide welcome relief from a day filled with nappies and dribble.

Emotions

Be open about the way you are feeling. Don't be ashamed to tell people if you are struggling or feeling sad.

Everybody goes through patches of feeling down and it's not necessarily postnatal depression. Your baby might be crying a lot, your husband or partner might not be as supportive as you expected and you might be feeling so many conflicting emotions.

It's important to talk about it, and not ignore these feelings. You need to take them all seriously, particularly if you suspect it's something more than the baby blues, and seek professional help.

Often there is a significant relationship element to deal with. It's not just about the mother and it being her problem. If you go to see a counsellor, do it together. That way your partner is aware of what you are going through. If your doctor tells you to get outside—exercise and get some fresh air for example—then your partner can be included or stay at home and mind the baby.

If you have had depression before you need to be aware that it might flare up. There is lots of help available, but people can't help you if you keep it to yourself.

Dealing with 'losing it'

If you, like us, start to seriously lose it one day with either your kids, your partner or just at home by yourself, here's some tips you may find helpful:

- Stop, breathe and reassess what you are doing
- Remove yourself. Put your baby in the cot so you know they're safe and go to another room where you can't

hear them scream. When you're calm and ready you can go back and comfort them

- Call a friend to come over to help
- Call a counselling service or hotline—they are in the phone book
- Lie down and have a nap if you can
- Have a long shower

Smacking

Smacking is something you're either for or against and is very often a last resort, sometimes something you do in frustration, and something a lot of us have done in anger. Current opinion is that smacking isn't a solution and that it provides a bad behavioural example to your child that hitting is okay. Try not to do it. If you find yourself resorting to it at all, or more often than you'd like, try some time out for the child (and you)—or put them in the now infamous 'naughty corner'. Even if they are young, try talking to them about what they've done wrong and why it's wrong, how they feel about it and how they've made others feel. It doesn't provide the immediate result that smacking can provide, but in the long term you'll build a better relationship with your child if you resist.

It's best to have a united front on this issue with your partner—if one of you smacks and the other doesn't the child will inevitably work this out. Talk about your approach to discipline before you get to the point of needing it. When they are little babies you're unlikely to need much discipline, just a whole lot of tolerance and love on your part.

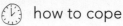

Seeking help

When things get bad and you really need to get outside help there are a number of ways to do it. Get a referral from your GP, call a local counselling or psychologist practice you know, or look up the phone book. Some people really are embarrassed about getting outside help—they feel it's an admission of failure, or that people will 'find out'. If you really are too embarrassed to sit down and talk to someone in person—or can't afford to—then call a counselling help line. They are *free* and *anonymous*—and they will listen!

Consider going to see a counsellor in person to talk through all the things that are worrying you—counselling services run by not-for-profit organizations are affordable and excellent value. And make sure you check out what government rebates are available which will reduce the cost.

Whatever you do don't suffer in silence for weeks, not coping and getting much worse. It's a hard first step but if you go and talk to someone about how you're feeling you'll end up being a whole lot better for it. You'll find that just talking will lighten the burden and help enormously. With the help of a professional counsellor or psychologist you can work through the problems and, eventually, sort them out.

Where to go for help?

If you don't know of anywhere to go for counselling or mental health support the first stop should be your doctor. Go and see them as a first stop. The federal government is now subsidizing counselling services, but you need a referral from your GP.

Call Relationships Australia who operate right across the country. It is a non-profit community-based organization providing professional services to support relationships (www.relationships.com.au 1300 364 277).

Do an Internet search for services that may be close to home—or look in the Yellow Pages.

> **For me, being a working mother** is extremely stressful, a lot of the time. I have a stressful job but I find being a mother even more so. Fantastic, but demanding. It's the descent into chaos that can't be controlled. It's the lack of personal space. It's the inability to rationalize with a small person. It's a battle of wills. It's the absence of time to myself. No time to read. No time to think. My stress levels rise and fall a lot. It depends largely on how much sleep I'm getting, how well I'm eating, how much I'm exercising, how much down time I'm getting—how nice I'm being to myself. I've found exercise is generally the key to undoing the stress at peak times. When I'm going into overdrive I know I've got to book some time off, make sure I go to yoga, try to get to the gym—take myself away from my kids and have a quick pedicure. I'm in no way athletic but exercise always helps.
>
> I know that some mums can cope with more 'face-time' with their kids than I can each and every week, in fact, they relish it. For me that just doesn't work. It makes me a worse mother. It makes me stressed. Something I'm happy to tell anyone who asks. So I work and I mother the best I can. In addition to weekends I have one day off a week to spend with my kids and work the other four. I try to get the stress levels under control. Try to balance it all as best as I can, which is pretty hard most of the time. But that's the best most of us can do. – **Jo**

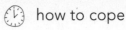

Coping with your return to work

Whenever you decide to return to work you'll be susceptible to guilt and anxiety. Guilt that you have to put the baby into childcare or leave them with a family member or nanny. Guilt because of the judgement of friends or family. Guilt that you should be there to share in the fun and the tantrums. That you may miss the very moment of your baby's very first steps.

But pulling at your heartstrings is the need to do something for your headspace, to breathe again, to feel a sense of achievement, to think—*to earn some money.* Managing that tug-of-war is the battle.

A few handy hints to help your return to work

- *Acknowledge the emotional stress* you're experiencing in going back to work. Talk to your partner about it. Talk to your girlfriends. Talk to a counsellor if you need to, but *talk.*

- You may still be breastfeeding when you go back to work and will need somewhere to *express and store breast milk.* Think about this before the first day so you have all you need with you to do the job—as well as a place to express. Talk to a few girlfriends who've done it before so you don't end up buying lots of expensive equipment and bottles that you'll never use.

- Be clear with your employer about what *new family responsibilities* you now have and what that might mean to your work life. Make it clear that you won't be staying back late as often but that you will be prepared to do work at home if it's needed.

- *Be flexible.* If you expect work to be flexible for you then you need to be flexible. Being able to be contacted via mobile or email out of hours will help.

- Get everything *organized for you*—in advance. Get your hair cut and, if you can afford it, something new to wear to work. Get a diary if you need one and anything else you'll need. Don't obsess about getting fit and losing weight right now, you've got enough on your plate. There will be time to do that later.

- Get things *organized for your baby*. Make sure you have supplies of whatever you'll need for your baby's carer or childcare provider—that may include nappies, sheets, formula or supplies of breast milk or solid food. They'll need a bag that will hold multiple changes of clothes, a sun hat and something warm in case it gets cold.

Single parents

Coping as a single parent brings a whole new dimension to the work–life balance thing. You have to do everything—or arrange others to do it for you. There are lots of groups and resources specifically focussed on helping single parents:

Parents Without Partners www.pwp.org.au

The Single Parent Bible provides resources and dating for single parents www.singleparentbible.com.au

The Single Parent Family Association website is at www.singlewithchildren.com.au

Being healthy

Yep, it's hard and yep there's no time, but it's just as important as before or during your pregnancy that you keep healthy, eat well, and do some exercise. Sorry to lecture. Exercise, post-baby weight loss and diet—it's all your choice and sometimes dependant on how much support you have (from family, friends and partner), on how much cash, or how much time you have and how busy

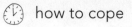

work is. But the sensible voice in our ear will tell all of us that doing some exercise every week, eating healthily and not carrying too much weight will make us feel better, less stressed and better able to cope with the pressures of balancing work and family.

Exercise

It's really important. Not just for post-baby toning—read more about that in Chapter 6—but to help keep you sane. All the medical advice will tell you that exercise is good for you and will help manage your stress levels. Medical research points to it helping battle depression. Some people aren't into running or anything too heavy-duty. Find something you like, from walking, swimming, yoga or even a visit to the gym. It's more likely that you'll do it if you don't have to rely on someone else—or fork out lots of money. That said, do what works for you—if that's a weekly game of netball or tennis then great. If it's a twice weekly power walk with a girlfriend all the better—you get to gossip as you de-stress.

Whatever it is, try to do it as often as you can manage, once or twice a week if you can manage it. Get your heart beat up for twenty minutes or more, and get a bit sweaty. The adrenalin rush, the headspace—just some time away from the kids—will do you the world of good.

Food and diet

Once you've had a baby the concept of a 'proper diet' for you often flies out the window. You're spending so much of your time organizing every one else's life that there often isn't much time left for you and your partner. The temptation is often to 'snack' on the foods you give your children—biscuits, quick meals and even lollies—or pop a spoonful or three of their leftovers in your mouth because you're hungry. Do that every day for a while and watch the scales tip. First there's the battle you have trying to lose weight just after the baby—but then there's the battle trying to maintain an equilibrium longer term.

> **When I'd just had** my first child I developed bad mastitis that stuck with me for nearly three months. To deal with the discomfort I put my son into the stroller and walked up the street to my local shops and happily had coffee and cake almost each and every day. One of life's small pleasures I assured myself. But rather than losing any of the weight I'd gathered during the pregnancy more piled on. After I recovered from mastitis, the task to lose the weight was doubly hard. Second time around I opted for walks rather than a daily cake hit. I'm not delusional, and still haven't returned to my pre-pregnancy weight or shape, but at least I didn't gain an additional ten kilos. – **Jo**

Handy hints—staying healthy

Set some ground rules for you, your partner and your family:

- When you're on maternity leave going out to a café with your mother's group or girlfriends is often a welcome break from staring at your four walls. But be careful how many calories you might be consuming and consider opting for a coffee only rather than the cake each time. You'll thank yourself for it later.

- If you're opting for the cake a little more often than you'd planned to then put your baby in the stroller, go for a walk, pop up to the shops to get some groceries or do an errand—but walk. You'll probably find that the baby will fall asleep and you can walk in blissful silence! Good for the waistline and great for stress levels.

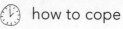

- Even though both parents work you should try to eat dinner as a family at least once or twice a week—if weekends are the only time you can manage it then so be it.

- Promise each other that you'll eat a proper meal as often as you can, plan ahead to have the ingredients in the house to prepare them and resist snacking or eating the children's leftovers.

- Keep a ready supply of fresh fruit and vegetables in the house, so you won't be tempted by your children's high-calorie snacks like dried fruits, fruit juice and chips.

- Have a plan when it comes to food for the week. Even go so far as devising a menu before you go shopping—it'll help you have a more balanced diet and save money. Think through what you'll have each night, write a shopping list and stick to it. Contemplate some vegetarian or non-meat dishes sometimes. You'll save money and eat more healthily.

- Make sure you've eaten before you set foot in the supermarket, otherwise you'll load the trolley up with rubbish you'll be depressed about later.

- Think about making larger batches of food, like pasta sauces, soups or stews and freezing them in smaller serving sizes so you have a week's supply of food. This is particularly easy during winter, but how many times have you come home and just snacked on rubbish or ordered pizza? Having something you can eat quickly that is healthy and doesn't cost a lot is a blessing!

'Mummy time'

Time for you is *so* important. We just can't emphasize how important it is. We can hear you say, loudly: 'I never get any' or 'I never get enough' or 'when?'. And to a huge extent it will depend on your support networks, whether you have a partner—or if s/he is a supportive one.

'Mummy time' can be something as simple as a half-hour daily walk, a bath once your children are in bed, two visits to the gym each week, a facial once in a while or a weekly yoga class.

Whatever it is you choose to do this time is *sacrosanct*—make it clear to your partner that this time is really important. If it involves you being away from the family make sure it's blocked out in the family calendar so your partner knows to keep time clear to be with the kids. Put it in both your diaries so it won't clash with anything else.

There needs to be a quid pro quo with this, of course, so you need to be available for 'Daddy time' as well!

Time out for Mum and Dad

Time out for both of you, together, is really important too. After months of sitting at home with a new baby it will amaze you to get out of the house and see people having fun and speaking to each other. If you can afford it, book in a babysitter regularly, say once a fortnight or monthly, to see a movie—or get the grandparents involved if they live close enough. It will be a revelation, we promise, and a great break from being at home every night.

It's important to remember that you both used to have a normal life talking about stuff before the baby came along. It is possible to have a night away from your child without talking about poo.

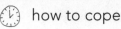

Sex—what sex?

Then there is the question of sex. How many times have you heard it said that after the birth of a baby it's all over as far as sex goes. Well, yes, it's true that there are physical demands that the baby's arrival will bring. And yes, it's also true that often it's the last thing on your mind for a while—but it's important that you and your partner work through this time to re-establish your intimacy together.

Often as women who juggle family and work we think we're invincible. We *can* do it all, we *can* have it all. And often in pursuit of this it is the relationship that matters the most to us—the one with our partner—that can suffer.

Order out of madness

We don't buy in to 'pregnancy brain', but life can get hectic when you're pregnant, working or after you return to work. It's important to at least *feel* that you have a grip on the world, even though you mightn't. One way of feeling in control is to make lists as you go, jotting down all the things you need to get done on a note pad dedicated for the purpose, or into a notebook or your diary. Don't get too anal about it—we can both recall moments of getting out of bed in the middle of the night to jot things on the list for fear they'd be forgotten in the morning.

But don't underestimate the importance of bringing a semblance of order to your otherwise disorderly life. It will free up your brain to do the important stuff like enjoy time with your children.

66 **We need routine** in our house in order to make it all work. Sometimes I feel like an army major, but it's the only way our family can manage, particularly with my crazy hours.

At work by 4.00 a.m., usually home by lunch time, school pick up, occasional afternoon sports—then the military precision kicks in. Dinner has to be underway by 4.30 p.m. and on the table by 5.00 p.m. I serve dessert just moments before the 5.30 p.m. conference call which buys me half an hour to discuss tomorrow's show with the team. After the first ten minutes of the six o'clock news it's bath time, stories for the kids and research briefs for me, then cuddles on the couch. Talia is in bed by 7.00 p.m., Nick at 7.30, clothes out for everyone for tomorrow, bag packed and off to bed myself.

Even as I write this I have to laugh at the organization of it all—I never used to be like this!

But ask any parent to pick the hardest part of their day and it will be the witching hour—and for me that has a very long phone call smack bang in the middle. Over the years I have wiped bottoms, cooked and fed spaghetti, scraped ice-cream off the floor, washed faces and shampooed hair, built Lego and dressed Barbie, all the while on the phone discussing global warming and footy tips. I think working mothers bring a whole new meaning to multi-tasking.

I have learnt the hard way that without order and planning it can all fall apart. And by the end of the day when I am as tired as they are, that can make for some emotional meltdowns. – **Mel**

" *I **used to work** in London with a woman who has gone on to become a very successful businesswoman and entrepreneur—and now a mother of three young children! I remember distinctly how Julia told me one day, before either of us had children, about the importance of 'list-making' and how it was the key to a successful woman.*

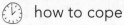

Her approach was to write a list of everything that needed to be done, crossing items off as things were achieved—and transferring any remaining tasks to the next day, so they'd all get done eventually.

I've never forgotten it, and pretty much adopt the same approach, jotting down things in my diary, and transferring them into the future so I know they'll get done, including stuff for the kids, work—anything, for that matter. – *Jo*

" *I remember to do things* at the strangest of times. I might be in a commercial break, or about to discuss welfare payments with the federal community services minister, when I suddenly think of the perfect present for that party on Saturday. I will be cleaning my teeth when that clanger of a question for the treasurer pops into my mind. I will be dozing off to sleep when suddenly the opening line for Friday night's speech takes shape in my head.

So I make lists. I have post-it notes everywhere. Little sticky yellow notes, in the car, beside my bed, on my desk, in the studio. My husband thinks I'm a complete scatter brain—but that's how my mind works. Anything and everything can run through my head when least expected. So I write it down. I have working friends who say focus is their biggest challenge—and especially when you first return to work. You try to concentrate on the job but your mind will wander. When is the next immunization due, I really should fertilize the garden and ring my aging aunt. Enter my lists! If I write it down immediately I can go back to what I was doing, safe in the knowledge that I won't forget to cook the chicken pastry triangles for my son's class Christmas party, or collect the dry cleaning or ring my girlfriend for her birthday. Now sorry Prime Minister, you were saying? – *Mel*

Outsourcing

No one imagines the huge change a baby brings. From a relative sense of calmness and order to complete anarchy—very quickly. Often a little, or a lot, of outsourcing is the only option to help restore order once you've gone back to work and time is precious. If both you and your partner work it's unlikely that you'll be able to do everything—manage the kids, work and keep your house as clean as you'd like it, the lawn mowed, or seeing an occasional movie that's not rated G. It's very probable that you'll need the occasional, or more regular, help of a babysitter, cleaner, gardener or nanny.

There's no reason to feel guilty about this. You're not lazy. You just have decided to throw some money at a problem that would otherwise create stress in your already hectic lives. Women of our mothers' generation who worked and balanced a family rarely sought such help—they'd think it just plain indulgence. Now families realize that it's often the best and only solution to maintaining their sanity.

And sometimes your partner mightn't understand the logic of your desire to have a cleaner—argue your corner and they'll come around.

How much money and how often will depend on your budget and how busy you are at work. Some homes with both parents working and children to juggle choose to have a range of help to get them through the week. This is a very personal decision and largely dependant on how much spare cash you have, balanced against how busy you are, and how important it is to you, and what you'll have to give up as a result.

" *Our cleaner comes once a week. Oh how I love that day. We wake up at 6.30 a.m., as we do each day, in a menagerie of craziness. Carefully negotiated breakfasts prepared for our*

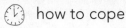

two-year-old daughter Frida, and five-year-old son Marlow. Associated guilt that they aren't eating properly. Nappies changed. Cartoons. A major feat not to get messy hands on my work clothes. Snatching a 'quick' shower that my husband argues is always at least fifteen minutes. Finding clothes. Negotiating drop-offs and pick-ups. Dealing with tantrums.

I return home on that day anticipating a state of Zen. When I walk through my front door my life resembles that of Princess Mary (I convince myself) for about a minute, though this is how it always is for her, all day, every day. New, crisp linen on the bed. Clothes neatly folded in washing baskets (well, Mary probably doesn't see the baskets). Mouldy food removed from the dark depths of our fridge. My pyjamas ironed! The assorted detritus of our lives in the lounge room diligently placed into ordered piles and placed out of sight. The floors cleaned. No human hairs on the bathroom floor. Wouldn't it be lovely if it could be like his every day? Dream on mummy.

Yes, financial compromises are made to have someone come and help us clean up our own mess, and yes we could do it ourselves and usually vacuum and/or mop the house ourselves at one stage during each week. But for our family, you just can't put a monetary value on it. We've decided that with both parents working because we enjoy it and need the income to pay the mortgage, we want to maintain our sanity, and spend the time we do get to spend together as a family without having to bother too much about household chores and have down-time together instead.

It's my once a week afternoon of bliss and I couldn't live without it now. I know that no matter how messy the house gets and how little time we have that it will be cleaned really well, and very professionally, that one time each week—and what a relief that is. – **Jo**

Time savers

- If you can afford to, have the dry cleaner wash and iron your husband's business shirts. Some even have a drive-through drop-off facility, or may pick up and deliver.

- Buy your groceries on the Internet. The first time takes the longest to set up your shopping list, but after that it's a breeze. And having them delivered to home is a godsend.

- Hang out a load of washing first thing in the morning— or even at night before you go to bed, then it's dry by the next afternoon.

- When you cook, make extra and freeze it. Instead of making one lasagne, make two.

- Freeze vast quantities of baby food. Mash vegies en masse and pack them into little sealed plastic pots. Or try freezing different ones into ice cube trays then you can easily mix and match.

Outsourcing—how to do it

To find paid domestic help—a nanny, cleaner, gardener or whatever—your options are to get a personal recommendation from friends or neighbours, use an agency which can be more expensive but is usually reliable, or to advertize yourself in the local paper (and you may get inundated with responses). However you do it, it's important to get references, particularly if they are looking after your children. Nanny/babysitting agencies usually carry out regular police checks on the staff they recruit which gives you peace of mind.

Whether it's a casual, more regular or permanent arrangement it's important to be clear on what's expected from the cleaner/ babysitter/nanny. For a cleaner, specify what jobs will be done

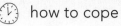

every time and what jobs done more infrequently. Can ironing or folding washing be included?

You need to pay the market rate, the agency rate or going price for the services. Undercutting paid help in your home undervalues the people you employ—basically it isn't fair—and you won't end up with the best people that way.

If you need to engage a nanny then you'll need to talk through what happens if you cancel them on short notice (are they paid?), how much notice you expect for time off, whether they will need holidays/public holidays. Generally, if you employ a nanny as a casual employee, you only need to pay for hours worked, and as a casual they are not entitled to paid sick leave or holidays. Domestic employees who do work for more than thirty hours a week need to be paid superannuation. You should also consider whether you need to deduct tax from any wages paid. The Australian Tax Office can give you information about your tax and superannuation obligations.

Once you've found a good babysitter keep them happy. Don't be stingy when it comes to payment, round up the money rather than paying exactly down to the minute. And be sure to leave some food and whatever magazines you have lying around when you go out. Go out as often as you can afford it, once a fortnight or a month is something to look forward to.

You should get domestic workers' insurance—this is relatively inexpensive and covers you for accidents any paid helpers may have in your home. Talk to your home insurer to see if they can arrange it for you.

66 **Kate McCabe, farm-based working mother of three**

As my babysitter leaves, I reflect on what has been a productive afternoon in our home office, but if I could just steal ten more minutes I could finalize that report. With my three young children contentedly playing, half an hour races by until I observe a precarious silence from my two-year-old. She strides up the hallway, proudly asserting, 'I go swimming Mummy', with sunscreen smeared head to toe and bearing her towel which she had located at the bottom of the basket overflowing from the last three days washed laundry having never quite found their homes. As I contemplate rewashing piles of sunscreen-coated clothing, I agonize over the emotional tug-of-war I feel everyday, searching for the perfect balance of allocating time for children, work, running an efficient household, husband, friends and myself.

Work is an outlet for me rather than a means of furthering my career prospects. My role is a far cry from the corporate world I envisaged during my university days, but it still provides me with some level of mental stimulus and sense of achievement. The flexibility of working from home, either at night or with a babysitter supervizing, allows me to be present to attend to my children's ever changing needs, during this short period of their preschool years.

While initially reluctant to engage hired help, in the form of cleaners and babysitters, they are now an essential part of our routine, and no longer feel intrusive. While formal childcare centres are not easily accessible in the country, reliable babysitters are, and close-knit communities mean you have first-hand knowledge of potential employees. Our location also enables us to rely heavily on family support from both sets of grandparents.

For me, maintaining a high level of fitness is absolutely imperative. It ensures I have energy to sustain busy days, refreshes my mind and enhances my multi-tasking capabilities. Living in the country, running has been the most time efficient way to keep fit and I aim to exercise three to five times per week.

Self expectations and standards need to be reassessed. An untidy house has become tolerable. Entertaining no longer involves deliberating over pages of *Gourmet Traveller* but rather, friends have learnt to expect the same roast beef on the Webber accompanied by an outsourced dessert.

The most beneficial 'me' time can come from the most unexpected sources. While I look forward and plan well in advance for a child-free shopping day in the city, I return home exhausted and frustrated at how little I've achieved. In contrast, after a weekly social basketball game (of which I have very limited ability) with girls of very different ages and interests, I come home from completely refreshed. The perfect ingredients for me being: physical exertion, social interaction, getting out of the house and expectation free.

A supportive partner

We all need a supportive partner, although some are obviously more helpful than others. We are both very lucky and acknowledge that we couldn't do what we do without our husbands.

Gone are the days when the men would come home, put their feet up and wait for dinner, whether their wives had also been at an office all day or managing the house and caring for five children.

Families today are built on partnerships and it's up to every couple to negotiate the right balance and make it work for them.

" *In her book*, What, No Baby? *Australian academic Dr Leslie Cannold says we need more of what she calls 'gorgeous men' in order for women to be able to achieve a better work–life balance. These are men who are happy and proud to leave work in time to pick up their children from childcare or after-school care, resist working on weekends, do the shopping, change lots of nappies—and push through the workplace stigma attached to these decisions.*

I'm married to one. I proudly claim that he's done more nappies than I ever will, folds the washing and does the garbage (while I pay the bills and do the shopping). He takes one day off a week to be at home with our youngest and works a Sunday night shift to make up the time—it hasn't impacted on his career and is in fact the sort of behaviour that is the norm rather than the exception at his company.

As I tell anyone who asks me why I've gone back to work '. . . my husband hasn't given up working because we had a child so why should I?' We're a team (well, most of the time!). We're both busy, we both work, both do other things. Support each other.

I work for a small global consultancy firm where 'gorgeous men' also proliferate. Colleagues who are also fathers all do their equal share of domestic work, share the collection of their children from childcare, take days off to look after sick kids. It doesn't mean endless days off work or slacking or not pulling their weight—sometimes it means that work is done late at night when children are sleeping.

Doing an equal share is as it should be, and male colleagues (or women for that matter) aren't held back for it and nor has it impacted on the company's bottom line. – **Jo**

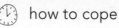

> *Andrew, Jo's husband:*

Somewhere in my distant memory—very much in the past—there is a recollection of a life before children. Back then it seemed to be all about me. My time was devoted to personal pursuits, be it work, travel or late nights out. The future was abundant and the present very much focussed on my desires.

Then the baby arrives.

With a beautiful wail our son took his first breath and I held him in my arms. Staring into Marlow's eyes I could feel my old life crumbling and a wonderful new life begin. The future had arrived and I promised myself to savour the present, the moment, the now.

Late nights out are replaced by late nights in, soothing Mum and our two children. I still need to perform at my best for work and somehow fit travel in, but my real desire these days is not so much about what I am going to do but rather acknowledging the present. Kid time is now blurred with my time. It really is true, they grow up fast and I don't want to miss it.

When I am at work I am focussed on what needs to be done and I strive for it. But I must also keep an eye on the clock. Our childcare options impose strict penalties for late pick-ups and there have been many evenings when I have felt deserving of a parenting medal as I successfully managed both work and childcare deadlines with seconds to spare.

Once home, United Nations-style negotiations (some-times with helmet and flak jacket) commence to organize dinner, bath and bedtime. Games are played, stories are read and silence finally envelops the house.

The pre-dawn cry of 'Dada' forces me from my new favourite hobby—sleeping—and signals the start of the morning shift: breakfast, getting dressed, organizing lunches, and heading out the door on time. Simple tasks I know, but just you wait.

Life often disrupts the routine. We talk things through as parents, not just as partners, we plan, we cajole, we chastise. Promises are made and broken, compromises are met and we somehow manage to work things out.

I even squeeze in the odd late night out, but the chance of a well-deserved sleep-in remains a distant memory.

Who's on your team?

When it's all crumbling around you and you're struggling to see how you're going to get out of the vortex, then think about who you can turn to:

One of your best girlfriends. These are the people who you can tell you're going mad and who won't judge you. Just disgorging this from the system will make you feel better, trust us. We're lucky when we find a kindred spirit and these friends should be nurtured at all cost! With any luck, you'll both be cooing over photos of your respective grandchildren in decades to come.

Family. It's sometimes a bit tricky, to be honest, even to ask for help from immediate family for fear you'll be judged. If you could do with some babysitting, so you can get out for a few hours, and if there is a willing family volunteer, take them up on their offer, even if you don't tell them how bad things really might be. They may guess, but will be unlikely to pry too far. But remember, often they've been there before and understand how difficult things can be to manage. Read more about turning to family for childcare in Chapter 7.

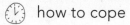

She'll turn up with a bottle of a wine and a barbecue chicken just when the afternoon has fallen into a screaming heap and you're having a bigger meltdown than the children. She'll whisk you out for a good power walk on a Sunday morning when she instinctively knows you need to escape for an hour. Or she'll let you borrow her babysitter, and she'll always cook extra when she's baking.

Motherhood can bring out the best or worst in women. There are those who make it a major competition—whose baby walked at six months, read at eighteen months and reel in horror when you admit to using a cake mix—then there are those who throw out a lifeboat as we ride together through the storm in the night. The latter are worth their weight in gold.

Never before have we so needed someone we can talk to—warts and all. In motherhood you will come to value your girlfriends in a way you never have before. A girlfriend is someone who won't judge you, who'll just listen with sympathy. Someone you can ring in a flood of tears when you can't handle babies, husbands or families and she'll tell you it's okay. She has advice when you want it, understanding when you don't. She might be from your childhood, or life after your baby—you might be lucky enough to have a few.

Be there for her as much as she is there for you. Life gets busy and we don't always see our friends as much as we used to or want to—but we can always manage to pick up exactly where we left off.

We can't parent alone—it's difficult and not nearly as much fun. **– Mel**

Resources list

- Parents Without Partners: www.pwp.org.au
- Relationships Australia: www.relationships.com.au
- A great Australia wide online resource is www.kidspot. com.au.
  It details literally hundreds of sites categorized by state with information about activities, parties, food, toys, sourcing equipment and clothes. Every resource or retailer you'll ever need to locate is here.
- A great Australia-wide site to help you locate a babysitter is: www.findababysitter.com.au.

✳ How to cope—handy hints

- Recognize that working and having children is stressful and will bring anxiety. Finding a successful work–life balance is really really hard.
- Discuss with your partner the whole co-parenting issue. It's essential to find the right balance for you both, given the changing needs of your growing family.
- Learn to live in the moment. Enjoy life. Enjoy your family time and your work time.
- Read some self-help books to inspire you.
- Do some exercise every week.
- Recognize when you need help for anxiety or depression—and seek it out.
- Talk to a good friend about how you're feeling, and the challenges of work and family.
- Take some time-out—have some 'Mummy time'.
- Consider outsourcing some domestic chores like cleaning, ironing or gardening if you have the cash.
- Find a regular babysitter and go out occasionally.

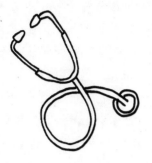

chapter 6

health—you and your baby

In this chapter:

- Checks and vaccinations.
- Breastfeeding—what suits you and how to manage it when you return to work.
- Sex and contraception.
- Getting enough sleep—for baby and you.
- Exercise and weight—what is realistic and what isn't.
- Baby blues—what's normal and what's postnatal depression.
- What clinic services are available to help you.

Having a baby is one of the most physically and emotionally demanding things you will ever do.

When you have your baby, naturally most of the attention is focussed on your little one—but don't ignore your own health and the need to get your strength back, preferably before you return to work. You will struggle to get enough sleep, and it will take a while to get back to feeling like 'you' again—don't compound these issues by ignoring your own wellbeing.

There are many professionals who will help you, from your doctor or midwife to your clinic nurse and physiotherapist. Not for one moment do we profess to have any medical knowledge, but from experience we do know birth is tough on your body no matter how smoothly your labour may have gone and how exhilarated you feel. It will take some time to recover, particularly if you had a caesarean. So be kind to yourself. You will be exhausted, you will most probably be pretty sore, you will have tender breasts as your milk comes in and as you get used to breastfeeding. You may be emotional, even teary. Just as your body was telling you to slow down in the weeks leading up to the birth, it will probably dictate the pace for the next few weeks as well.

Health checks and vaccinations

Both you and your baby will be advised to have a number of tests. The nurses in hospital or your midwife will guide you through some of the early ones. Your baby will have the Newborn Screening Test which checks for congenital problems, the first of the prescribed immunizations and a dose of Vitamin K before they leave hospital. The next vaccinations are suggested when your baby is two months old, then four, six, twelve and eighteen months, four years, mid-teens and late teens.

If you want your son circumcised, you will need to find a doctor who performs this operation as many don't. Nor do some hospitals. It's a good idea to discuss this with your partner before you give birth so you are both clear on your position. If you do want to go ahead, it's not widely done in the first few days after birth anymore. It is regarded as a surgical procedure and is more commonly done during the first year. You should talk to a member of the paediatric staff before you leave hospital.

Handy hint—immunization allowance

The federal government pays every family an immunization allowance of a few hundred dollars. To receive it you need to provide proof to Centrelink that you have all your baby's immunizations up to date before they turn two, and provide your Medicare number. Check with Centrelink about how you can register to get the allowance.

Breastfeeding—how to know what's right for you and how to get help

Breastfeeding can take some getting used to. It doesn't come naturally for all women and nor is it the pain-free serene experience that you might imagine. Each feed can take a long time and for many women it can hurt, at least initially.

At best, you and your baby will get it together from the first moment and it will be a comfortable, natural experience. At worst you could develop sore cracked nipples or get mastitis.

We all know it's good for your baby, particularly in the first few weeks, and nurses suggest you give it a go for at least six weeks. There is a lot of help available. Your midwife will be a great source of information as will your local clinic nurse. You can also hire private lactation consultants who can come into your home. The Australian Breastfeeding Association has counsellors available by phone twenty-four hours a day.

But as with every part of having a baby, be prepared to adapt and ask for help. For some women, breastfeeding just doesn't work for them no matter how hard they try and how much guilt and pressure is lumped on them. Others can be surprised at how smoothly it goes.

66 Get as much help as possible. Even pay for advice if you have to.
    – *Catriona Dixon, mother of two*

66 I saw a lactation consultant. If you need help, get it.
    – *Sue Vercoe, mother of two*

66 If you were a man and you wanted to learn to play golf you'd hire a golf pro!
    – *Feyi Akindoyeni, mother of one*

Deciding to do what feels right for you can be hard because this is such uncharted territory, and you will feel pressure from most medical professionals to persevere. You will also obviously want to do what is best for your baby. But a happy, healthy and unstressed mother is more important than anything else.

66 **Katrina Hobday, full-time mum, mother of one**

I, like many mothers, knew the benefits of breastfeeding but I, like many mothers, had trouble. When my son was born I spent the first week in constant tears and felt like I was failing my baby because I wasn't giving him the best. My family finally convinced me that a happy mum is just as important and I decided to bottle feed with expressed milk (for at least the beginning weeks). This enabled me to relax and with a bit more persistence I was able to breastfeed, although feeding remained my biggest concern with being a first-time mum and it wasn't until my son was two months old that I was finally happy with our feeding technique. I live in a rural area and found help was limited. I want other mums to know that something that seems so natural isn't easy and a happy mum is just as important.

> *I had problems breastfeeding exclusively with both my children as my supply wasn't enough to allow them to gain the weight they needed. With Frida this was worse and she began to lose weight fairly rapidly. I persisted for over two weeks with a gruelling regime of first feeding, then expressing to stimulate supply and provide her with more milk. Each feed took close to two hours and left little time for anything else including sleep—driving me mad and making me stressed. So I combined the breast with formula bottle feeds almost from the start. With both children this had the benefits of helping them sleep better (formula is said to be heavier), gain weight normally, and allow me some flexibility I might not have had if I had solely breastfed. It wasn't what I had wanted to do, but hey, it was my only choice, and once I stopped bashing myself up about it I knew it was okay. – Jo*

> I remember the agony of my milk coming in. No one tells you how much it hurts. I had a shelf of bosom!
> *– Sharine Ruppert, mother of four*

> I sat in bed topless, I was in so much pain.
> *– Sue Vercoe, mother of two*

66 **Voula Serbos, marketing manager, mother of two**

I had intended to breastfeed my first child, Isabella, but it just didn't go the way it was meant to. My milk didn't come in until day eight which meant for the first few days my baby was hungry and cranky, so my paediatrician suggested supplementing her with formula. In the meantime we kept trying. She was sucking so hard she was making me bleed profusely, but still no milk came. The midwives tried to stimulate my flow and I was hooked up to machines, but still no milk, just blood. It was very unsettling and very emotional and I was forced to stay longer in hospital.

Day six came and I was sitting there that evening, still trying, still hooked up to the machine and still no milk when I just lost the plot. The nurse came to check on me and in a flood of tears I told her 'I can't do this' and she said 'Honey you don't have to'. So she took me off the machine, told me everything would be okay and put Isabella on full formula.

So with my second baby, Yasmine, I was not prepared to return to that trauma. I told everyone when I went into hospital that I had no intention of breastfeeding, it was even written on my birth plan. I was given a tablet to dry up any milk. This time I felt relaxed, in control and completely at ease. The nurses were supportive. All they wanted to know was which way I wanted to go. Because I said I wanted to breastfeed first time around, they persevered and tried to do all they could to make it happen for me. So the second time, when I said no, they were all okay with it. I always thought you had to breastfeed, but it's not always the best solution for every woman.

Breastfeeding and working

Now is the time to start thinking about whether or not you want to continue breastfeeding after you return to work and how you will manage it. You have a couple of options—you can feed your baby entirely with your milk, by expressing during the day and feeding that milk to your baby via a bottle when you are not there. Or you can opt for a combination of breast milk and formula, maybe feeding your baby when you are with them and using formula at other times.

❝❝ **Kerrie Goodwin, clinical nurse specialist**

The older your baby is when you return to work, the more success you will have if you continue breastfeeding. Once they are about six months old, your baby won't need as many feeds and should have a routine established which will make it all much more manageable. It's also easier for you if you miss the occasional feed, particularly if you go back to work part-time.

What you do and where you work will also influence your plans. You may simply not be able to slip away and express milk privately or comfortably for your baby, nor have enough time in your day. On the other hand, your workplace may be flexible enough to allow you the required space and time, or you might work from home.

One other thing you will need to take into account if you are feeding during work hours is that some babies take their time over meals. You could be occupied for up to an hour, but then again dinner may be over in twenty minutes!

> *I returned to work when Talia was ten weeks old. My seemingly awful hours actually proved a blessing in this regard. I weaned her onto a bottle of formula for the 7.00 a.m. feed about a week before I went back, knowing that would be the one feed I would miss and to give my body enough time to adapt. I didn't want leaks on air! I would breastfeed her at 3.00 a.m., shower and leave for work at 3.30 a.m. It worked pretty well except the odd morning when she would sleep past 3.00 a.m.*
>
> *What would be a blessing for most mums saw me pacing the lounge room, bursting at the seams. And Murphy's Law is such that the moment I had finished expressing she would wake up. Anyway, I'd host Sunrise from 6.00 a.m. to 9.00 a.m., then make it home just in time for the 11.00 a.m. and subsequent feeds. Luckily for both of us we had a good routine going as this was our key to managing. I did a bit of travelling in the months immediately after returning to work and managed to express the excess milk as I didn't want to affect my supply. But I did find this the toughest part. As one who produced an abundance of milk, one skipped feed and I was in agony.*
>
> *I am thankful I was one of the lucky ones for whom breastfeeding came naturally. Both of my children were super guzzlers and, if anything, I initially worried they weren't getting enough, given the average feed was over in ten minutes. But they both grew like weeds and my clinic nurse assured me they were just not ones for wasting time.* – **Mel**

Where to get more information?

The body responds amazingly to demand and supply. The less you feed your baby, the less milk you will produce over time, and vice versa.

There are shelves of great books out there to help you. We swear by Robin Barker's *Baby Love*—apart from everything you need to know about the first years of your baby's life, it also has some great information regarding feeding and managing.

You can also get plenty of information from the Australian Breastfeeding Association and your local clinic nurse.

" *I found the key to managing was to establish a routine as soon as possible, and I more or less let my babies determine it. On a piece of paper I would note down the time of every feed and the time and duration of each sleep. Over a few weeks a pattern would begin to emerge and this gave me an indication of when my little ones were at their hungriest and when they tended to sleep the best. This let me structure my day around them—keeping both of us happy. My two children responded well to routine and still, to this day, it's the only way we manage.*

Oh and one other tip—if you alternate breasts for each feed wear a bracelet or a ribbon around your wrist that you can swap easily to remind you. You may laugh now—but trust me, your memory will fail at 2.00 a.m. after only two hours' sleep. – Mel

Mastitis and nipple care

Mastitis is an infection in the milk ducts in the breast. It usually enters your system via a cracked nipple, develops rapidly and can leave you in agony. You need to treat it immediately, usually with antibiotics, and if you do so it calms down quite quickly. Your doctor will advise you on the best course of action.

You can continue to breastfeed even through severe mast-ititis, but some women do give up and go onto the bottle. This is best discussed with your GP before you decide which way to go because to stop feeding can make the mastitis even worse. It can be of particular concern when you return to work and may find yourself missing the odd feed, as it's usually caused by a blocked duct or poor drainage. Some women are simply more prone to it than others and may find it recurs. Good hygiene and washing your hands a lot during the day minimize the likelihood of contracting mastitis.

When breastfeeding you also need to be aware of proper breast care, so you can avoid things like cracked nipples. It's an old fashioned remedy but women still swear by it—rub a little of the milk at the end of the feed onto the nipple and let it dry naturally. There are also a number of different creams available from the chemist, but talk to your doctor or nurse. They may recommend a nipple shield to help you feed if you have severe cracking—a plastic cover that protects your nipple, but still allows your baby to feed.

66 **I got mastitis** in the first week after the birth of both my children. With my first child I tried to treat it naturally and followed the advice of a doctor who suggested applying cold cabbage leaves. But for me this remedy, which often works wonders for many, was used too late, the infection had already taken hold.

I ended up taking about twelve courses of antibiotics in a row and having the puss in my breast drained by a breast surgeon three times (I won't go in to any more details). The antibiotics I was first prescribed didn't get it, and it wasn't until the breast surgeon ordered a biopsy of the infected puss that they determined what medication was needed to get rid of the infection. It went on for four months—I kept breastfeeding throughout the ordeal as I was determined not to give up—put on some weight as the only solace

I had from the constant discomfort was a daily coffee (and cake) at my local café.

*With my second baby I noticed the readily-identified redness and lumpiness in the first week. Within the hour I was at the doctor's door demanding the strongest antibiotic available. It was gone within forty-eight hours and nipped in the bud, thankfully. – **Jo***

Breastfeeding is different for every mum—for some it's simple and natural, for others it's difficult and heartbreaking. However you decide to feed your baby, do it calmly and with advice. If breastfeeding works for you, it can be the most wonderful bonding experience between mother and child, but if it doesn't you need to do what keeps you both happy and healthy.

If possible, just try to sort it out before you return to work for both your sake and your baby's. When you return to work you will need to give your body time to adjust to any changes and you will want your baby settled too. Get them used to drinking from a bottle as early as possible, even if it's with your milk. You don't want a baby rejecting a bottle the first time you leave them in someone else's care. That's an added stress neither of you need. You'll find more about managing breastfeeding and working in Chapter 8.

*I **decided to return** to work earlier than I planned with Frida, my second baby, when she was just three and a half months. Work was busy, I needed the stimulation and I was only going back two days a week—a perfect combination to help my sanity and stem the boredom of being at home seven days a week. As she was still being breastfed multiple times a day—and I had decided to go back early only two weeks before I returned—I faced the decision of* *weaning, which for me wasn't an option, or expressing a number of times each day. So as we didn't have a private room at work, I did a combination of expressing twice a day and popping home to feed her, as I luckily lived only a short drive from my office. The guilt was a lot less the second time around, we engaged a temporary nanny for two days a week until we could get a childcare place, and Frida coped well. – **Jo***

Sex and contraception

Breastfeeding is *not* a form of protection against pregnancy. So remember, you can conceive the moment you have unprotected sex. Most doctors suggest you delay intercourse until after you have been given the all clear at your six-week check-up. At this point you can talk about contraception and what will suit you best, particularly if you are breastfeeding. If you are keen to get things started prior to this time, talk to your doctor or nurse before you leave hospital.

If a woman has experienced a particularly severe tear during childbirth, she can develop pain with intercourse for a few months and very occasionally a fistula, an infected abscess, between her vagina and bowel. Your doctor will check the healing at your six-week check-up, but problems can still develop after this when you have intercourse. Always check anything that doesn't feel right. Don't be embarrassed or think you are the only one who has experienced difficulties.

Sleep

If you used to think staying out late with friends made you tired—you ain't felt nothing yet.

For most new parents, it's all about sleep, or the lack of it. Mums and dads with newborns have a sort of exhausted, desperate look in their eyes that we all recognize. Unless you're one of the few lucky ones, you will never have enough sleep. You will feel tired for the next few years and if you are about to return to work that can be a real worry, particularly if you operate heavy machinery, or need to smile and be nice to people.

A lack of proper sleep is also one of the reasons your baby may be unsettled and crying, so this can really become a vicious cycle for all concerned. With babies' brains taking in three times as much in that first year as any other year, it's no wonder they need their rest.

Obviously, trying to get your baby into a sleep routine as soon as possible will help—but every baby is different. Some sleep all night from the word go, others take years. Sorry!

Handy hint—sleep and noise

Keep the noise levels around your house normal. The more babies learn to sleep in a normal environment in the early days the better. A completely silent home is never sustainable.

If the lack of sleep is getting the better of you, seek some help early on. Remember you're not alone in this and help is available. You can start with your local baby health clinic. Some run settling classes that might be of help, or even chat to your clinic nurse and ask for their advice.

There are organizations which offer telephone helplines in each state, such as Tresillian or Karitane in New South Wales, and Mothercraft Home service in the ACT. Tresillian have a national twenty-four-hour advice line available (1800 637 357) who will answer your emotional phone calls in the middle of the night. They also provide centres with trained staff where you can literally move in for a few days while they try to help sort you and your baby out. Don't leave it for twelve months if you need help. Seek help early and get some sleep!

There are also plenty of books available, sleep experts who will move into your home and whole websites devoted to this one issue. There are also private mothercraft nurses who will stay with you for a few hours through to a few days, depending on your need and what you can afford. You can locate these through your baby health clinic.

Contact your local hospital, GP or baby health clinic to see what is available in your area.

Use whatever help you need. Don't be afraid to call out for help. If someone asks if they can do anything for you, ask them to sit with your baby for a while so you can have a nap, or better still, do one night on duty, because without sleep you will find it hard to function, cope or even survive.

How to get your baby to sleep (so you can sleep too)

Sheyne Rowley, baby sleep expert, offers some advice.

1. Work with their body

Work out your child's individual sleep needs by keeping a diary for at least a week and working out the average sleep they need over a twenty-four-hour period. Your six month old may need thirteen hours a day, while another may need sixteen. Based on this, you can adopt a routine to suit your baby's actual needs and prevent cat napping during the day and night waking.

2. Lock it in Eddie

Establish consistent waking and settling times each morning and night. This way you are not creating a sleep debt by providing compensation sleep-in after a poor sleep session.

3. Positioning for success

Teach them to lie down and be still. Excessive rocking, jiggling, patting, pacing or swinging a baby while they are awake can create an over-dependence on perpetual motion, and prevent them from falling asleep independently.

4. Cot play

When a baby has difficulty settling, parents put them into their cot after they have fallen asleep, or stay with them until they fall asleep. When they wake up and find they are alone they cry and usually get picked up again, so the only associations they then develop with their cot are unpleasant. In order to learn how to fall asleep on their own, they must first learn how to be in their cot awake. So make time for cot play, open the curtains, turn on the light and provide toys for them to enjoy. Stay with them initially but gradually practice leaving the room using a short-term absence cue such as 'I'll be back' and a big smile. This will help them get used to you leaving the room when they need to put themselves to sleep.

5. Transferable sleep routines

Develop a little sleep routine with verbal cues that your baby recognizes. Sleep time is a vital part of you preparing to return to work. Establish a relaxing ritual that your baby's new carer can easily imitate so baby's sleep conditions stay predictable when you aren't there.

6. Catering to their needs

It's natural for a baby to become dependent on a set of conditions to fall asleep, but if you become their only sleep association (rocking, patting, feeding) then your baby will be forced to call on you every time they need to go to sleep and this can mean an overtired baby and mother.

7. Making sleep snuggly

The ideal temperature of a baby's room is nineteen to twenty-two degrees celsius. For the first twelve months, most babies need to sleep swaddled in light clothing or a sleeping bag. Day sleep and the final night cycle from 4.00 a.m. onwards are their coldest sleeps, so ensure they are dressed in appropriate sleepwear as a child under two is unable to keep bedding on them for warmth. Hormones and adrenaline mean the initial night sleep is their warmest, so keep the bath at a pleasant temperature without overheating them and don't place extra blankets on until you go to bed. Setting a heater timer to come on for an hour at 3.30 a.m. to take the chill out of the room is also useful on cooler nights.

8. Beware of light

Our body is tuned to respond to the sun and light naturally. If your child is having a difficult time going to sleep, or staying asleep, block out excess stimulation such as light.

9. Balance their nutrition

The right dietary balance will make a big difference to your child's sleep. If they are refusing solids because they are having too many milk feeds, they won't sleep as well. Low iron levels, vitamin deficiencies and too much sugar will also have an impact.

10. Play that dreams are made of

Provide a day rich in challenging developmental floor play with age appropriate toys and discovery opportunities to promote great sleep.

11. Days to promote sleep

The best pattern is a busy, stimulating morning of play at home with a good nap, then a relaxed and enjoyable afternoon out. This will promote better night-time sleep.

For more detailed advice see Sheyne's website, www.australian babywhisperer.com.au. She also has a book coming out in 2008.

Your health

Every baby needs a healthy mother. So as well as trying to get enough sleep, don't forget to take care of yourself. Don't let going back to work and juggling a busy timetable distract you from looking after your health as well as your baby's.

Always talk to your local doctor or nurse if something doesn't feel right.

Brace and sneeze

There are a few health issues that new mothers face—and obviously these need to be discussed with your doctor or nurse. One of them is urinary incontinence where any exertion such as laughing or sneezing can cause leakage. This can be a problem if you have had a few children close together. The World Health Organization recommends that for a woman to maintain her optimum health she wait one year between giving birth and conceiving the next child.

If incontinence is a problem for you talk to your doctor and they will probably refer you to a physiotherapist or local women's health centre to get information and instruction in pelvic floor exercises.

But even before you leave hospital, you'll probably find that the one exercise your doctor or nurse will talk about is one that strengthens your pelvic floor muscles. This is particularly important in the early days after giving birth. If you are having trouble working it out, a physiotherapist can help.

Exercise after childbirth

Physiotherapist Liz Millard has written the following guidelines for exercise after childbirth:

Returning to your normal level of fitness after having a baby is important, but it must be done gradually.

Pelvic floor exercises can be started straight after the birth. Gentle walking is okay, but leave other exercise until after the six-week check-up with your doctor. It is fine to go swimming in salt water, but avoid chlorinated pools for the first six weeks especially public ones because of the small risk of infection. Remember some people wee in pools!

If your stomach bulges down the middle when you raise your head or try to sit up, it means your stomach muscles have separated. If this happens, practice pulling your stomach muscles towards your spine and holding for a few seconds without moving your back to help bring the muscles back together. Avoid sit-ups for six weeks to let your stomach muscles come back together.

Check with your doctor first, but most sports can be commenced six to eight weeks after a normal vaginal delivery or two to three months after a caesarean.

Pelvic floor exercises

The pelvic floor muscles are a sling of muscles running from the pubic bone to the tailbone. They help support your bladder, uterus and bowel and assist in control of the bladder and bowel.

Pregnancy and childbirth can weaken these muscles, which may lead to an inability to fully control the bladder and bowel. During pregnancy some fifty per cent of women are likely to have bladder leakage if they cough or sneeze (stress incontinence), and some of those will be unlucky enough to have that continue after the birth. That is why it is important to start your pelvic floor exercises as soon as possible after the birth.

How do I do pelvic floor exercises?

Sit or stand and tighten the muscles around your urethra, vagina and anus as if you were trying to stop yourself from passing urine or wind. As you tighten, lift upwards and inwards with the muscles around your vagina and at the same time draw in your lower stomach muscles. Hold for several seconds—up to ten seconds, ten times in a row. Don't hold your breath.

An easy way to remember to do them is to do ten at a time when the opportunity arises (for example, watching television, standing up in the kitchen, feeding your baby, stopping at the traffic lights, and so on). Nobody knows you are doing them.

Remember that if you don't use it you lose it, so you have to make it a daily habit.

Watch your back!

The effect of pregnancy hormones combined with your changing body shape act to weaken the back and stomach muscles. This can cause back pain. For this reason it is important to start strengthening your stomach muscles after six weeks and maintain good posture in order to look after your back and prevent injury.

Be careful with lifting anything heavier than your baby. Always keep your back straight and bend your knees. When changing your baby stand or kneel to keep your baby at waist height e.g. on the kitchen bench or washing machine.

When feeding your baby, sit in a comfortable chair with a pillow behind your back for support and a pillow under your baby to bring the baby to breast height.

Remember, at six weeks you are only about ninety per cent physically recovered. After six months there will be no further improvement. What you see is what you get. This also applies to other problems such as haemorrhoids, varicose veins and back pain. So if you are still experiencing back pain or stress incontinence that has not eased since the birth of your baby, see your GP first and then contact a physiotherapist.

Handy hint—pelvic floor exercises

Buy a packet of coloured sticker dots and put them in places where you will be standing for any length of time, such as above the sink or in the laundry. They will remind you to tighten your pelvic floor.

The baby blues

Finally, but possibly most importantly, don't forget your emotional wellbeing. Eighty per cent of us will get the baby blues. For some it strikes right on cue on day three after the birth where you find yourself crying for no apparent reason. You may find yourself in tears on and off for weeks as you adjust to your new role and your hormones adjust to theirs. We talked more about this back in Chapter 5. So be aware that you might cry occasionally, but also be aware that if you suspect it's something more serious you need to talk to someone.

There is a difference between feeling blue and feeling black. One in seven women develop postnatal depression, although it's suspected this figure is closer to one in five as a lot of women are reluctant to reveal it. And it can strike at any time during the first year. For some women it develops even before they give birth.

Partners can help here. If you sense that your partner is having more than a bad day and if you have any doubts, talk to her and seek some help.

Your GP and baby health clinic are good places to start.

Symptoms of postnatal depression

- Feeling sad most of the time
- Loss of interest in things that used to be enjoyed
- Chronic exhaustion or hyperactivity
- Feeling unable to cope with daily tasks
- Loss of confidence or self esteem
- Anxiety/panic attacks
- Negative or morbid thoughts
- Thoughts of self harm

The Beyond Blue website has more information as well as a list of services available in each state.

www.beyondblue.org.au

New mums are proud and we all want to manage properly and show the world how well we are doing. There is an enormous amount of pressure to be a good mum from ourselves and others. But being a good mum is making sure you are well enough to care for your baby.

If you are depressed, don't try to hide it and hope those feelings will just go away. Put your hand up and ask for help. Reach out to your partner, your family or your friends.

Feelings

66 **Anne Hollonds, from counselling service Relationships Australia**

Be open about the way you are feeling. Don't be ashamed to tell people if you are struggling or feeling sad.

Everybody goes through patches of feeling down and it's not necessarily postnatal depression. Your baby might be crying a lot, your husband might not be as supportive as you expected and you might be feeling so many conflicting emotions.

It's important to talk about it, and not ignore these feelings. You need to take them all seriously, particularly if you suspect it is something more than the baby blues, and seek professional help.

Often there is a significant relationship element to deal with. It's not just about the mother and it being her problem. If you go and see a counsellor, do it together. That way your partner is aware of what you are going through. If your doctor tells you to get outside, exercise and get some fresh air for example, then your partner can be included or stay at home and mind the baby.

If you have had depression before you need to be aware that it might flare up after you have a baby.

There is lots of help available, but people can't help you if you keep it to yourself.

Belinda Lee, editor, mother of two

I was so unprepared for the enormity of my emotions after my baby was born. I had had a difficult and dangerous pregnancy. First there was joy and relief after my baby daughter's release from hospital after being born two months' early; but then came an overwhelming sense of fear. At its worst, I was afraid to go out of the house with my new little baby. Once an independent, successful woman, I lost my confidence to do the smallest things—to go to the shops or use the telephone. The anxiety—an unidentifiable sense of fear and dread—stopped me from going out, and the deep sense of sadness cloaked the happiness I knew I should be feeling. I had no family close by to support me and, having recently moved interstate, had no close friends nearby; this just made my loneliness worse.

It took a while for me to recognize that what I was experiencing was not normal new-baby adjustment. I thought that this was just how it was with a premature baby and that I simply had to get through it. Somehow, once I had acknowledged the possibility of 'postnatal depression', I felt relieved. I knew I had to get help. Joining a mothers' group at about this time helped me enormously in re-establishing a social network. My partner did all that he could—listening to me, doing the night shifts with the baby so that I could get sleep, just holding and supporting me—but I needed expert held too. My GP was responsive and encouraging and, with anti-depressants, I was soon back to the light-hearted me who could truly enjoy my new little girl.

I was apprehensive that I would experience postnatal depression with my second child, but it didn't happen.

Looking back, I am so fortunate that I caught it early; leaving the depression untreated could have made the situation a lot worse.

Find someone you trust to talk to. That may be your partner, it may be your doctor. Just don't let it affect your relationship with your baby or your family.

Weight

Like most new mums you may be wondering when those last three or thirteen kilos will melt away. Don't beat yourself up over this. Sure, we all want them gone ASAP, but every woman's body is different. Victoria Beckham is not average.

The recommended average weight gain during pregnancy is about twelve to fourteen kilograms, but this can vary widely.

Some women lose this weight during the time they are breastfeeding, others only start to shift the kilos when they wean their baby. Just remember it took nine months to make your baby, it will take at least that long for your body to return to normal. Although bear in mind it will probably never be quite the same again—after all, you have produced a child. It takes three months alone for your fluid levels to get back in balance.

One thing every medical professional will reiterate is *do not diet* while you are breastfeeding. Your body is working hard to produce milk so think of it this way, your baby is living off you. Don't let vanity interfere with you or your baby's health. We know we've heard it all before, but damn it, its true—eat sensibly and exercise. A healthy diet will make you feel better and be better for your milk supply, and regular gentle exercise is as good for your head as your waistline.

Studies show that women who exercise during and after pregnancy have more energy, less stress and fewer physical complaints than women who don't. Recent British research has also found that holding on to that extra weight can make it harder to conceive your next child. Most mothers wait six weeks after giving birth before doing too much, but gently walking can be managed straightaway.

If you're keen to get back to something a little more vigorous, or you are in a particularly physically demanding job, have a chat to your doctor about what you can do and when it is wise to start.

When you are keen to get moving, plenty of gyms have childminding facilities. Or you might like a mums-only exercise group. 'Prams in the Park' in Melbourne is just that—a team of mums with prams exercising in the park. You can find similar groups like Mums Squad in Sydney. An Internet search will find locations and times and other similar groups in your area—or you can think about starting your own.

At the end of the day, our bodies are made for making babies and they bounce back pretty quickly. Just do yourself a favour and listen to what your body is telling you.

Stretch marks

About half of us get stretch marks and while there are loads of oils and creams on the market, the jury is still out on this one. But the main consensus is rubbing oil on the area during your pregnancy and immediately after may minimize long-term marks.

If it doesn't work, then think of them as a badge of honour!

First aid

If you have never done a first aid course, now is a good time. You could get your mothers' group together and have an expert come into your home to teach you. Just knowing a few key things that could save your baby's life will leave you feeling much more confident.

It's also a good idea to put together a basic first aid kit. Your chemist should sell them or at least help you put one together. You can also contact an organization like St John's Ambulance service.

If you leave your baby in someone else's care when you return to work, ask them what first aid knowledge they have and if they have a kit handy. If they are in your home, make sure they know where the basics such as thermometer or bandages are and who to call in case of emergency.

Support

You might notice a couple of key messages we keep coming back to in our book.

- Go easy on yourself

- Don't try to be supermum

- Find support

You are not alone in this parenting experience. Outside of your personal circle of family and friends there is an enormous range of services for your baby, you and your family unit.

A great place to start is your local early childhood centre. They usually offer a wide range of services from mothers' groups to parenting classes. They are your first stop to keep an eye on your baby's physical development once you leave hospital, monitoring their weight and growth but beyond that, your local clinic can provide reassurance and help.

Services vary from state to state, but generally your clinic can arrange for a community health nurse to visit you; they hold information evenings covering topics from sleeping to intro-ducing solid food; they screen new mothers for postnatal depression and domestic violence situations, and get you started with a mothers' group.

Mothers' groups were discussed in Chapter 4, but never underestimate the importance of this support network. It's a great place to swap tips, ask questions, feel normal and make some new friends.

Clinics

Kerrie Goodwin, clinical nurse specialist

There are a number of key times to visit your local clinic or GP—within the first month, again between six and eight weeks, six to eight months, one year, eighteen months and annually until they turn five.

Clinics tend to look at wellness compared to doctors who look at illness. We also look at the wellbeing of the whole family, not just your baby. If there is an issue that needs addressing and we can't help you, we can direct you to someone who can. We are there to offer reassurance and help to parents, particularly when it's your first baby. For your next one, we can help with the adjustment to parenting two children. We encourage you to fly with your own confidence and do what you want to do.

Resources list

There are dozens of books that can help you, but here are a few of the ones we've trusted:

- *Sheyne Rowley's Dream Baby Guide* by Sheyne Rowley (to be published in 2008)
- *Baby Love* by Robyn Barker
- *Touchpoints* by American paediatrician T. Berry Brazelton
- *The Baby Book* by Karitane

Websites

- www.australianbabywhisperer.com.au run by Sheyne Rowley
- www.karitane.com.au
- www.cs.nsw.gov.au/Tresillian
- www.charlotteswebdirectory.com.au is a comprehensive online resource for families and details useful health related sites.
- www.breastfeeding.asn.au
- For further information or pre- and post-pregnancy exercise classes: www.lizmillardphysio.com.au
- www.mumknowsbest.mumspace.net is a website that supports new mothers and deals specifically with postnatal depression.

*Health—handy hints

- Breastfeeding. If it works for you, give some thought to how you will manage it once you are back at work.
- Talk to your doctor about contraception, as breast-feeding won't prevent you conceiving baby number two.
- Make sure you get enough sleep in order to function properly at work and home. Easier said than done, we know.
- Find out what local services are available in your area and use them. Your Early Childhood Centre is a great place to start. There may be a wealth of free classes and information evenings that could be helpful.
- Be kind to yourself and your body. It has just done something incredible. It will take a little while to get over the birth, but if you don't feel right, get checked.

chapter 7
childcare

In this chapter:

- Choosing the right childcare for you and your baby.

- Finding a centre and when to book in.

- How to find a nanny or babysitter and what to ask in the interview.

- Grandparents as carers.

- How to manage the tears (baby's and yours).

Once you have decided to go back to work, deciding who will care for your baby in your absence is your next toughest choice. It can be an emotional decision and there are so many options, all ranging in price and convenience. It's a matter of finding what works best for you and your new baby and what makes you feel the most comfortable. You can choose from a daycare centre, family daycare, work-based childcare, a private nanny, grandparents, friends—or a mixture of two or more of these. There are a number of choices and they all depend on the hours you work, what is available, what you can afford and where you live.

Daycare

Daycare centres are either privately owned or run by your local council.

Long daycare centres usually operate from about 7.00 a.m. to 6–7.00 p.m. forty-eight to fifty-one weeks of the year, and are staffed by early childhood teachers and trained and untrained early childhood staff.

Never underestimate how tough it can be to get into the childcare centre of your choice, and how long the waiting lists will be in areas where demand is high. *Put your baby's name on that list as soon as possible because waiting times can be a year or even two in some areas.* In some places it's advisable to do it as soon as you find out that you are pregnant. You will probably have to pay a booking fee and if you can afford to, it's a good idea to put your name down at more than one place.

You will most likely find one particular centre you like best, but be prepared to accept your second or third choice if the offer comes up and coincides with your need—even if it means a little bit more travel time each day. Once you have a place, you can always move your child later if a spot becomes available at your first choice.

Finding the right centre can take a bit of leg-work and is best done while you are pregnant. Have a look in your local phone book or call your council and get a list of all the centres in your area. You might consider an area closer to work too.

You will also find a number of handy websites such as www. careforkids.com.au. It lists your local childcare centres and even has a vacancy alert system. Our advice on finding a place is to be vigilant and keep in touch yourself. Don't rely on them to call you—if you are in an area of high demand it's best to call or even drop in regularly.

Mandi Wicks, mother of two

One of the biggest challenges we face is living so far away from our families. We are constantly torn between living in Sydney and loving it and missing our parents in South Australia and feeling guilty for depriving them of watching our kids grow up. We have had to create other foundations. We have always had a nanny at least one day a week because we wanted and needed another person in their lives—someone they know and love and who can step in when the curveballs strike!

When Henry was born at 29 weeks, we would've fallen apart without all the support from our friends. Luckily, our family also drew up a roster system and flew to Sydney as needed.

During the past five years Nick and I have foregone family time to ensure our kids have access to Mum or Dad as much as possible. Nick worked weekends and had days off during the week and I had weekends off. It's great that the kids have Mum OR Dad for five days a week and we both have full time jobs. But it leaves us with only small windows of family time that we absolutely cherish.

I'd be lying if I said I didn't have any regrets. However, they are fleeting moments because I know we are incredibly fortunate to have two wonderful kids who we love more than anything else. Corny but true! It's the old 'glass half empty, glass half full' analogy. They are both healthy and happy. I know the madness won't last forever . . . working long days, racing home for dinner, bath and bedtime, and then working late nights on the computer.

Regular breaks are essential—a long weekend here and there and a week off every four months or so. At work, try negotiating for more annual leave rather than more money.

My mum is a wise old owl; she says:

1. Don't skimp on childcare if you can afford it. If you are going to work full-time, ensure your kids get the best care you can afford rather than saving every penny for a rainy day.

2. Don't feel guilty about getting a cleaner every few weeks if you can afford it.

3. Once you get home from work—switch off for the kids' sake. Drop the brief case, whack on the tracky-dacks and focus on the kids. They deserve your attention—the washing, dishwasher etc can wait! Kids also know when your mind is elsewhere and they resent it. When you are with them, be with them, in body and mind!

Word of mouth is also a reliable way to find a centre. Ask friends, your local clinic, even your local school, work colleagues or your mothers' group, as some may have older children already in care. Then visit the centre to see if you like it. Make sure it's clean, organized and well resourced. How many staff are there? What is the staff turnover? Do you like the director you meet and the teachers you see? Do the children look happy and attended to or do they have snotty noses and smelly nappies? Do the staff look happy? Is the centre properly accredited?

You also need to find out what the centre provides—some supply everything from nappies to food, others will leave it all up to you.

Those run privately tend to be more expensive than those run by your council, but higher fees do not necessarily mean better quality. The most important factors are the teachers and the quality of care.

Long daycare centres—pros and cons

Long daycare is great for just that—the length of time it's open. But it can be hard to access.

For

Hours. Long daycare centres open early and close late to give working parents more flexibility. You may have to pay penalties, though, if you are running late to collect your child at night.

Stimulation/socializing/activities. Centres usually have learning plans with structured play and children seem to enjoy the company and stimulation of other children. Lots of mums we know leave the particularly messy paint and playdough for kindy!

Against

Demand/accessibility/waiting lists. It may be difficult to get your child in. Some have waiting lists up to eighteen months long—or longer.

Cost. Some private centres in high demand areas can charge hefty fees.

Illness. Be prepared for your child to come home with some sort of bug almost every week. You will see snot for most of the first year. Still, doctors say kids either cop it in the first year of daycare, or the first year of school.

Tears. Be prepared for your child to take some time to settle in. Some adapt immediately, others will cry every time you drop them off for the first six months. As heartbreaking as it is, it doesn't necessarily mean you have chosen the wrong option. Crying is normal, and a lot of children stop the moment you have left. Just chat with the teachers, ask how long your child cries after you've gone and if they haven't settled after a period of time they may like to call you. Pay attention to how your child is when they get home at night. If they are still distressed talk to the teachers and they will let you know if it's going to work out or not—or they might suggest other strategies that you might think about. Oh and be prepared for your *own* tears. Waving goodbye can be gut-wrenching.

> " No one ever tells you how hard it is to drop them off and hear them cry when you leave. I feel so awful every time. The adjustment is definitely hard for us both.
> *– Emma Angel, mother of one*

Mercedes Soldo, Administration Assistant at the Thomas Carlyle Children's Centre offers the following suggestions for approaching daycare:

- Put your name down at a minimum of three centres. Take the first place offered to you—you can always move your child later.

- Keep in touch with the centre. Ring regularly to gently remind them you are still waiting. Go and visit if you get the chance.

- By all means list your day/s of choice, but accept what days are offered. Once you are in, it's easier to change or add more days as preference is given to current attendees. Stay in touch with other parents and if you hear someone is leaving ask for their day. But always ask. Don't leave it to the centre to ask you.

- Start your child at the centre before you return to work so you can both get used to it. It can be hard for little ones to adjust, but never underestimate just how hard it will be for the parent.

- Leave as many phone numbers as possible with the centre to contact you or your partner.

" *My son started at daycare one day a week when he turned one. As I start work very early I was spared the morning drop off. Nicholas cried every time for about the first six months. And I think my husband cried just as much once he made it to the car. We agonized over our decision—but the staff assured us Nick settled within moments of John leaving. Poor John used to hang around outside and peek in the windows just to be sure.*

I had the happier job of picking him up. But if ever the routine changed and our roles reversed the tears started again. We were honestly torn for a long time but knew he really was okay. Years later when my daughter started it was completely different. She carries her bag, waves goodbye and runs off to play with her friends. – **Mel**

Coping with separation

" **Psychologist Jo Lamble offers advice for coping with the separation.**

As you walk away from the centre with tears rolling down your cheeks, remember that you're crying because you love them and they love you. You're crying because you have had to make the decision to leave them in someone else's care and you made that decision for all the right reasons. Being upset and feeling guilty doesn't make it a bad decision. After an hour or so, ring the centre to check on how they're doing. Nine times out of ten, they have settled right down and you can look forward to that wonderful reunion at the end of the day.

Some long daycare centres will also have a number of occasional care spots available each day. You will just need to check the centre's policy for allocating these. For example, you may have to book up to two weeks in advance. Find out how flexible they are, particularly if you have a job with changeable hours. Other centres are solely occasional care.

" Donna Saltram, grocery store cashier, mother of two

It's very hard being a working mum but it's been a lot easier to cope with my mum around, if it wasn't for her I couldn't work because on my money childcare is too expensive.

A woman I work with was so desperate to come back to work she has had to rely on family daycare because she has no family in Australia—they are all in Vietnam—but that's still expensive for her.

I went back to work when my first child was four and my second child was three months old—I only did one day but relied on my mother to be the carer. I'm Lebanese so my family is very important to me.

I wanted to go back to help pay our mortgage and living costs and it's good to get out of the house.

I work for a small family-run chain of grocery stores and the owners and my supervisor are really supportive. They are really flexible when I ask for time off and with the rosters, so that's been a great help.

Family based childcare

Family daycare is where a number of children are cared for in the home of a registered carer. These homes will usually have only around six children at a time, and can also provide before and after school care for older children. Your local council coordinates the strict selection of carers and monitoring of their homes and can help you find a family daycare home in your area.

Some parents love this family home environment for their child. The child receives personal attention, they play with a small group of children, and the hours are sometimes more flexible than formal childcare. Some parents talk about the close bond their child established with the family daycarer. But you will need to assess the home's suitability for you and your child. Does the family daycare 'mum' have a similar approach to you?

Is their level of hygiene the same as yours (within reason if you tend to be rather particular in this area!)? Are the kids happy, fed and clean? Is the house safe? Do they have pets you are not comfortable with?

66 **Angus Trigg, consultant, father of two**

Go and meet the potential carer when a place opens up— make sure you are comfortable with them, their family, any pets and the safety of their house.

In my view, family day care is really best for younger kids between six months and three years. The younger ones get more individual attention and it's not as intimidating for them as a big childcare centre. If you have a great carer, your child can build a really positive relationship with someone new, outside the family. It also tends to be cheaper, and you know the carers have the experience of their own kids under their belt.

As they get older I think they need more excitement and stimulation from other kids their age. It may be better to go to a bigger childcare centre then. You will also find the styles and attitudes of all carers are very different, and you may get one that doesn't end up working out.

There can also be a problem if younger infants are mixed with children of different ages. A six-month-old has very different needs to that of a two-year-old. I'd say avoid any carer who has more than four children and all of differing ages.

Work-based childcare

Some employers provide work-based childcare on site or at facilities nearby. These are usually bigger companies or government departments, but even some smaller to mid-range employers now understand that they can retain valuable staff by providing quality childcare for their employees.

Work-based childcare is usually subsidized and one advantage is that you will know many of the parents and children using the centre because you work with them.

A word of warning though, if your workplace provides childcare don't assume that you automatically get a place. As soon as you are pregnant, and perhaps even before you have told all your colleagues, consider putting your name on the list to avoid disappointment. It's best to find out how many places are provided, what the cost is, what days are available, what days you'll be needing and how long the waiting time is as soon as you know you'll be needing to use the service.

Some employers allow you to salary package childcare costs or will provide discounted fees. Find out about this early, so you are prepared for the additional expenditure each week once you are back at work.

> I had a friend answer the door at 11.00 a.m. in her dressing gown with a cocktail in her hand. She knew then she needed to find some daycare.
> – Feyi Akindoyeni, mother of one

Nanny

Having a nanny care for your newborn in your own home can be very comforting. If they have had lots of experience and you have had none you may even learn a thing or two.

It also gives you a little more flexibility if you do shift work, odd hours or tend to travel for your job. There are many benefits, but it also tends to be costly. Also, inviting a nanny into your home to care for your baby can take some getting used to—they essentially become an intimate part of your family. You need to trust him or her, like them and relate to them.

There are a number of ways to find a nanny. You can check the 'Work-wanted' column of your local paper, place an ad yourself, or go through an agency. The first two are certainly the cheapest ways, but be prepared to conduct a lot of interviews to find the right person.

Going through an agency is the most expensive option—agency fees can be anything up to two thousand dollars—but it can be the safest. The agency will interview potential nannies, conduct police checks, and provide you with a list of candidates to interview. The agency can also help you draw up an employment contract to agree on arrangements such as salary, hours and leave entitlements.

If you employ someone directly, you need to be aware of your obligations as an employer. You are required to provide pay advice records, group certificates and superannuation if your nanny works more than thirty hours per week.

You may also want to conduct a police check. The federal government's Institute of Family Services website has some information that can help you.

For police checks go to the federal government's Australian Institute of Family Studies website at www.aifs.gov.au and look for more information under their link to the National Child Protection Clearing House. Or you can get there directly via www.aifs.gov.au/nch/policechecks.

The Australian tax office website has information on employing household staff (www.ato.gov.au).

It's also advisable to have insurance that covers domestic employees in case they are injured on the job. This is relatively inexpensive and taken out annually so talk to your insurer.

Choosing a nanny

66 **Angie Kelso from the Nannies and Helpers Agency, Sydney says that there are a couple of things to look for.**

A good nanny will always get down to the level of the children immediately. She will talk to you at your level and children at theirs. You also need the right personality mix. A nanny may have the best references, but if you don't like her or your children don't, it won't work. You will also need to ensure that you and the nanny agree on discipline. Make sure she follows through on your family's criteria.

Finally, if you decide to go through an agency, use a reputable agency that has been around a long time. Establish a good rapport with your agency. If your consultant knows exactly what you want, you are more likely to find just the right person.

Pros and cons of a nanny

For

- Your child is in its own home, own bed and own routine.

- You can make the most of her knowledge if your nanny is experienced.

- Hours are more flexible than a childcare centre. They can stay on if you have to work late or start early. They may even be able to stay overnight if you travel.

- They might do other chores around the house while your baby is sleeping.

Against

- Cost. This is the most expensive option. Nannies range in price from ten to thirty dollars per hour depending on experience. Although, if you have more than one child it could be cheaper than a childcare centre. You could also investigate sharing with another family.

- Communication. There will be times when you don't see eye to eye on issues.

- Continuity of care. Your child will probably get attached to their nanny. There will be some adjustment if she leaves.

- Red tape. Issues such as insurance, super, pay, and tax can be complicated.

66 **Jackie Frank, magazine editor, mother of two**

The secret of successful motherhood, for me, is all about honesty—being upfront with yourself and those around you about how hard it can be—and about when you need help. I chose to have children and stay in the workforce and, let me be honest, it was the hardest thing I ever did. When I launched *marie claire* twelve years ago, I had very little experience of what would be involved in that gargantuan task. Long hours, financial pressures, staff issues, circulation targets . . . and, month after month, my staff and I give birth to our own baby, a new issue. It's undoubtedly a labour of love. But it's nothing compared with the pressures, fear and sheer slog that go into having and raising children. And while no one can prepare you for that experience, a little honesty would work wonders.

Everyone always asks how I do it, I've even heard the word 'superwoman' bandied around; well let me tell you there is no superwoman. She is a fraud, born out of a conspiracy of silence by women who are too ashamed to speak up and say, 'this is *hard*!'. Trying to live in her image is what makes us so miserable. I think there are many mothers who don't tell, won't tell or simply refuse to believe the reality of their own life and so create a face, different to their own, which they present to everyone. I've never been able to do this, but now I've learnt that's a good thing.

I know I'm very lucky to have a full-time nanny and a supportive husband who shares the parenting role. But I want to dispel the myth that any choice—full-time mother, work–home balance—is easy. If someone tells you that they have it all under control, they are lying! By pretending they are effortlessly coping, women deny each other the sort of honesty and support that would help lighten the burden.

The demands on us—as mothers, partners, employers, employees—are enormous. Knowing to ask for help when you need it isn't a weakness but a strength. And saying no once in a while doesn't hurt, either.

Funnily enough, it's a word you end up using a lot as a mother—experts say that for every 'no' you tell your child, you should say 'yes' five times. Perhaps the opposite applies in the adult world—saying no I can't go to that function, no I can't stay late, no I can't drop in to that launch gives me more precious time with my children before they go to sleep. They are my priority—my husband and I make sure that between us, we don't miss a school function, a good-night kiss. I try to include my kids in my work life, too, so they understand what I do. I've even taken them to Fashion Week—and they do a mean runway show at home!

What to look for in a nanny

- Do they come in and comment on your child first or your house?

- Do they make an effort to interact with your child? Bear in mind a lot of children will be shy and probably not let her anywhere near them. Does the nanny at least try to engage, but without pushing too hard?

- How do they intend to fill the day—walks to the park? Craft? TV?

- If you want them to take your child to any activities, do they have a safe child seat in their car, or do you need to provide one? Will you need to provide a car?

- Do they know first aid and CPR? What will they do in case of emergency or if your child gets sick?

- Discipline. Are her techniques the same as yours? You may want to ask about her policy on smacking.

- Set clear ground rules from the beginning. What you want her to do, what do you *not* want her to do? Do you require her to clean up before you come home? Do you want her to do any extra housekeeping duties? If so, does she want to be paid extra? And when will she do them? Do you want her doing the ironing while your baby is awake, or only when it sleeps? Is she prepared to do some grocery shopping and prepare the dinner sometimes?

- Is she happy for a week/month trial to see if the situation suits you both?

Nanny interview questions

- How much experience has she had? Ask for her CV and references and use them.
- What are her rates? What holidays will be paid and what will happen if you need to work on a public holiday?
- What discipline techniques does she use?
- Do you want her to do housework/cook meals/other chores?
- Do you want her driving with your child? Will you or she provide the car and/or car seat? Check the details on her drivers licence.
- Does she have her own children? What will she do with them if they are sick or on school holidays?
- How punctual and reliable is she? You need a backup plan if she calls in sick.
- What is her emergency and first aid plan, particularly if your child has special needs.

Share a nanny

Sharing a nanny became an affordable option for new mums, Regina Fikkers and Melissa Donnelly, when they both returned to work at the same time. They both wanted to have their babies cared for at home but found the cost prohibitive—so they split the bill and used alternate houses each week.

They found the most challenging part to be the three-way communication between both families and the nanny. Melissa says the key to managing it all is to have everything on paper and to have a clear set of guidelines to accommodate two different families' needs and expectations.

'We drew up a formal agreement for our nanny, but we also drew one up between ourselves covering everything from holidays to what will happen when one of us has our next baby.'

The women outlined how they wanted their children cared for including issues such as time-out techniques, sleeping routines and diet.

'We didn't know each other that well in the beginning so wanted to make sure our children were being looked after in the way we both wanted them cared for.'

They also addressed more complicated issues, such as dispute resolution, particularly if one family wanted to change the arrangements and the other didn't.

'We set clear boundaries from the beginning.' The advantages included the obvious cost savings, but the women also found there were non-financial benefits. 'If one child is sick, or you are held up at work, there are four parents between us to help out. We also liked having them in our own home, but we particularly liked creating our own support network.'

It's important to find a nanny who fits comfortably with your family, but it's just as important that your nanny feels the same way. Carmel Wall, a nanny to two children, explains 'It's important to work for a family you love and want to be committed to. When we first meet, I'm interviewing you and the children as much as you are interviewing me. I won't take a job if I don't like the children or their parents. I feel like part of your family, almost like another grandma.'

Au pair

You could also look at hiring an au pair, although this may not be the best option for you if you are after full-time care. An au pair is typically a young overseas student who moves into your home for up to a year, or longer.

They require meals and accommodation and in return will care for your children for between twenty-five and thirty-five hours per week at a rate usually under ten dollars per hour. They become part of your family and can provide wonderful cultural benefits to your children. But because they usually study during the day, the preferred hours of work can be mornings or afternoons, so you will need to take this into account to see if it suits your hours of work. You can try an au pair or nanny agency.

Grandparents and friends

For many working parents this is an option either on its own, or worked into the mix with those mentioned above. It's a handy choice if you return to work part-time or on a casual basis.

It can work very well, but it can also be a minefield of problems. Just make sure you set clear guidelines from the beginning. As much as grandparents adore their grandkids, they can also grow to resent becoming the primary carer.

You need to work out:

- What you expect from them, particularly in relation to hours.

- Do they want to be paid?

- Transport. Do the children go to their house or vice versa?

- How to assess when it's no longer working, or how to change the arrangement when either party is unhappy.

- Discipline. Particularly what to do if grandma is not raising your child how you would.

- Food. Do you have clear ideas about what your children should eat? Your parents' lolly policy may be a lot more liberal than yours.

" Voula Serbos, mother of two

Voula leaves her two daughters with their grand-parents three to four days out of five, and she admits this is the only way she and her husband are able to work full-time.

She travels about half an hour to drop them off on a Monday morning before driving another forty-five minutes in the opposite direction into work. She then brings them home on Tuesday night. They go to daycare on a Wednesday then her youngest spends Thursday and Friday with Voula's mum, her older daughter spends the two days with her other grandmother.

There is a lot of travelling and some very early starts, but, 'This is what we have to do to work. I'm lucky to have mum. We couldn't afford a full-time nanny, and daycare doesn't fit with my hours and amount of travel.'

Voula packs their bags, gets their bottles of milk ready and wakes them up, loading both girls into the car by about 6.15 a.m. to begin the morning journey.

'They are used to it. It's their routine and it works for us. It's a lot of juggling and I get a lot of criticism from other women, so I don't discuss it with them anymore'.

'I'm a really good weekend mum and that's okay with me. I need help bringing up my kids.'

Does she ever want to stop it all and stay home?

'Yes. I cannot shake the guilt of not having been there. I feel guilt at not having been with them day to day.'

As comforting as having the grandparents can be, there are inevitable compromises and areas of disagreement, such as maintaining routines, how you want them brought up and missing major milestones.

'It can be hard to tell mum things. But we did set very clear ground rules in the beginning. She is great now at not giving them lollies and chocolate, but they do get a few too many iceblocks. She sticks to the girls' sleep routines and I think that helps her manage her own home—she's realized the benefit for both her and them. This was hard in the beginning as she would let them sleep late in the afternoon. What she didn't see was the impact that had on the evening with us—that they wouldn't go to bed until extremely late—making for a really cranky household. We managed to break that habit by having her experience first-hand the impact of it.

And there are other things, like every time they take them to the shops they buy them a little toy and my parents don't get that that's not what you do. So when we take the girls to the shops on a weekend they expect a toy and tantrums can ensue. For my parents it's about love and they justify it by saying it's not expensive—it's just a one-dollar toy. But to the child, it's "we're going to the shops and that means I am going to get that toy I want today and tomorrow I can get the other one . . ." You've got to watch what you are training them to expect.'

But at the end of the day, Voula knows if they can't be with her, then grandparents are the next best thing.

'They get 24/7 love and care. I trust them implicitly. The grandparents are also spending that time with their grandkids. It's the extended family network—they are constantly with a family member—it's just that we are not all under the same roof. I wouldn't change it for the world.'

Grandparent classes

Robyn Thornton, grandmother of four, comments 'It's been thirty years since I had children and a lot has changed!'

Robyn did an evening course at her local hospital in preparation for her new role as a grandmother. Herself a mother of three, she certainly knew what to do, but acknowledged that a number of practices had changed.

Under the guidance of a trained midwife using a baby mannequin, the grandparents were guided through today's techniques from wrapping, how to prevent SIDS, using disposable nappies, feeding and managing allergies, even first aid.

'The room was full of husbands and wives and single grandparents—all there because our sons or daughters or daughters-in-law are working and we want to be able to help.

'There were a lot of men there who had invested a lot of time and money in educating their daughters and didn't want to see that all go to waste—so they want to be involved with their grandkids. The grandmothers wanted to update their skills.

'And it wasn't only the practicalities that were discussed—part of the evening was devoted to understanding the extra pressures on mums today and the different lifestyle, particularly when both parents work.

'The group also discussed handling the new parents/ child relationship and seeing their daughter now as a mother and realizing you are there as a support person—her way is the only way.'

How to find a babysitter

Any parent, in paid or non-paid work needs a few trustworthy, reliable babysitters. A good one is worth their weight in gold.

Word of mouth is great here. Ask your friends. Do a bit of detective work in your neighbourhood—who has older children, maybe the lady who lives a few doors up and whose children have all left home might like a bit of extra cash herself. You could post a notice at your local high school, university or church. School students can be cheap, but probably won't drive. It can put a fizzer on a big night on the town if you then have to drive the babysitter home. And they may not have any experience in dealing with very small babies.

Handy hints—finding a babysitter

University students make handy babysitters. They often have flexible timetables which can be useful if your regular carer is unavailable. They may also be free to help out during the day or the late afternoon 'rush hour'.

Keep all the numbers of babysitters you have used in the past somewhere handy—stored in your mobile phone, or in a personal phone book. That way if you need one in a hurry you'll have lots of numbers to try.

Questions to ask your babysitter:

- What previous experience have they had? Do they have references you can check? (and *do* check them).
- Do they know first aid? What will they do in an emergency?
- How will they discipline your child, if required?
- What rate do they charge? You can pay anything from five to twenty-five dollars an hour depending on age and experience.
- Do you want them to do any extra duties? For example, if they are giving the kids dinner do you expect them to clean up after?

Make sure you run through your child's routine with your sitter, particularly how to resettle them if your child wakes during the night. You will also need to show them where everything is that they will need, such as the telephone, heating and door locks. Run through house rules in relation to things such as smoking and having company. You might even have them come and mind your child while you're there. That way you can watch them interact and you can feel comfortable before you leave them alone.

Babysitter checklist for your fridge

Leave a list of your numbers for your baby's carer somewhere handy—maybe a list stuck to the fridge with numbers for you, your partner and a couple of backup people they can call upon if they can't reach you. Include:

- Your mobile number
- Your street address (important if the sitter has to call an ambulance or fire brigade)
- Where you are going
- Maybe a landline number—the restaurant or a friend's house
- Second contact if you can't be reached
- Phone number and address of the nearest hospital
- Phone number of the poisons line

Predictable patterns

66 **Sheyne Rowley, baby expert or 'Australlia's baby whisperer'**

Heading back to work and leaving your baby with someone else can be extremely challenging for you and your little one. Just as your day is filled with reminders of them, their day is filled with reminders of you.

These come in the form of routine events throughout their day, so teach your new carer some of your little rituals so your baby can predict their day even when you aren't there.

Create a predictable pattern around leaving for work. Try to leave at the same time and follow the same ritual of saying goodbye. Your little one should always be given the opportunity to warm up to the idea of you leaving, and have something to look forward to as you leave each day. A special bye-bye song and tickle that makes them laugh, or a little stamp or lipstick kiss on their hand will ensure this event is pleasant and stress-free for all.

Create a predictable pattern around coming home from work. This can often be a more difficult time of the day for your baby as they are tired, so being able to prepare themselves and look forward to your arrival is important. Try to come home during the same event so your baby and their carer can work towards this time every day. This will empower your baby with a sense of control over their day.

Stay in touch with your baby and their activities while you are not there. Develop a diary where you and your baby's carer share information on patterns of eating, toileting and sleeping for each other to work off. Track general mood and management needs of your little one through the day and night to help maintain consistency.

For more information see Sheyne's website www.australianbabywhisperer.com.au or read her upcoming book *Sheyne Rowley's Dream Baby Guide*.

Preschool

Preschool may seem a long way away—years in fact, but while you are on your hunt for a daycare centre it may be well worth looking into preschool. Some schools require enrolment early on, others don't take bookings until your child turns two. At least pick a few that interest you and find out their enrolment policy for when the time comes. Some also offer long daycare hours.

Support

The most important thing you can set up around you is a good support network. Gone are the days, unfortunately, when we raised our children ten minutes from our own family home. For a lot of working families, grandparents are interstate, siblings and childhood friends might live on the other side of the city.

Get to know other parents through your mothers' group or your childcare centre. Offer to help them out when you can and they will be able to return the favour. There will be times when you are running late from the office and will need someone else to pick up your little one. There will be days when your nanny calls in sick, or the grandparents have other plans. If you hire a nanny, keep a few of the other applicants' names up your sleeve if your first choice doesn't work out, can't make it some days, or one of your friends is looking for a carer.

Your local council is a good place to find out about other services that may provide you with some support and new friendships.

Playgroup. These are informal gatherings for parents, carers and children aged up to five. They are run by parents and usually meet once a week for a couple of hours. It's a great chance for parents to meet one another, talk and share their experiences.

Libraries and toy libraries. These are exactly as you expect. A place to borrow books or toys, keep little minds stimulated and save you a fortune.

As a working mother you will realize you can't do it alone. Girlfriends, colleagues, family, neighbours—nowadays we create our own 'village' to raise our children.

Resources list

For useful websites to help you locate childcare, try these:

- www.findababysitter.com.au
- www.CareforKids.com.au
- www.kidspot.com.au

✳ Childcare—handy hints

- While you are pregnant spend some time deciding on what type of childcare you want for your baby. What will suit your hours, your needs and your baby's and what you can afford.
- If you want a place in a daycare centre, have a look at as many as possible and put your name on the waiting list right away.
- Give some thought to preschool and at least determine when your child has to be enrolled.
- Start building your support network. Other parents, babysitters, backup carers for days when your primary method of care isn't available or suitable.

chapter 8
returning to work

In this chapter:

- Exploring options for your return.

- How to negotiate with your employer—how far can you push it?

- Other options such as part-time work or working from home.

- How to keep breastfeeding when you return.

- How to get out the door on time!

66 *For a lot of working mums* there comes a time when you realize something has got to give. For me it was flying to Melbourne to host a spring racing carnival lunch and trying to combine work, travel and breastfeeding. I wasn't rattled by the smirks and chatter among the security staff as they slowed the conveyor belt and chuckled over the contents of my handbag—lipstick, wallet and breast pump—it was

sitting in the ladies, knowing I had missed the 11.00 a.m. feed and trying to relieve the agony while the floor manager was calling me up on stage.

There are some things that can't be rushed! Nothing like being dressed to the nines, about to face three hundred of Melbourne's most stylish, and suffering the indignity of a public loo and a manual breast pump—best not to drip on the silk blouse. There had been other moments before this—we took Sunrise *on the road each Friday for a month the week I returned from maternity leave. I had managed to store up enough milk for what was only ever about twenty-four hours away from my four-month-old baby, and the mad dash to express just prior to going on air was made that little bit easier because I could confide in my co-host David Koch—himself a father of four. He happily made excuses why I was always running a little late.*

I wanted to return to work. I love my job. But I can tell you it wasn't easy. The lack of sleep nearly killed me. I struggled with the hours, I struggled with my emotions, I struggled with my weight, but I knew what I was doing was right for me and would eventually get easier. My husband took a month off when I went back after having Talia—and I simply could not have done it without him. That first six months was tough, but we don't regret it for a moment. Sure, a few extra months off would have been nice, and maybe I would have breastfeed my baby for longer than seven months, but we knew it wouldn't be that way forever. – **Mel**

To return, or not

How do you know if or when you are ready to return to work? Can you afford not to? How many days do you want to come back to and in what capacity? Should you continue to breastfeed or wean your baby first? Will you get enough sleep? How will you manage it all?

There are so many questions and for most of them you may not have an answer until you get there. Many a mother has changed her mind and she has every right to!

First of all you need to decide if you want to return to work. If so, will you slip back into your former role and manage it around your new baby? Maybe you want to return, but on a part-time basis, or as a job-share with a colleague? Maybe you simply have to keep working, so now it's a matter of finding how you can manage it to best suit you and your family.

This is the time to assess your priorities, both personally and career wise and decide what makes you happy, not just what pays the bills. These are questions not always answered on maternity leave or even before. How you feel as a pregnant woman can be very different to how you feel as a new mother holding your tiny baby in your arms.

Our advice here, as with anything, is you can change your mind. Okay, so quitting after a week back at work might put a dent in your long-term career plans, particularly with that company, but you'll be happier if that's what you want, or find you need to do, at the time.

On the other hand, it might all go a lot smoother than you expected. You could be lucky enough to have a little one that sleeps through the night straightaway and you might be keen to get back into the office earlier than you anticipated. Or you might negotiate an arrangement that allows you to work from home a few days a week, which could have a big influence on when you return.

And don't do all this alone. Share the decision-making with your partner. It is a partnership and you'll be spending many sleepless nights together in the early days so making a decision about your future workload that you're both happy about is really important. You'll probably want to canvass how your decisions will impact on your partner's workload as well as your joint financial needs and goals. After all you're a family now and really soon there will be one more person to think about.

Your career goals may also come into play here. Sometimes it's helpful to talk to other working mothers in your office to find out how they managed, and what sort of reaction they got from the boss. Not that this would necessarily change your mind about starting a family, but it may help you determine how to approach the situation.

It may mean you look at changing roles or even jobs before you fall pregnant to something that has a little more flexibility. It may mean a rethink of the promotion that is coming your way if it means longer hours and more commitment. It might be something you consider postponing for a few years. But on the other hand, if you have a good support network around you, there may be no reason to turn it down. Yes, life will be tough for a while as you negotiate how you juggle both, and yes you will be exhausted.

There are a lot of things to think about. Talk to as many people as you can and consider all your options and what will work for you and your family before you make a decision.

" Natalie Barr, mother of two

I ran back to work after four months of maternity leave. I admire women who stay at home with their children, but I was never one of them. I loved my baby, but I hated being a stay-at-home mum. I felt trapped and bored at home. Although there was a lot of washing, ironing and cooking to do, I wasn't satisfied and, right or wrong, needed to get out and work. I'd spent twenty years working my way up the career ladder and decided I could do both and I still believe that. The house would be cleaner if I stayed at home, the kids might know their abc's a little sooner and the meals at night would be more imaginative, but I have been prepared to sacrifice that to have both. Some women have told me that's selfish—maybe it is—but that's the decision my husband and I have made, and we're happy with it.

" **Clare McHugh, CEO of the Metropolitan Aboriginal Land Council, Sydney, mother of one**

Finding a balance between career and family is difficult for most working parents and I was no different.

I was torn between the need to bond with my new son and the need to return to work to pursue my career goals. I think every working woman with a desire for children and a career will understand this inner conflict.

The world around us changes so rapidly and professionally there was a fear of taking any lengthy time from my profession.

I have been fortunate to work for an employer who has the foresight to recognize that family commitments should not come second to professional commitments and that the two can coexist. The Metropolitan Aboriginal Land Council is an Aboriginal community-controlled organization based in Redfern of NSW where there is a strong emphasis on family and community by the current board. In traditional Aboriginal cultures family, extended family and community has always been central to our way of life.

Myself, and two other young Aboriginal women in the past two years have returned to work with babies four months old. It is not unusual for the office to be full of children of all ages particularly after school hours.

I returned to work with my son after four months' maternity leave. I needed to be certain I had all my strength back and was completely rested to ensure I would be capable of upholding all my responsibilities and obligations as both mother and CEO. Under no circumstances would I have accepted the offer to return to work if I was not ready to give a hundred per cent to both roles, this would not have been fair for my son or my employer.

In the earliest stages I still experienced moments of panic, worry and uncertainty about how I was managing both motherhood and career. I was worried about how others would react when I arrived with my son in a boardroom, whether they would be put off or not take me seriously as CEO.

The Chairperson, Rob Welsh, sensed my concern and reminded me that as an Aboriginal community organization we operate differently because we are culturally different— one of the major differences is our obligation to family. I think Rob enjoyed the culture shock many non-Aboriginal people experienced when we arrived with a baby at meetings. It was like a quick lesson for others of the difference between cultures.

I am always reminded how lucky I am and how different and unique it is to take babies to work when the people you meet are constantly amazed and thrilled to learn this is the norm.

There are enough hurdles to overcome when tackling motherhood and a career. Not having to worry about keeping the two roles separate makes life much easier.

For me at the core of being successful in both my role as mother and CEO is a good support network, a strong commitment to both roles and lots of passion for what I do. I have been blessed to have a loving and dedicated partner who is an attentive father to our son. Without his ongoing support I am sure things would have been more difficult. These elements helped me prove to myself it is possible to juggle both roles. The icing on the cake for me has been to inspire and open the eyes of the people I meet in my day to day dealings that it is not necessary to choose one role over the other.

There is a great need for workplaces and employers to be more innovative and show greater leadership when it comes to matters of accommodating family commitments and obligations. The benefits for the company include among other things greater employee satisfaction which can only be a good thing.

Emotions

There are a lot of practicalities to take into account when you decide to return to work, but don't forget to allow a little time to remember yourself and your feelings. Leaving your baby for the first time will be emotional. You will probably have tears, pangs of guilt and be ringing the carer every ten minutes. The only way to alleviate at least some of these feelings is to have confidence in what you are doing, why you are doing it and who is caring for your baby. This is why it's best to organize as much as possible well before your return so you are comfortable with your decisions and confident that it will run smoothly.

On the other hand, you may feel completely liberated as you jump in the car, crank up the radio and head back to a world that doesn't revolve around sleep times and milk!

66 If you work there's guilt, if you don't there's guilt. Everybody feels this way. Whatever you do, you'll question whether your decision is right or wrong.
– *Catriona Dixon, mother of two*

66 Either you are going to question your choices or others will. Just be sure in your decisions and make sure your partner stands with you.
– *Sue Vercoe, mother of two*

When you apply for maternity leave, leave a little room in the back of your mind for the unknown. It is difficult to know how you will feel until after your baby is born. You may be completely satisfied with the length of time you have taken off and be ready to return, but then again many a tough career woman has changed her mind.

Legal entitlement

- You are entitled to fifty-two-weeks' unpaid leave.
- You can extend parental leave only once within the fifty-two week period, provided fourteen days' written notice is given to your employer. Any further extension within or after the fifty-two-week period is at your employer's discretion.
- You can only shorten parental leave with your employer's agreement, and you need to give at least four weeks' notice.
- There is more detail about your legal rights in Chapter 9.

Never underestimate those factors which you cannot control. You may have a smooth birth and a baby that sleeps all night.

Or you may have complications in labour or a baby that needs extra care. You could be one of the fifteen per cent of new mothers who suffer postnatal depression. You may have an unexpected caesarean, and find yourself unable to drive for six weeks. Such a major operation can take its toll on your body.

The message is—try to remain as flexible as possible. Go ahead and make your plans, but leave a little room to move. For career women used to controlling the situation, having the biggest one taken out of their hands can be pretty daunting.

66 *John, Mel's husband:*

If you're ever in doubt about your worth to an employer, the quickest way to find out is to ask for 'flexibility' after you've had kids! This request can be more daunting than asking for a pay rise.

When we had Nicholas, Mel had six months off work, so the transition for me in the workplace was quite subtle. I tried to get home earlier and even scaled back the amount of travel I was usually required to do, but it wasn't a radical change.

Once Mel returned to work it became a bit harder. I spoke to my boss at the time and reassured him that despite maybe needing to travel less frequently, or head home at 5.00 p.m. my work would still get done and I would pick up any extra slack at home or on weekends. And essentially that's what happened.

Luckily for me, I had/have a good boss who agreed and went along with my predictions that it wouldn't impact my work life whilst I suspect he knew that it would. And it did, but not to the detriment of my role.

When we had Talia it was a whole different story. Mel only had three months off work as Sunrise was on its climb in the ratings. I saved up my holidays and took a month off work when Mel returned, so that at least one of us was home for those first few important and exhausting months.

Once I went back to work and Mel was doing her strange early hours, it was a whole new ball game. I figured that since it didn't matter what I looked like at work, I would try to be the one who got up during the night. It also meant that travelling for work became more complicated and Mel needed the extra support at home with two kids, especially at the end of the day when she'd been up since 3.25 a.m.

Again, my boss was great. Do the best you can, get what you can done and if there's a shortfall, we'll address it. I'm pleased to say that with his support and understanding, and my commitment to get the job done in return, things worked out pretty well. I didn't necessarily work any harder or longer, but I did get a whole lot more efficient.

Ironically, the biggest adjustment in this process for me wasn't my employer, but getting used to it myself.

When to return

The Australian Bureau of Statistics has found the average length of time taken off with a new baby is around seven months. Just eight per cent of women are back within four months. Around half come back when their child is between one and two, and most of those who return in this time take a part-time position.

Your timetable could depend on any number of factors, not least being your job. Some women find the decision is not theirs alone. You may run your own company, have no access to paid maternity leave or job demands that dictate your return.

Building in flexibility

Spontaneity is about to get a whole new meaning. Instead of connotations of flying off to the mountains for a romantic weekend away, it now means cancelling that meeting at the last minute or clocking on late for your shift because your baby is sick or the sitter can't make it.

A working mum needs as much flexibility as possible and this is something best negotiated before you take leave.

Maybe you can float the idea with your boss of one flexi-day a week or even a fortnight. You may hardly ever need it, but if you put your claim in early you avoid any surprises down the track. Try to pre-empt what you may require as much as possible and do the ground work before you take time off to have your baby.

66 Donna Kennedy, hairdresser, mother of three

Donna Kennedy returned to work within the first week after giving birth to her two youngest children. Owning her own hair salon meant she was keen to keep the business ticking over, but it also gave Donna the flexibility to bring her baby to work.

Each baby got used to the noise of the salon during the nine months in the womb and had no trouble settling in such an active environment.

'I felt isolated at home as everyone I know works. I was bored and lonely so was happy to return to work and bring my baby with me.'

Her daughters slept in a portable carry bassinette on a day bed in the salon.

'Our clients love it. They all shared my pregnancies and couldn't wait for the baby. They are upset if they come in and she is asleep.'

Donna found it manageable for the first three months, but once they required more stimulation she left them with her mum before ultimately finding a childcare place.

Donna's top tips

- Delegate tasks as much as possible—both at work and at home.

- You can structure your first three months around your baby more than you realize, particularly if you work for yourself. At that age they can't go anywhere or touch anything.

- Don't over-handle your baby. Get them used to lying down and sleeping on their own. Don't pat them off to sleep and create extra work for yourself.

Full-time or part-time—or other options?

Returning to work full-time, or at least full-time in the office, may or may not be for you. This is where technology and the changing face of work environments have played a big role in giving working mothers so much more freedom. Depending on your employer, you have a number of options from full-time to part-time, flexitime, job sharing, freelancing, working from home or a combination of any of these.

❝ **Nicole Sheffield, mother of four**

Get ready for the question 'what are your plans after the baby arrives' as soon as you announce your pregnancy. It was asked more of me than the standard 'when are you due?' or 'what do you think you're having?'! And it doesn't just come from your boss—your work colleagues and staff will also be interested.

As the pregnancy evolves, your emotions and intentions change, so I always waited until around the six-month mark before making my plans.

I have always felt it essential for me to return to work after three months—even if it was part-time—to ensure I kept my profile and position. The sad thing is while we are entitled to twelve months, waiting a year for many small-to-medium size businesses is a big ask. After a year they have someone else in the job and a system that is working effectively, and I worried that I wouldn't have a job to come back to, or at least comparable to the one I had left.

Remember when negotiating your leave, that it's a business. So work out what you want and then work out what the business needs. You know your job better than anyone else—so be involved in the plan. Ultimately, everyone is replaceable so have the philosophy that no one is going to do you a favour—they're a business and they really do not want any interruptions, so make it painless for them and in turn it will be less painful for you.

Nicole's top tips

- *Stay in Control*. Do not give up on work up as soon as you announce your pregnancy. I have seen it too many times, women who are so caught up in having a baby they make comments like 'I don't care what happens, I'll be out of here in three months'. We may feel like that from time to time, but try to stay focussed.

- Ensure there is a *good handover*. With my third child I went into early labour whilst driving to work. Luckily I had been doing a handover for a month with all key staff so my disappearance was not such a shock.

- Ensure the person looking after your workload is someone you can *trust*, that way you will feel more comfortable and relaxed. It will also minimize the changes when you return.

- Try to *stay in touch*, so they remember you exist. However don't ring the office every day, you need to take time to get into baby mode too.

- Suggest a *gradual come back*. The best model for me was no contact for the first six weeks—for my own sanity! Then touch base with the office and do some work from home. After three months I returned for two days and took work home, then I went to three very full days with more work from home about a month later.

- *Stagger your days.* If you are working part-time—try not to work three days in a row. People think differently if they see you around the office as much as possible. I started off working Tuesday to Thursday then realized quickly that if someone needed something and the request came through at 5.00 p.m. on a Thursday I had to say I'll get that back to you on Tuesday—which seems like ages to those working five days a week. I changed to Tuesday, Thursday and Friday which doesn't seem as long when you say to someone 'I'm not around tomorrow but I'll do it first thing Thursday'. It also seemed to reduce the amount of take-home work I had as well.

- Finally, be nice to other women in the same position as you. I've had two people in my team fall pregnant and I've ensured that they could come back three days and have the same position as when they've left, because I think women have to look after each other!

66 *Both times I've returned* to work I've eased in gently. Coming back at first two days for a few months, then three and finally settling on a permanent four days each week.

Because my partner is able to have a weekday off each week I have Fridays off and spend it with my two-year-old daughter, doing the grocery shopping and walking my son to school and collecting him at 3.00 p.m.

I work at a global consulting firm that advises large blue chip companies, but they have a refreshing mind-set on work–life balance. We work in project teams, so they firmly believe that individuals can work three or four days a week and manage it perfectly well with four or five consultants across the company working in this way. Team members support each other and clients are usually aware you're not around—and they cope too. Access to email at home has been a godsend. And while I don't do a day's work on my day off, I always log in a few times to respond to emails or deal with urgent things that may come up.

It works well. I deal with the guilt of working better, stuff gets done and I get to spend some daylight hours with my children apart from the weekends and be involved with things at our local school. – **Jo**

66 Kalinda Cobby, lawyer, mother of one, step-mother of one

I was a partner in my firm when I became pregnant, so rather than having to deal with a boss I had to convince/negotiate with all my partners, all of whom were male. Their reactions differed from congratulations to reserve. We talked through the logistics and fortunately one of them was familiar enough with my work and clients to assume the burden of my absence from the office.

I did, however, fail to deal with my employees' perceptions that I may not return to work which left them concerned with their own job security. In retrospect I should have spoken with each of them in the same way that I had with my partners.

My mother worked full-time throughout my childhood, so it simply never occurred to me that it was not a normal thing to do. To a certain extent I did not so much choose to work full-time as fail to consider that I could work part-time.

Both parents, though, must assume equal roles. Partners must adapt and compromise just as much as we expect work colleagues, employees and clients to.

It is possible to have it all, but you must prioritise. You may not be able to go to work, volunteer for canteen duty, help with reading in your child's class, lobby for political change, have an immaculately clean house and cook gourmet meals every night, but you can do some of each occasionally. It is a matter of balancing your life and continuing to re-balance it.

My son recently asked 'Why can't you pick me up at three o'clock like all the other mummies do?'. But I think working can make the whole mothering experience better. You don't micromanage them. You enjoy your time.

How you will work, when and where, needs to be negotiated with a number of people. Not the least being your boss. And this is best explored before you take leave, so you at least know what options are available to you.

You'll find help on how to have this conversation with your boss and how to achieve the best possible outcome for you both in Chapter 2.

But this is a family decision, your plans also need to be negotiated with your partner. Your decision to work will ultimately impact on more than just you, particularly if you travel or do shift work. We go into more detail about the conversations that you need to have with your partner in Chapter 4.

       My early-morning starts work well for our two children. We have afternoons together, dinner together and go to bed at the same time. As parents we are happy with this, but my hours have certainly meant some major adjustments for us as a couple and for my husband in his workplace. John usually eats alone, it's killed off our social life as I'm in bed by 8.00 p.m., and he has reduced his travelling as it means we have to find someone to stay overnight. On the plus side we never argue over the remote!

       John has managed to shift his whole working day forward so we can have a few hours of family time together at night. He starts early so he can be home in time to help bath the kids while I do an evening conference call to plan the next day's show. My hours have meant some changes not only for him, but also his company and that's where we appreciate the flexibility of his boss. John takes the kids to school and preschool two mornings a week which means he doesn't get into the office until 9.30 a.m.

       If I get called away from home to stand outside a mine in Beaconsfield or fly to LA to interview Tom Cruise, it's John who has to pick up the slack, and it's his boss who allows him to do it.

       We regularly stop and check it's still working. We know it's not easy and we know we are making some sacrifices, but we also know it won't be like this forever. **– Mel**

Rethinking your career

Having a baby can also offer some women the opportunity to rethink their career. Now might be the perfect time to change

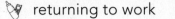

jobs, so you can work from home with hours that suit. Jobs such as direct selling, bookkeeping, data entry, telesales and the Internet industry offer this sort of flexibility, as do teaching, childcare and cleaning.

> ## Kaylene Ferguson, cleaner, mother of three
>
> Some professional women may have questioned what I was doing—my clothes stained from Domestos, hair tied back and my pink rubber gloves covered in Gumption as I scrubbed another bath clean.
>
> But I never did.
>
> My kids will always come first. So if that meant forfeiting my career as a skincare specialist with cosmetics company Clarins to ensure I was there to support them at a swimming carnival or to help out in the classroom with reading or book club, then I'd do it.
>
> The reality is that some mothers have to work. My husband Kendall is a bricklayer and, as many other families involved in construction or trades know, if it rains, you don't get paid.
>
> I tried to juggle my position with Clarins, servicing my clients, organizing promotions and wooing new customers, with my role as a mother to three growing children and wife to a busy husband. But it just didn't work, I could do neither to the standards I set myself.
>
> So, I went out cleaning. It started as a bit of a joke at first when I suggested to a girlfriend I'd take on the job after she sacked her cleaning lady. My career path took a new turn, instead of making people look and feel more beautiful, I would do it to their homes instead.
>
> For me it meant no more weekend work, the flexibility to take the kids to and from school, attend athletics

carnival, netball games, school concerts—and still earn the money we needed to keep our family budget out of the red.

It isn't glamorous and it is hard physically, but my kids are my priority. My career can wait. They won't be young forever, and I am prepared to make what sacrifices I need to be the best mother I can.

Seeing their faces light up when I am there for them always confirms I made the right decision.

" *My son, Marlow, recently got the whole work–life balance thing. Sitting in the bath he said to me 'Mummy, you and daddy have to work so we can live and buy things, don't you'. And while it isn't that simple, as there's guilt and career aspirations that come into play for working mothers— children really don't have to feel second best in the whole deal, if we take the time to explain why we work. – Jo*

Staying at home

The cost of childcare may also force your hand in the decision-making process. Sometimes the cost of putting your little one into care all but cancels out your weekly pay packet and may outweigh the benefits of working full-time. We talk more about budgets and reaching this decision in Chapter 11.

Or it may be more emotional than this. You may find your desire to be at home full-time with your new baby completely negates any desire to return to the workforce—at least for the time being. You may want to step back from your work and career for a few years—at least until your child or children are all at school.

> **Monique Tompson, freelance events manager, mother of three**

Monique Tompson had been successfully combining motherhood and a career as one of the best event managers in the country for nearly six years when she decided she needed to get some balance back into a busy family life. Her last big event was the Nicole Kidman/Keith Urban wedding, when she decided to pack it all in. Both she and her husband Andrew worked long hours and in the end something had to give.

'I wanted a break. I hardly had any time off with our first two children. When you run your own business, work is a constant presence. I needed to be able to completely switch off this time around. It was a difficult decision because I enjoyed my work, and the financial impact was significant—choosing to forego that second income was something that we didn't do lightly. But it has made a world of difference, I got a bit of life back.'

It means some sacrifices, the renovations will need to take a back seat, the family income is reduced—but Monique says her girls, aged three and five, are so happy.

'They were announcing to everyone, even the man in the butcher shop: "My mum doesn't work anymore!", "Mum's mine now!"'

'Their routine is based a lot more around them now rather than my work. I hate to recall this now, but Eliza spent the first few months of her life in the office—we used to call her the boardroom baby!'

Monique says it's changed the whole family dynamic for the better.

'I am the main disciplinarian now. I am not conflicting with a nanny or any other carer. They listen to me a lot more. I think I was the world's crankiest mother and wife. Now it's so much easier.

'We want more kids. Andrew was always a fantastic support, so this change also gives him the chance to concentrate further on his career and I can support him from home more. How very traditional!'

Traditional maybe, but Monique acknowledges it's what her family needs right now and she knows they are lucky enough to be able to do it.

So does she miss work?

'Not yet as I am still doing the odd project for select clients, but I anticipate I probably will. The beauty of my business is I can come in and out on a project by project basis. I also want to do a bit more pro bono charity work, but if ever I leave the house dressed in my work clothes I get the full Spanish Inquisition from the kids.

'It is right for us now. I wasn't ready to give up a few years ago, nor could we have afforded to. It's all about timing.'

66 Lois Oakey, intensive care nurse, mother of three

Working night shift, juggling hours, managing permanent sleep deprivation and pre-planning is how Lois Oakey managed to continue her career and raise three children.

'Before they started school I would do evening duty, dropping the children off at crèche on my way to work.' Lois would work from 1.30 p.m. till 10 p.m. and her husband Alan would pick them up on his way home from work.

'I had the meals already prepared so he only had to bath them and put them to bed.'

Once they started school Lois moved to the night shift in order to be there for afternoon activities.

'I'd give them dinner then put them to bed and start work at 9.30 p.m. working through until 7.30 a.m. I'd be home by 8 in time to take them to school and drop my youngest off at kindergarten for the morning, then I'd come home and sleep for a few hours.

'Of course I'm always tired—but this is the choice I've made. I think you're tired anyway as a mother! If I got four hours' good sleep I could manage that. If you can have quality time with your children, then everybody is happy.'

With all her children at school, Lois went back to uni to complete a science degree in order to continue her climb up the career ladder.

'I never felt I made the wrong decision. I could always see the light at the end of the tunnel. I was never going to give in. I don't think the kids missed out on anything and they are all pretty well adjusted. We managed all the afternoon activities—ballet, sport and music. I had the time to take them because I was there during the day.

'I wanted to be there to take them to school each day and pick them up—but we also wanted a bit more money to cover things like excursions and after school activities.'

Claudia Keech, motherinc.com.au, mother of one

My life was one big Hollywood story prior to the birth of my son Callan. I worked as an international marketing consultant in Los Angeles. I all but worked and travelled 24/7.

I drove a convertible, attended great parties, caught limousines, helicopters and planes—all for work. I was launching products, movies and people from Australia into the USA. My clients wanted me everywhere at once and I was!

I continued consulting on my return to Australia, setting up an extensive home office and working for Time Inc. on their sponsorship of the Commonwealth Games and the public relations for *Who Weekly* magazine.

Two years later I was married and Callan arrived in January 1995, but my best laid plans fell apart. I had intended on taking three months off, but my temporary replacement took another job the day before I gave birth and Callan arrived with both colic and reflux!

Never one to give up, and having never been a mother before, I really thought I could do it all. I just went back to work, used the money I saved from my replacement and hired a mothercraft nurse to help me with Callan's reflux (I really needed help to manage his diet and erratic sleep patterns) and worked from home.

Our early years together were not dull. Callan's first birthday was in Hollywood at a Who Weekly movie premiere. He quickly learnt to smile to the right people as he hopped on planes, usually in a super hero suit which doubled as pyjamas.

Many working mums leave their babies behind with a nanny, but I couldn't do it. I wanted him with me whenever possible.

Unfortunately I became a single mum by the time Callan was eighteen months of age, but as I had always been the major breadwinner in the family, my role in that instance did not change. I began consulting and over the next few years the perfect working balance seemed to be there, but something didn't feel right.

I was totally and utterly exhausted. In retrospect I realized Callan had not slept through a night for three years and my working mum role was just not working for me. It was time to make a change.

With regret I resigned, took a six-month break living on the smell of an oily rag and moved into a tiny apartment. It gave me time to breathe financially, and got me thinking about motherInc, the first online magazine for mothers. Something mums can now tap into at home, whether they are up feeding in the middle of the night or trying to understand their child's homework. motherinc.com.au was created because I felt it really was time to recognize that motherhood today is a career choice in itself and that we don't throw out our make-up or desire to look and feel good when a baby arrives.

My home office continues and now it really works. Callan has sports commitments every moment of the day, but the fact that I have great women who work with me—all mums, all part-time, means I can dash out the door to watch him play and I don't miss a thing. I realize I have created an enviable situation. Not everyone can work for themselves and few mums have the freedoms I can give myself and my staff. But this didn't come easily. I was never going to be labelled a poor single mum. I wanted to work to provide for my small family and provide a great role model to my son—to let him know that it's okay for mums to work, if they need to or choose to.

Without Callan there would have been no motherinc. com.au. The business has won local and international awards and all because a little baby arrived with reflux!

If you do think the time has come for a complete change you could have a look at some recruitment sites to see what sort of part-time work is on offer. It's also worth looking at mother-related sites such as www.motherinc.com.au. Or for more ideas, see also the US based site www.workingmother.com and their magazine.

Like Claudia, some great business ideas have come from mothers who want to find a way to work from home—and some of the ideas they have come up with are quite innovative. Party products, monogrammed baby clothes, catering, wedding or baby photography—the list is endless, as is the wealth of information out there to help you get going. You will find plenty of publications covering this in your local bookshop, such as *Show Mummy the Money* by Sonia Williams and *Let Go of My Leg* by Kirsten Lees.

" Jacki Stevens, caterer, mother of three

I had been running a thriving café and catering business for a number of years when I fell pregnant with Lachlan. I knew I wouldn't be able to continue running the business, work such long hours, manage staff and cope with a new baby, so we put the café up for sale. But demand was still there for my catering and before I knew it I was taking on the odd job and it grew from there. I was making biscuits, then Melbourne cup lunches, and it just continued.

The juggle was a lot easier with one child, but I just take each job as it comes and make sure I'm organized. I always sort the children first and that makes the catering a lot easier.

I run the business with my sister Victoria. She has two small children, so we manage them all together. Mum is also a big help, as is my husband. His support is vital, especially when I dash off to the shops when I need something at the last minute or deliver food at all hours. We actually delivered sandwiches on the way to hospital to have Emily!

The business is totally part of our family life—and that's the only way it works for us. Most jobs can be done with the kids around and they understand what mummy does and when we are having a cooking day. Other jobs require more concentration so I'll work after they have gone to bed, or I'll get up at 3.00 a.m. and get organized before my husband Nick goes off to work. I make the most of my time. If I have a quick ten minutes I'll throw a cake in the oven.

I have to be organized as well as flexible as both of my roles are 24/7.

Most clients know I have kids so they're okay when they call to place an order and there are children screaming in the background.

Jacki's top tips

- *Passion.* You have to love what you do. It's a job but also so much more. I'm never going to make a million dollars from it, but I enjoy it. Cooking is part of our life and the kitchen is the centre of our house.

- *Integration.* Gelling the business into our daily life makes it easier to manage. I know some home businesses say keep the two separate, but for us it works to combine them. The business is there for when I have the time. Any second you get you grab. While the pasta's boiling for dinner, I can quickly do a quote. The laptop is on the kitchen bench near the phone.

The Internet has opened up a world of opportunities for women wanting to work from home.

" **Delia Timms, www.findababysitter.com.au, mother of two**

Like so many new mums, Delia Timms found returning to her job as a speech pathologist wasn't justifying the enormous cost of childcare. She was also having difficulty finding great babysitters and nannies, so Delia quit and started her own small business from home. Her website www.findababysitter.com.au introduces parents to babysitters and nannies. Carers can post their details on the site, and parents can also post their requirements. The site grew quickly, going national within six months and exceeding all expectations.

'The biggest challenge was taking a financial risk and letting go of a "paid job". However once the first steps were taken it was actually really empowering to take responsibility and work towards an exciting goal!'

Now Delia finds the hardest part is separating work from home life. 'Running your own business can be all consuming. You need to plan how you will balance the demands of family and work to ensure you manage the competing priorities.'

Delia's top tips

- Arrange dedicated child-free time to get work done. Working from home is still work.

- Conduct thorough market research to identify a genuine need—ask 'what is the problem others are experiencing and how can I solve it for them'?

- Choose to build a business you are passionate about, because you will live and breathe it.

- Identify your strengths, get expert advice and outsource as necessary.

- A good idea alone is nothing without great implementation—implement it right.

- Believe in yourself and your business.

Your return to work may also be determined by a number of factors outside of your immediate control. There is the issue of finance. A lot of women work simply because they have to. Seventy per cent do so to pay the mortgage, not because they have a dream job. You may have a single income, be a single parent, or need your wages to supplement your partner's to cover the bills.

Single parenting

Single parenting in itself throws up a lot of challenges—finances and childcare are but two. Becoming a single parent often means rethinking the flexibility of your job.

Justine Kelman, real estate valuer, mother of two

It's a juggle to manage full-time work commitments and those of two school-aged children—it's even harder when you have to do it all on your own.

Justine found changing jobs was the only way for her to make it work. As a real estate valuer, she was working for a firm that required nine-to-five hours and she was finding it impossible. So she took a gamble and went out on her own, contracting her services to a number of companies.

'I have to work, and I certainly work longer and more hours this way, but I can do it during the times that suit me. It's much more flexible.'

Justine inspects properties between dropping her children off at school and picking them up. Afternoons are filled with sport or ballet, and after the children go to bed she gets back to work, typing her reports well into the night.

'I get through so much more work because I am disciplined and I know I only have limited times in which to get it all done. I want to do it for my kids and provide a good environment, and I think it encourages them to work hard at school when they see me working.'

When she does have a late appointment, it's other mums who help her out. 'There is a strong mums' network of support and we take it in turns to help each other. They are my main backup, and I couldn't do it without them.'

Justine's top tips

- Get flexible hours. Change jobs if you have to. This is particularly vital if you need to take your child to the doctor or attend a school concert.

- Take time out for yourself. Do this at least once a fortnight. Call on your ex-husband, mother or anyone who'll take the children for even just a day to give you some time alone to regroup. Being a sole carer can be so draining and constant, you simply need a break sometimes away from them.

- Have your weeks organized to a 'T', theirs and yours. Everything from activities to friends visiting. It sounds boring but it works.

- Have a cleaner if you can afford one. You'll struggle to manage it all otherwise.

- Discipline. It makes your life easier when everything runs to plan. Discipline can be hard when you have no other parental backup.

Working also gives some women their own identity and a sense of satisfaction. It may be as simple as having a job they love and a career they want to continue.

> *I am lucky enough to have a job I love. Even if I won lotto, I would continue to work. That's not to say the 3.25 a.m. alarm doesn't sometimes get the better of me—but on the whole I actually look forward to going into work, seeing my colleagues and doing my job. Spending as much time as I do with my children though helps my balance. But time with my husband is my biggest challenge, as is my social life. It's pretty non-existent at the moment, but god bless girlfriends who continue to love me and always pick up where we left off. Having said all that, at the end of the day I also know my job doesn't define me. If I felt it was no longer working for my family, or my children were suffering, I would walk away. I would quit in a flash and cut sandwiches. As a family we constantly reassess that balance. – Mel*

Working and breastfeeding

If you return to work while you are still breastfeeding your baby, you may want to give some thought as to how you will handle this.

We talked about the practicalities of breastfeeding and working in Chapter 3, and how to make it work for you, but you also have to give some thought to how and where you will feed.

Will you continue all feeds from the breast, or just those while you are away from each other? If you have childcare at work, or your baby will be coming to you, is there somewhere you can feed in private and comfort? If you want to express milk during the day, is there somewhere appropriate you can do this and then store the milk safely and hygienically?

" **When I was planning** my return to work at a small inner-city office I'd been happily working at for many years, the last thing I considered was that I'd need to use a very attractive plastic breast pump to express milk in order to keep up my supply. I'd planned childcare, I'd bought some new (larger) work clothes, had my hair cut and felt (vaguely) respectable again. It was liberating. I was excited about the prospect of engaging with human beings. Being able to use my brain. But as the day drew closer the challenge of how I'd manage to maintain my milk supply dawned on me. I bought the necessary requirements and then I realized—I'd have to express in the toilets.

Unsatisfactory as it was I chose a toilet on another level of the building so at least my co-workers didn't have to listen to the resultant squelching and slurping noises emerging from the cubicle next door. I then diligently brought the milk back and popped the bags in to the *communal freezer—you never waste a drop of expressed milk, I can tell you!*

It wasn't perfect, but hey, it was the best I could do in the circumstances, and it meant I didn't have to stop breastfeeding and feel even guiltier. – **Jo**

Whatever you decide to do, our advice is decide before you go back to work. Give your breasts, body and mind, as well as your baby, enough time to adapt to the changes. If you choose to wean, do so ahead of your return. Make sure your baby is used to the bottle well before you are no longer there as a baby who rejects a bottle is not a stress you need the day before heading back to the office. Believe us, you will have enough on your mind! Another option is to reduce the number of breastfeeds to two or three a day in preparation for your return, and then express once or twice a day depending on how much milk you have, to keep up your supply.

Someone like your local clinic nurse can be a huge help here—talk to them about what you want to do.

You'll also find a lot of books to guide you through dropping feeds or maintaining your supply.

A great one is Robin Barkers *Baby Love*. It's full of fabulous information on how to handle your baby in its first year—we swear by it!

66 **Nicole Sheffield, mother of four**

The hardest part of returning to work before the three to four-month-mark is managing breastfeeding. Most workplaces do not appreciate the whole 'I have to cut this meeting short as my breasts are going to explode' comment or the leakage through the top when you've realized you've just had a let down.

Nicoles's top tips

- Get comfortable with the breast pump before returning to work. I tried two before I found one I really liked. At home I used an electric pump, but at work the power points were in open plan areas not appropriate for 'pumping'.

- Ensure the baby is able to drink from a bottle easily. The first time I left Zac he had never had a bottle before and it took him a while to get used to it—upsetting for baby, carer and mum!

- Find a room where you are comfortable expressing. In my workplace every office has glass walls so the only place I had privacy was the sick-bay or toilets—both rather gross, but I made sure that my breast pump was well sterilized before using it and that the areas were clean.

- You need somewhere to store your milk. I found putting it in the work freezer was key. Obviously no one wants to see your bottle or breast pump when they go to get their lunch, so keep it in a sealed bag that people are not likely to check. I had a breast pump and bottle stolen because I had them in a David Jones bag—someone obviously thought it was something yummy from DJ's food hall and took it home. Imagine their shock! Clearly, they were too embarrassed to bring it back and just threw it out. So I learnt my lesson and ensured that all future breast 'equipment' was in a zippered bag that in no way could be confused for food.

- Finally, to avoid the embarrassment of leakages, schedule regular expressing times in your diary. That way you can ensure you are not at a meeting on the other side of town at a time when you know you need to be 'pumping'.

Returning to work and adapting to the changes

Having a baby can bring the greatest joy into your life—but it also brings with it some considerable changes.

We've all heard a pregnant couple boast their new baby won't change their life.

'We'll still go out to dinner,' they say with such confidence, 'we'll simply pop the capsule under the table. It will just have to fit into our lifestyle.' Any parent who's been there just smiles knowingly.

The reality is a baby will change your life, in many ways. It will no doubt curb your social life, your love life and impact on your career.

Don't think that you can just go back to the way things used to be. The goalposts have moved. Babies get sick, you will be exhausted, work will demand more than you can give, and most importantly you now have a little person who you want to shower with love and attention and time. This book is all about helping you find the right balance—as long as you remember that any scales always require adjustments.

> ## Quick tip
>
> Warning—this time can be really emotional for you as you quickly realize that your relationship with your baby is changing from one where they were totally dependent on you. Keeping a stiff upper lip probably won't work. Talk to girlfriends who've been there before you and have a good cry. It'll make you feel better.

Going back to a changed workplace

With the way businesses change so quickly, you may also find your job quite different if you return after twelve months' leave or longer, rather than just a few months. The company may have changed, the staff may have changed, your boss may have left, and technology might have been updated. If you are taking an extended leave it may be worth popping in once in a while to see what is happening and staying in touch with colleagues.

You may also need or even want some retraining if you are out of the work force for a while.

And don't forget to factor in to your budget a wardrobe update if it's been a while since you've had to wear office attire.

> **Anne Laurie, office administrator, mother of three**
>
> I'd been out of the workforce for eight years and felt completely out of touch. Prior to having children I'd been a graphic designer and studio manager, but to return to that field was just too hard. I couldn't afford to get new graphics software and retrain and I didn't necessarily want the pressures associated with that type of work again. So I started selling ENJO, a range of cleaning products. The company was a big support, providing equipment, software and training, all the help I needed to get going.
>
> There were instant rewards with this type of selling and I could work the hours that suited me, mainly evenings and Saturdays. That was especially handy with young kids and it enabled us to avoid childcare costs.
>
> There were a few changes at home though—I went from doing everything in the house, to having to walk out the door and leave a lot for my husband Cameron to do. It was a big mental challenge. I tried to organize everything,

and slowly started to relax about it and enjoy work from a social point of view. It was somewhere to go where I didn't talk about the kids. I felt important.

After a while, though, working nights and weekends put too much of a strain on our family. So I took an office job during school hours. It gave me routine and stability, a reliable income, superannuation, and I built up a nice rapport with my colleagues.

The regular hours also made family life so much easier. Sam in particular found it tough when I was doing evening and weekend work and wasn't around as much. I was burning the candle at both ends, Cameron had to do a lot more at home and that became an added pressure. By doing regular office hours he's not affected. I manage everything at home as I used to.

It's a big factor to take into account—how much time your husband has to change his routine when you go to work. Some men struggle to manage the increase in their workload.

It's almost easier to return when the kids are younger because it becomes part of their routine. Sam was seven and really noticed the changes. I no longer have time now to prepare dinner ahead of time, so I can spend afternoons playing with the kids. Now we all come home together and I run around doing dinner, the washing, tidying up and running the children's bath, homework, stories and bed.

It just means I have to be really organized and schedule our lives. We have a weekly planner with all work and play activities and a family jobs roster.

You may have been out of the work force for a while, you might even be feeling a little nervous, but don't underestimate yourself and your abilities, or the new project management skills you have acquired in your role as a mum.

The perfect time manager

> **Geoff Morgan, Director, Morgan Investments Pty Ltd and Talent2 Recruitment**
>
> My perfect model for a great time manager is a working mother. If you ask any working mother how they spend their day then invariably they are up early making school lunches or dressing children for childcare, doing washing and often getting their husbands out of bed too! Working mothers should value who they are and value their skills because they have a lot to contribute to the workforce.

Managing colleagues

You may also find colleagues' attitudes have changed, and there are some who no longer think you can handle the job. Those without children, in particular, are more likely to underestimate just what a busy mum can really handle.

Work relationships

> **Anne Hollonds, from counselling service Relationships Australia**
>
> It is inevitable that those without babies will think they carry all the load. So it's up to you to demonstrate you can do the job. Working mums learn very quickly to be multi-skilled. Don't be apologetic.
>
> You might also find yourself skipping Friday night drinks, keen instead to get home to your family. But at the same time you don't want to be perceived as not being part of the team.
>
> Maybe you could develop other team rituals, or tell your workmates you can only attend once a month. Be overt. Tell them things have changed, but you are still part of the team. But remember socializing is still an important part of your work culture.

You may not want to do as much, but sometimes it import-ant. This is one area you may need to find a compromise.

How to get out the door on time

One last thing to remember as a mum, in paid work or not—gone are the days of getting out the door in under fifteen minutes. Never again will this be simple and quick—particularly if you have to drop a baby off at childcare or grandma's.

The key, as with so much of being a working mum, is to be organized. Prepare as much as possible. Have the work done before you have to rush—because believe us, it will be the one morning that you are dressed in a white silk blouse and have a very important client meeting that your little darling will vomit on you.

The smaller they are the easier it is—no battles over clothes, pigtails or cleaning teeth—but even at this size they can still throw a major spanner in the works.

Getting out the door top tips

- Do as much as you can the night before. Pack your baby's bag, lay out their clothes, leave two options if the weather is changing.

- Then pack your own bag, lay out your clothes, find the keys, wallet and mobile phone.

- Set the breakfast table, turn the dishwasher on, wash and hang out a load of clothes.

- Dress yourself last. Wait until your baby has finished feeding, dishes are cleared and hands washed. This will minimize mess on you! Always have two options clean and ironed in case of the inevitable poo/vomit incident.

- Use bibs. They are so much easier to pull off as you walk out the door so you can at least create the illusion your baby is clean.

- Once your baby gets a bit older you can make games of the morning routine. Some kids' music on a CD in the car can also be a handy incentive to get things moving. Just remember, the more they are involved, the more likely they are to follow instructions.

- Share the duties. Maybe you can achieve more at night and your partner is fresher in the morning. Maybe you bath, put to bed and pack the bags at night, he gets baby up and dressed in the morning.

- Fill the car with petrol when you are alone—even if it's not empty. It is so much easier and quicker to dash in on your own than bundle your little one in and out of the car. And that's the last thing you want to be doing when you're in the middle of morning or evening rush hour.

- Routines help. The more organized you are, the better and the smoother things will run. Children react to your stress. If you are frazzled they will be too.

- Most importantly though, cut yourself some slack. No one is supermum. Some mornings it will run to plan, other days it won't. Don't have unrealistic expectations.

- When its goes smoothly smile in the knowledge you are the best mum ever! When it goes completely pear shaped, try to smile and remember even Carol Brady would have had bad days (and she had a live-in nanny!).

If, when or how you go back to work may be among the toughest decisions you will have to make. You may find it simple, but your girlfriend on the other hand may be thrown into dissaray.

She might completely change her mind and reassess her career goals after childbirth. As with the birth itself, prepare to remain flexible where possible. And remember, if you are unsure, apply for a longer maternity leave or come back earlier if you feel ready.

Resources list

- Check out www.mumsinbusiness.net which offers seminars and training for mums so they too can have their own business.

- *Show Mummy the Money* by Sonia Williams.

- *Let Go of My Leg* by Kirsten Lees.

✳ Returning to work—handy hints

- Discuss with your boss before you take leave what options you may have upon your return. Consider working from home, working part-time or job sharing.

- Have as much as possible in place before you return— eg childcare, feeding routines—to make the transition easier for you and your baby.

- Leave a bit of room to move within your maternity leave. You have the option of taking longer or shorter leave if you change your mind.

- Look at what other work options are available that might suit you, at least in the short time. Or make some changes in your current job that will make life easier when you return.

- Discuss it all with your partner and family. Maybe they can make some changes to help you manage it all. Maybe your partner can cut back some hours or days, maybe you start earlier in the day or work later and they do the opposite.

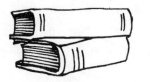

chapter 9

the law and working mothers

In this chapter:

- You've found out you're pregnant, but when do you need to tell work?

- What are your legal rights at work while you're pregnant, negotiating your return to work and once you do go back?

- Changing your will to include your new child.

- What options you have to appoint legal guardians.

- Some of the legal obstacles you may face and how to deal with them.

Note: Government's change and with them laws can too. We are not legal experts so the following information is correct right now but it's always best to make sure you know your legal rights if you ever have a problem. We have provided a number of resources at the end of this chapter that will be able to provide further information—or you can always contact your state or federal member of parliament as well.

Being pregnant, giving birth and spending maternity leave at home with your new baby can be a wonderful time in your life. It is also a time when as a working mother-to-be you'll need to devote some time to negotiating a variety of things—from maternity leave to your return to work, maybe considering a move to part-time work, and ensuring the job you return to is what you expect.

Most of the time this goes smoothly and is hassle-free, but sometimes less than fair employers may try to use your pregnant status or your return to work after maternity leave as an excuse to give you the short shrift. Read on to find out exactly what your legal rights are, how to negotiate, and what you can do about it if you've been treated unfairly.

Where do I find the law on parental leave?

The law dealing with parental leave (which includes maternal, paternal and adoption leave) is spelt out in the *Workplace Relations Act*, and is part of the Australian Fair Pay and Conditions Standard, known as the Standard. This Standard sets out key minimum entitlements for employees which cannot be taken away. It sets out what your rights and obligations are, as well as those of your employer.

You may be entitled to additional benefits over and above this minimum Standard depending on your employer, and these may be contained in your employment contract, workplace agreement or company policies.

When to tell work you're pregnant

You've just found out you're pregnant and feel like shouting it from the rooftop. Pause right there! Not only do you not have to legally tell work for many months—there are a range of reasons why you shouldn't tell them for a while. Apart from the possible risk of miscarriage in the first three months, you need to be clear in your own mind what possible impact the pregnancy may have on your work. Do you want to continue in the same role? Is going part-time for a while an option or what you want? Who will replace you while you are on maternity leave?

Before you have the inevitable 'I'm pregnant' conversation with your boss you need to know your plans for maternity leave and for your return to work. You also should have a view about the impact of your absence on any particular projects you may be working on and who should replace you.

You do not legally need to tell work that you are pregnant until ten weeks before the expected date of birth, when you must give your employer a medical certificate confirming that you are pregnant and providing the expected due date. You also need to formally apply for maternity leave at least four weeks before the first day of the leave you want to take.

In reality, most women will show way before the six-month mark, but this means that you can leave it for as long as you feel comfortable within this time frame. For most women this is usually around the three to four month mark. Sometimes nausea, repeated visits to the bathroom or quaffing lots of dry ginger ale will give the game away, but try to stop yourself from telling colleagues until you are good and ready.

Your rights while you are pregnant

If you are pregnant and you have told your employer, and your doctor thinks it's unsafe for you to continue in your position because of illness or risks associated with being pregnant, you're entitled to be transferred to a safe job. If your employer doesn't think there is any safe job available you're entitled to paid leave until the start of your maternity leave. This paid leave doesn't reduce the total period of parental leave you are entitled to.

You are also covered by anti-discrimination laws which are discussed later in this chapter.

Your leave entitlements

Before you have that conversation with the boss or negotiate your time off, you need to know whether you have any maternity rights, and what they are:

- To be eligible to apply for parental leave, you need to have at least twelve months of continuous service with your employer before the birth of your baby.

- If you're employed as a casual you're entitled to parental leave providing you have worked on a regular and systematic basis for at least twelve months before the due date.

If you are not entitled to parental leave under the Standard, perhaps because you haven't worked the twelve months to qualify, you may want to try to negotiate some unpaid leave with your employer.

Under the Standard, parental leave provisions include:

- Up to fifty-two weeks total of unpaid parental leave for parents to take on a shared basis to care for their newborn child or newly adopted child under the age of five years. Other than one week at the time of the birth (or three weeks in the case of adoption), both parents can't be on parental leave at the same time.

- You can start your maternity leave at any time in the six weeks immediately before your due date. If you continue to work during that time, you may be required to provide a medical certificate to say you are fit to work in your current job.

- You are not legally required to take maternity leave, but if you take leave you must take at least six weeks' leave after the birth and take the leave in one continuous, unbroken period.

- Special maternity leave can be recommended by your doctor for a pregnancy-related illness or in the event that you have a miscarriage.

- One week of paternity leave is available for male employees taken within the week his partner gives birth.

The Standard doesn't recognize parental leave for lesbian couples. While the partner who gives birth to the child is entitled to maternity leave, the Standard only provides paternity leave to leave taken by a male employee after his spouse gives birth. Same sex couples will have to try to negotiate an arrangement with their employers.

In the case of adoption, you are entitled to up to two days of unpaid pre-adoption leave to attend any interviews or examinations required to obtain approval for the adoption.

Paid parental leave

Women in Australia have no entitlement under the Standard to paid maternity leave, although figures show that thirty-eight per cent of female employees reported they had access to some form of paid maternity leave.

Generally, this applies to public sector employees and those employed by large companies.[1] In some companies, only senior female staff are entitled to paid leave as well as their statutory leave.

Quick Tip

Your employer might have more generous leave provisions in a policy, workplace agreement, or as part of your contract of employment. This could include some paid parental leave. You should ask your manager or HR department for information about what is available to you.

Applying for leave

Under the Standard there is a number of things you must do to qualify for parental leave. In reality, a lot of employers are quite flexible, but you must check what the expected procedure is where you work and make sure you dot the i's and cross the t's so you can get the arrangements you want.

By law you need to do a number of things:

- Provide a medical certificate from your doctor to your employer no later than ten weeks before the expected date of birth (where possible).

- Apply formally for parental leave four weeks before the first day your leave starts by providing a written

1 See the Human Rights and Equal Opportunity Commission (HREOC) report 'A time to value: A proposal for a national paid maternity leave scheme', 2002.

application stating the dates for leave. You must also provide a statutory declaration setting out the period of any other leave, and details of any paternity leave your partner is going to take.

- If your partner intends to take additional paternity leave after the short period at the time of the birth, he must give his employer ten weeks' written notice and provide his employer with a signed statutory declaration detailing leave periods (yours and his), stating that he will be the child's primary caregiver and that he will not do other work inconsistent with his employment while on parental leave.

Different rules apply to you if you give birth prematurely.

While you are on leave

You can extend parental leave only once within the fifty-two-week period, provided fourteen days' written notice is given to your employer. Any further extension within or after the fifty-two-week period is at your employer's discretion. You can only shorten parental leave with your employer's agreement, and you need to give at least four weeks' notice.

You can take other leave (for example, annual leave) for the birth or adoption of the child in combination with parental leave. The fifty-two weeks of unpaid parental leave is reduced by other leave you may take as you only have a right to take fifty-two weeks in total between yourself and your partner.

There may be other rules that apply to you because of your particular workplace agreement—you should make sure you understand what they are before you go on leave.

Returning to work—your rights

Returning to work can be a tricky thing to negotiate and you often don't know how you'll feel until you get there and how much time you'll want off. Giving yourself some flexibility is all well and good, but you need to know exactly what you are entitled to. More often than not your employer will remain open and flexible, but if they aren't, be equipped with information about your entitlements.

If you take parental leave you're entitled to return to the position you held before the start of parental leave or if that position no longer exists, to a position nearest in status and remuneration to your former position. Sometimes there has been a restructure while you have been on leave, and a question arises as to what job you should come back to.

Cynthia's experience

Cynthia Thomson was returning from her second period of maternity leave with Orica. She was returning full-time. While she was on leave her sales patch had been allocated to another employee, and Orica had also rearranged the sales territories slightly. On her return, she was told she would be looking after a different set of customers.

The Federal Court decided that the job she was asked to do was significantly different in terms of tasks, duties, responsibilities and status, and in effect a demotion that would not have occurred unless she had taken maternity leave. Orica argued that as her title and remuneration were the same, there had been no demotion or discrimination and she was returning to the same position. The Court decided that Orica had discriminated against Cynthia on the grounds of sex and pregnancy, and had effectively dismissed Cynthia by not following its own Family Leave policy.[2]

If you were full-time before taking leave, there is nothing in the Standard which allows you to return part-time; however, in some circumstances, the refusal to allow part-time work can amount to discrimination on the grounds of sex and pregnancy. Some workplace agreements, particularly in the public service, contain a right to part-time work, but this is rare in the private sector. If you aren't sure whether this might apply to you, find out.

Beverley's experience

Beverley Bogle was employed as a Charge Nurse. After she adopted a child she asked to return to work on a part-time job-share basis. Her employer said she could either come back full-time as a Charge Nurse, or part-time in a lower graded position. The Western Australian Equal Opportunity Tribunal decided that she had been discriminated against as the requirement to work full-time was not reasonable in all the circumstances. The Tribunal believed that her employer had failed to conduct any proper analysis or evaluation of her proposal to job share, and by forcing her into a part-time role of a lower grade, denied her a number of benefits including access to opportunities for promotion, denial of her usual salary and loss of status. Her employer was ordered to reinstate her, trial a job-share of the Charge Nurse position and pay her financial compensation.[3]

---

2 The case is *Thomson v Orica Australia Pty Ltd* [2002] FCA 939. You can read the decision on-line at www.austlii.edu.au/au/cases/cth/federal_ct/2002/939.
3 The case name is *Bogle v Metropolitan Health Service Board* (2000) EOC 9193–069.

Factors that the courts and tribunals have taken into account in deciding whether it would be discriminatory or not to insist on a return to full-time work have included the size of the employer, the nature of the job, whether other people have worked part-time, and whether the employer has a policy that promotes flexible work practices. Each situation will be different, however, and if you want to return to work on a different basis you should be prepared to support the idea in discussions with your employer.

You should discuss your plans for your return at an early stage with your employer, preferably before you take maternity leave. Be prepared to put the case for why it would work in your job—don't expect your employer to suggest part-time work or job-sharing. If necessary, be prepared to suggest a trial period for the arrangements to be evaluated. Whatever is agreed to, make sure you get it in writing—you don't want to find that your manager changes while you are on leave and there is no record of your employer's commitments.

Depending on the nature of your work there may be a number of options you could consider such as:

- Permanent part-time

- Job-sharing a full-time role with another part-timer

- Guaranteed start and finish times

- Working from home exclusively or on some days only

Flexibility works both ways—consider how you can make a flexible or part-time arrangement work for you *and* your employer or consider purchasing additional leave.

Maybe you can check your email at home, or make yourself available by being contactable on your mobile. Just make sure you don't end up doing a full-time workload with a part-time pay!

For more information about your entitlements

Useful contacts include your HR Department, your union, the Office of Workplace Services, the Human Rights and Equal Opportunity Commission and state and territory anti-discrimination bodies. Contact details can be found at the end of this chapter.

Discrimination and your rights at work when pregnant

Generally, employers must treat pregnant employees the same way as they treat all their other employees. They must do this whether you are permanent, full-time, part-time or casual. They can only treat you differently if there's a legal reason for them to treat you differently.

For example, it is generally against the law not to hire you because they think you might become pregnant.

Remember that employers cannot dismiss or retrench you because you are pregnant—this amounts to an unlawful dismissal, and gives you a right to lodge a claim in the Australian Industrial Relations Commission to seek re-instatement and/or compensation. Your employment can still be terminated while you are pregnant or on parental leave, but only if it would have been anyway, maybe as part of a redundancy program, or for poor performance.

There are also Commonwealth, state and territory laws which make it unlawful to discriminate against a person on the basis of their pregnancy or potential pregnancy.[4] This includes behaviour, such as:

4 See the HREOC publication, 'Pregnant and Productive: It's a right not a privilege to work while pregnant', 1999.

- Harassing you, or allowing other employees to harass you, because of your pregnancy

- Not providing you with larger sizes of uniforms—if they normally provide your uniform

- Transferring you to another job 'out of sight' because you're pregnant—unless you willingly agree to the transfer

- Transferring you to another job where they think you will be safer—unless there are valid medical or safety reasons

- Denying you training just because you're pregnant

- Stopping you being promoted just because you're pregnant

- Not giving you the same or a similar job when you return from maternity leave. If you've been working regularly for twelve months with the same employer, you have the right to take maternity leave and return to your job afterwards.

However, in some states the law allows employers not to hire a woman if she is pregnant at the time of application or interview.

The anti-discrimination laws also make it unlawful to discriminate on the grounds of pregnancy in areas other than employment. These include:

- When you get, or try to get, most types of goods or services—for example, from shops, hotels, entertainment venues, banks, lawyers, government departments, doctors or hospitals

- When you rent, or try to rent, accommodation—for example, a unit, house, commercial premises, hotel room or motel room

- When you apply to get into, or are studying in, any educational institution

- When you try to enter or join a registered club, or when you're inside one

It is also against the law to treat you unfairly or harass you in any of the above circumstances because you have a relative, friend or associate who is pregnant.

Sex discrimination

As well as it being unlawful to discriminate against you if you are pregnant, if you are treated differently because you are a woman, this may amount to sex discrimination. The courts have stipulated that being pregnant and having the responsibility of caring for small children is a characteristic that relates to women generally. If you are denied part-term work, or some flexibility in your working arrangements because you have taken time off on maternity leave, this could amount to sex discrimination.

Carer's responsibilities discrimination

If you are treated unfairly or harassed at work because you are responsible for caring for or supporting a child, or have responsibilities to care for someone else, such as aging parents, you may have been unlawfully discriminated against. For more information, contact the anti-discrimination bodies listed at the end of the chapter.

What can I do if I think I have been discriminated against?

You should check with the Human Rights and Equal Opportunity Commission, or the equivalent state or territory body to get some preliminary advice about whether your treatment was unlawful.

If what's happened seems to be against the law, you can try talking to the person or organization that you think has discriminated against or is harassing you. The organization may have a policy on these issues and/or a process in place to deal with grievances. You can also get help from other sources such as trade unions, if you are a member, a community legal centre, or a private lawyer. If talking to the person or organization doesn't work, or isn't appropriate, you may decide to make a complaint to HREOC or the anti-discrimination body in your state. It won't cost you any money, and you may be able to avoid using a lawyer.

To make a discrimination complaint

If you want to make a complaint to HREOC, or the anti-discrimination body in your state, it must be in writing and it is best if it is signed by you—explaining why you think you have been discriminated against. There may be a time limit for making the complaint—you should check with the relevant body. Anti-discrimination bodies will also accept complaints on your behalf from your lawyer, or organizations such as unions and other representative bodies and, in some circumstances, you may also be required to show that you consent to the complaint being made on your behalf.

After you make a complaint, it will be investigated, and the parties will be invited to participate in a conciliation conference to try to reach an acceptable settlement. If the matter is not resolved at conciliation, you can decide whether to pursue the complaint further. This usually involves more formal court proceedings, and there can be costs associated with taking these steps. You may want to get legal advice before you make the decision to take your complaint further.

Privately-agreed settlements and court outcomes can include payment of monetary compensation for any financial loss, a component of compensation for pain and suffering or distress, and a wide range of other orders including an apology, agreement by the company to provide further training or a commitment to develop better policies.

What do I do if I've been sacked?

If your employment has been terminated for an unlawful reason, such as sex, pregnancy or family responsibilities, you should contact the Australian Industrial Relations Commission. The unlawful reason only needs to be *a* factor in the decision to terminate, not the *only* reason. Any claim for unlawful dismissal must be lodged within twenty-one days from the date of the termination. The Commission can order re-instatement or compensation.

Louise's experience

Louise Laz was employed as the personal assistant to the Group Managing Director of Downer Group. Although the hours of the job were 8.30 a.m. to 5.30 p.m., at the interview she told her employer that she could work back past 6.00 p.m. on nights when her husband lectured provided she was given some notice, as she had to make arrangements for her young son to be collected from childcare.

Some time later, her boss found a replacement who could always work longer hours and her employment was terminated, with one of the reasons given that she was not always able to work past 5.30 p.m. when he wanted her to. The Federal Court decided that a significant reason, if not the sole reason forher termination, was because she was unable to work the hours her boss demanded because of her family responsibilities—and that her termination was unlawful. The Court decided that Louise Laz should be re-instated and paid back-pay for the period from termination to the date of the judgment.[5]

Considerations when drafting a will

Having a baby is an exciting time. The need to make a will or to revise your current will is not something which often springs to mind. Many people put off making a will believing that their estate will go to their spouse and children anyway.

So why make a will?

The laws of intestacy (that is, when someone dies without leaving a will) provide for the property to pass to your next of kin, but to people and in proportions you might not necessarily like. Making a will provides you with the freedom of choice to determine who you would like to make gifts to and what you would like them to receive. Dealing with assets is simpler, quicker and cheaper if you have a will. If you don't have a will, a family member or other people (in certain circumstances) will have to prove who your next of kin are to a court.

5 *Laz v Downer Group Ltd* [2000] FCA 1309, available online at www.austlii.edu. au/au/cases/cth/federal_ct/2000/1390.

Who should you appoint as your executor?

In your will you must appoint an executor. You can appoint your spouse or partner or one or more of your adult beneficiaries. It is always wise to appoint an alternative executor in case the first one you appointed dies.

What provision should you make for children in your will?

The first thing you need to consider is how 'children' should be defined in your will. You can of course name your children in your will but you may wish to provide for any future children you may have.

All states and territories have some general status of children legislation which includes adopted and ex-nuptial children. You need to keep this in mind when making a gift to a class of beneficiaries as opposed to naming each individual beneficiary. A specific clause can be included in your will to exclude ex-nuptial children or relatives who may claim through them, but there is no guarantee that this clause will be effective because the general status of children legislation has been carefully drafted to prevent people disinheriting any ex-nuptial children.

A child conceived but not yet born may be included in a class gift to your 'children'. If you have foster children or step-children you would like to include in your will, then these children need to be specifically included.

Some thought needs to be given to how gifts to minor children—or children younger than a specified age, say eighteen or twenty-one or twenty-five years old—will be managed until they reach majority or the specified age.

The will should include specific powers for the executor to be able to make payments from the child's share to the guardian or person with whom the child resides, which is to be used for the child's education and advancement in life and other benefits.

Without these powers in the will, the legislation relating to the payment of gifts to minors is quite restrictive. If the share which your child is to receive is not large, it may also be useful for your executor to be able to pay the gift out in full to the guardian or to the person with whom the child resides.

If any of your children have a disability, or may become financially unstable, suffer from an addiction, become bankrupt or be involved in family law proceedings, you need to consider the benefit of creating a protective trust or discretionary trust in your will. This means that the gift you make to any of these children in your will will not be paid out to them immediately but will form part of an ongoing trust which will be managed for its duration by your executor.

If you belong to a blended family where you have a second spouse but have your own children from a prior marriage, you need to ensure that you make provision in your will for your children as well as your current spouse.

It is a good idea to have an ultimate beneficiary or beneficiaries who would inherit your estate if all your children die before you do or die before reaching a specified age.

What options do you have to appoint a legal guardian?

One reason many people consider it important to have a will is to appoint a guardian to care for their minor children. Unfortunately the decision to appoint a legal guardian of your minor children is not that simple. Care needs to be taken about your choice of guardian, as only the Supreme Court has the power to change the appointment.

Every state and territory has legislation which gives each parent the right to appoint a guardian or guardians by will or deed to care for their minor children after the parents' death. The legislation also provides for a parent to appoint a guardian to act with the surviving parent of that child. The issue is made more complex because the Commonwealth Family Law legislation provides that parental responsibility is left to the parent of the child. There appears to be no room for another person to exercise parental powers over the child unless the surviving parent consents to this arrangement.

When drafting a will to appoint a testamentary guardian it should be made clear in the will if the appointment is only to take effect when there is no surviving parent, or if the appointed guardian is to act jointly with the surviving parent. If you consider appointing more than one guardian you should consider what may happen if these guardians develop conflict over the care of your children. It may be wiser to appoint one person to act as the guardian of your children with a substitute named in case that person is unwilling or unable to act.

When appointing a guardian in the will, powers need to be given to the executors to ensure that adequate funds are available so the guardians of your minor children do not suffer any financial hardship as a result of caring for your children. A clause should be included in your will to provide for your executors to be able to make loans or use up as much of your estate as is necessary to provide the care for your children. Another possibility may be to make a substantial gift absolutely to the guardian of your minor children. If you adopt this approach you must be aware that you are placing your trust in the guardian to use the gift for the care of your children.

One final consideration is whether you should provide a separate statement expressing your wishes for the care of your children known as a Statement of Wishes. You might like to cover such issues as your child's education, religion, and other family values which are to be taken into account in their upbringing. This document is usually prepared at the same time as making your will. It provides some guidance to the executors but it is non-binding.

Other hurdles

Being gay or lesbian parents has its own hurdles. While discrimination on the basis of sexual preference is unlawful, in reality public behaviour and attitudes can be a whole different story.

66 **Feyi Akindoyeni and Kate Deverall, research director and political adviser, mothers to one**

We were together eight years when we decided to have a baby together. As lesbian women this required a sperm donation and a decision on how one of us would conceive. Kate decided to have the baby and we decided to use IVF to conceive, using Fertility East in Sydney who were very professional and provided an excellent counselling service that ensured that everyone participating in the process, including the sperm donor, was happy. Luckily, Kate conceived in our first round of IVF.

During the pregnancy we didn't encounter any prejudice against us. The hospital and the other eight straight couples in our prenatal class were all really friendly and welcoming. It was undoubtedly the topic of many dinner party conversations of some of our friends but no one said anything to us directly that we took offence to.

One thing we'd suggest to others going through the same process is that the partner who did not give birth to the child should report the birth. You get your name on the birth certificate this way, alongside the birth mother who is on there already. We didn't do this, but we didn't know what the rules were at the time.

We've had to clarify a few things with first childcare and now school—if Kate wasn't available, for instance, could Feyi take her to hospital. Somewhat surprisingly there was never any issue with private health cover—adding on the partner and child's name just wasn't an issue. Superannuation, though, is another story and remains a big problem for us.

✱ Your legal rights—handy hints

- Know your rights—make sure you understand what you are legally entitled to, and what your employer can and can't do.
- Make sure you comply with the notice requirements, and give your employer a doctor's certificate ten weeks before the due date, formally apply for maternity leave at least four weeks before you intend to start the leave, and notify your employer of your start date four weeks before you intend to return to work.
- Discuss your return-to-work plans early and get any agreement with your employer in writing.
- Be prepared to put forward the business case for why any flexible working arrangement will work.
- If you and your employer can't agree to arrangements for your return, consider making a complaint to an anti-discrimination body—although these can take some time to resolve. If you have to go back to work full-time

and you don't want to, make sure your employer knows you are unhappy about it and are challenging the decision.

Useful contacts

Human Rights and Equal Opportunity Commission (HREOC)
  Phone: (02) 9284 9600
  Complaint info-line: 1300 656 419
  General enquiries and publications: 1300 369 711
  Website: www.hreoc.gov.au

ACT Human Rights Office
  Phone: (02) 6205 2222
  Website: www.hro.act.gov.au

Anti-Discrimination Board New South Wales
  Phone: (02) 9268 5544 (general enquiry service)
  Toll free: 1800 670 812 (for rural and regional NSW only)
  Website: www.lawlink.nsw.gov.au/adb

Anti-Discrimination Commission Queensland
  Phone: 1300 130 670
  Website: www.adcq.qld.gov.au

Office of the Anti-Discrimination Commissioner—Tasmania
  Toll free: 1300 305 062 (statewide)
  Website: www.antidiscrimination.tas.gov.au

Victorian Equal Opportunity & Human Rights Commission
  Phone: (03) 9281 7100
  Website: www.humanrightscommission.vic.gov.au

Northern Territory of Australia Anti-Discrimination Commission
  Toll free: 1800 813 846
  Website: www.nt.gov.au/justice/adc/index800.html

Equal Opportunity Commission of South Australia
  Toll free: 1800 188 163 (statewide)
  Website: www.eoc.sa.gov.au

Equal Opportunity Commission of Western Australia
  Toll free: 1800 198 149 (statewide)
  Website: www.equalopportunity.wa.gov.au

Office of Workplace Services
  Phone: (02) 8293 4683 or 1300 724 200
  WorkChoices Infoline: 1300 363 264
  website: www.ows.gov.au

Community Legal Centres—see your phone book for listings

ACTU
  Toll free: 1300 362 223
  Workers' Hotline: 1300 362 223 (for help with a workplace issue)
  website: www.actu.asn.au

Australian Industrial Relations Commission
  Phone: (02) 8374 6666
  Website: www.airc.gov.au

chapter 10
baby etiquette

In this chapter:

- How to deftly deal with those helpful strangers keen to offer advice and lay their hands on you, or your baby.

- How and when to accept offers of help from relatives, and how to politely decline them.

- How to manage the expectations of your immediate family alongside the interests of your new family and work.

- How to manage work situations with a new baby and how to handle difficult colleagues.

- Eating out with your baby.

- Travelling with your baby.

All new parents have to deal with it somehow. Your baby is public property—or so mere strangers, distant aunts and your mother think. How many times have you heard the banter from a great aunt or new grandmother: 'I forgot just how small they were', or 'Don't you just love that new baby smell' (and secretly you wished they go off and smell someone else's baby!).

Everyone loves a new baby. And from the moment the baby is born managing and politely refusing help or social interaction from strangers through to grandparents is a challenge.

Add to this personal challenge your return to work—made harder as you manage difficult colleagues and the pressure of being seen to 'pull your weight'. This chapter will help you negotiate your way through this etiquette minefield—so read on.

How to handle hospital and the thousands of visitors

The etiquette challenges begin just minutes after the baby is born. Do you *really* need your entire extended family standing at the foot of your hospital bed when you are exhausted and have just gone through a seventeen-hour labour? Well, no, but how do you tell them?

In our view you should set the rules and even better if you do it before you go to hospital. If family is important to you welcome them in, but make sure they aren't all there at once and encourage just one visitor at a time.

Here are a few handy tips we've picked up from girlfriends— some of them we wished we'd thought of when we were in hospital!

- It's not your job to entertain visitors when you're in hospital—you're trying to learn breastfeeding and it's all daunting and you're exhausted. So blame your baby or the nurses. Get your partner/husband to be the policeman. Ask people to check with him before visiting. Tell your friends if you don't want visitors.

- If you don't want any visitors, just say no. You and the baby aren't going anywhere—and believe us they won't have grown in a week, so wait until you are feeling up to it and at home before you entertain.

- Consider spending one week by yourselves as a family—no visitors. Get the hang of things, get into a routine and try to get some sleep—then open the doors and say 'hi' to family.

- Call out for help in hospital. Buzz that buzzer! Use all the help and expertise available.

- Once you've left, use midwives as a resource. Call them if you have a question and ask for information.

- Do not rush home from hospital. Stay as long as possible if you are able to rest. Especially if it's not your first child.

Being polite to nosey strangers

I was shopping for shoes just before I returned to work after my second child, Frida was born. She was nearly three months and still a babe in arms and had just had a bottle. The matronly Italian shop assistant, a grandmother of five herself, insisted she needed to 'be burped', promptly picked Frida up, placed her face down over her knees and proceeded to slap her very firmly on the back, many times. Never mind that Frida had never been burped before. I was horrified, with visions of projectile vomit shooting all over the collection of beautiful Italian shoes and the assistant. Would have served her right, I thought. As politely as I could I reclaimed the child and even managed to buy some shoes—they were on sale after all. – Jo

How many times have you heard a complete stranger tell you that your daughter is 'such a Daddy's girl' or that she *definitely* looks like you. Or tell you that's not the right way to wrap your baby when you know what works for your own child. How the hell would they know, you think, and quite rightly.

And so begins the world of intrusive strangers, neighbours and local shopkeepers. You'd rather not have to deal with them at all, but within reason you have to, for politeness' sake.

It's always hard to know where to draw the line. Taking verbal advice from the woman across the road is one thing—you can usually suffer most things for a few minutes before you excuse yourself to feed the baby or change a nappy. But what do you do when they start to intrude further by placing their hands on your child to demonstrate their point?

It all depends on how well you know them, how mad they are and what the circumstances are. You'll need to make that call at the time, but usually and luckily your child will start to cry providing an instant excuse to snatch them back. Unless they are particularly mad or you judge them to be potentially harmful for your child at that moment—if they smoke near them for example—then we'd suggest just grinning and bearing the advice for a few minutes before you politely excuse yourself—in the interests of good neighbourliness—and retreat home.

Advice from family and strangers

People will always give you advice. Just smile and nod. As a new mum, don't take criticism to heart. Things have changed in the ways of parenting, from swaddling and breastfeeding to how they sleep. Not everyone you meet will accept that.

If someone's comments make you feel worried or unsure of yourself, find a person you trust who you can call and ask for help or advice.

The importance of your family

Every family is different. Some of us have a huge extended family that we love spending time with, go shopping with and see every week—we wouldn't be without them. Some of us have small families, and some of us have families interstate or overseas. Some people may be estranged from theirs or not see eye to eye with them.

Whatever your situation, never is family as important as when you have a little baby. They'll be as proud as a button that their 'little girl' has now started a family of her own—and they'll want to help you. How that works will differ in each situation, depending on how close you live to one another, how much time your parent/parents in-law have and how much help you need.

The issue of how help is offered—and accepted—needs some thought from both sides. It's important that if family are involved in your weekly routine or childcare needs that you talk through the ground rules early on—just so any differences in childrearing, routines etcetera can be ironed out and to avoid problems later on.

How to ask your family for help

No matter how big or how small your family is, you'll want them around some of the time after you have a baby, believe us. Often a new baby can be the rapprochement of a difficult mother–daughter relationship or can be the ice-breaker for a family that doesn't always get on. A new baby is always loved and adored, cuddled and kissed.

But how do you ask for help when you've lived away from home for years, been your own person and haven't needed the help of extended family since you were at school?

Well, there's a lot to be said about broaching this topic while you are still pregnant. Start by asking your mum and dad or parents-in-law how they'd like to be involved with your family after the baby is born. How often they want to catch up, babysit or be available for childcare down the track. If this sort of open-ended conversation would be tricky for you and your family, then consider dropping hints—or telling them more directly—about what you hope their role will be. You can drop into conversation 'when we start going to movies again' or 'maybe you could mind the baby one afternoon a week while I'm on maternity leave to give me a break?'. See how that is received and if the response is positive then perhaps discuss it more fully together. In that way you'll have come to a mutually convenient view which won't overly impose on their life, but will help you out enormously.

Don't forget that while your parents/parents-in-law/ extended family *will* want to see your newborn they all still have their own lives to live, jobs to go to, friends to see, and so make sure whatever you decide is something that they are happy with and can cope with alongside their other commitments.

Managing offers of help from family

Not meaning to be ungrateful, but you probably won't want your mum there *every* day after you come home from hospital. And not all mums will want to be there either. We've heard so many stories of women whose mum flies in from interstate or overseas just days after the birth 'because you just won't be able to cope alone dear', planting themselves with you for a week or two.

Those first few weeks can be *really* exhausting, yes, and you can go mad just dealing with sleep deprivation and the demands of the baby's feeding schedule. But a lot of families really want to keep much of all that to themselves—it's such a precious time. So many women, and men too, would like to preserve those treasured early days for themselves, even becoming a little protective of their new family. But how do you deal with the kind offer/s of help?

You may just adore your mum or mother-in-law, but we suggest that you decide well in advance what the limits are, when you want them around, if you want them staying at your place or somewhere else, and then tell them your decision—well before the baby is born. It will save tension or delicate negotiations just after the birth, which is the last thing you need when you're exhausted.

If you want only your mum or mother-in-law around for a weekend a few weeks after the birth, say so. Don't be pressured into a situation that you and your partner/husband will find uncomfortable just to make immediate family happy. It's a hard one to navigate and the last thing you want to do is offend anyone who just wants to offer their love and support, but it's equally important that your new family finds its own feet and gets to know one another. With the support of close friends, your partner and the local baby clinic, you *will* be able to manage.

> ❝ Remember, you are a family now and your family must take priority. As the lioness you must protect your baby and you.
> – *Catriona Dixon, mother of two*

> ❝ You need to find a way to make it all work. Remember family members are just as excited as you are. They want to be part of your new baby's life.
> – *Sharine Ruppert, mother of four*

Socialising with family—on your terms

It's a difficult line to walk most of the time. Your immediate family will have dreams of playing happy families with you, picnics by the beach and frolicking in the sun while watching your baby grow and develop. You will occasionally want to call on them for babysitting, but you want to keep intimate moments with your new family off limits some of the time. How do you do it?

Sometimes close family will want it all their way—they want you to be available every few weekends for a 'baby viewing', but are reluctant to be available to babysit at night. In our experience, making it very clear, very early, that you won't be available all the time is the best way to manage it. If you need an excuse, come up with one. You shouldn't have to have an excuse, but if you do it makes it easier to have thought up a good one in advance. Tell them that you're seeing friends or shopping, but make it convincing.

It's very much a generational thing as well. Your parents will often not understand the pressures that you and your husband might be under—working long hours, sometimes taking work home, logging on to email from home and weekend work. And sometimes no explaining will help them understand. It's hard enough managing your new life, work and less sleep. You should be the arbiter of how much time you spend with your extended family—not them.

As part of the 'have it all' and 'do it all' generation of women, we often drive ourselves into the ground and are really stretched, with not enough time to spend with our husband or partner and baby let alone time to see extended family. In our view, times have changed. You make the rules. There are obligations to family and, yes, close family should be part of your life. But on your terms. You have work and family to juggle and you need to work out the best way of doing that for yourself, without pressures to fit in lots of extended family outings that you really don't have time for.

A lot of women will come from families where their extended family is an integral part of their life, families that can be relied upon for full-time childcare if needs be. You can read more about grandparents and family helping with childcare in Chapter 7.

It may take some time to manage these new relationships with close family but in your own interests it's best to set parameters early on and things will just fall into place and the pressure will subside from a weekly call to one every few weeks. And you'll be happy you stood your ground.

Once you've established some ground rules and they're working well then time spent together will be wonderful. You'll be chilled, because it's under your control and your extended family, aunts, uncles or grandparents, will be deliriously happy because they'll be seeing their precious nephew/niece/ grandchild! Sorted.

What every grandmother should know

Country Women's Association, 1939

The newly-made grandmother (everyone talks of a newly-made wife, or mother—why not grandmother?) must prepare herself for shocks, said a grandmother speaking of children. She will see the most fantastic plans of infant welfare tried by her daughters and daughters-in-law. Her most cherished precepts and laws will be flouted, and if she is wise she will hold her tongue. She must never forget that, however modern her outlook may be, she herself is necessarily a back number. Her daughters and her daughters-in-law hold all the trumps, and it depends on them as much as on herself whether she can establish relations with her grandchildren which will improve and ripen as the years go on. Unless a grandmother always remembers and recognizes that the responsibility for the children is in the hands of their mothers, not in her own, she will never be given the opportunity of getting to know them well.

Your baby and work

You're planning your return to work or you're already back—and it's a minefield of baby-etiquette dilemmas. Here are some hints on how to manage them.

Bringing the baby into the office

It's a hard call and depends *very* much on your office and company culture, but bringing your baby into the office has its pros and cons. Some places will be much more supportive of this than others. In legal firms or merchant banks you can almost bet it's a no-no. But if it's your own business or a small, family-run company, a political or creative environment then it could be entirely possible.

Pros:

- In the early weeks you can have the baby with you and breastfeed as required.
- You and the baby don't go through the trauma of separation quite so early.
- It's cheaper than formal childcare.

Cons:

- The baby doesn't get into as regular a routine as it might at home or in childcare—unless you have a quiet place for it to sleep.
- It depends on how flexible your work schedule is in accommodating the constant, and fluctuating needs of a baby.
- Your time will be split between the baby and work—and as a result you probably won't do either as effectively as you may have hoped.

- The noise and distraction can be stressful on your work colleagues and cause unspoken resentment toward you.

- There are lots of options to explore here, and it's best to be frank and open with your employer about what you're hoping to do. Many employers wouldn't object at all to the baby being brought in for a feed once or twice a day—most people *love* seeing new babies. But having a baby with you all day is another thing. In the end, it's up to you, what sort of workplace you have and how flexible they are—*really*.

Read more about returning to work in Chapter 8.

66 *When my first child, Marlow, was six months old I returned to work just two days a week initially, my husband was able to take paternity leave on those days to look after him. Although I'd left some expressed milk and he took a bottle and solids by then, Andrew brought him in to the office once a day for a feed—which I did sitting at my desk. My colleagues loved seeing a little baby and it was good for Marlow and me.*

Don't feel that you have to wean because you're going back to work—there are lots of options to consider. And most workplaces will probably be more flexible than you think. Breastfeeding in public is entirely legal in all states of Australia and no one can stop you—breastfeeding at your place of work is something you'll need to play by ear. – *Jo*

Skiving off?

A lot of you have been here. And you know the score. It's nearly five, childcare closes in an hour and you need to get the car and drive across town to pick up your baby. You exit discreetly, hoping that your colleagues won't notice or disapprove. Others at your office—mostly childless and single—will still be there at 6.00 p.m. or later.

How you manage this can be hard. There can be lots of guilt involved for some of us. If you work at a big city law firm then it's almost de rigueur to be there until after dark, and back again before the sun comes up. If you've returned to work early and have a small baby at home or in childcare waiting for a breastfeed, then staying late will be emotionally and physically difficult—apart from a distressed child your breasts will ache. You are, after all, a parent and someone needs to pick the baby up from childcare or relieve the babysitter or nanny.

Calling on grandparents or other friends or family when you are particularly busy on a project can work some days. If that will work for you and them get them a baby seat and a key to your house, so they can help out at late notice. Make sure they know the baby's routine, how to mix up formula, and how to bath and put them to bed. Make a list of this information and display it somewhere prominently so they can rely on it when they need to.

And although you may have family or friends you can rely upon occasionally, the reality is that it's your new family that has to take on these additional burdens and juggling for the long term, so the sooner you can recalibrate your and your partner's work patterns and your work colleagues' expectations, the better off you'll be.

Babies thrive on routine, so the quicker you establish one when you're back at work the better for everyone. If that means logging on and doing a few hours of work from home later in the evening each day after the baby is in bed, then so be it. Work colleagues will soon cotton on to the fact that you aren't skiving once emails regularly arrive at 11 p.m.—you just work different hours, and work differently, to them. Particularly intransigent colleagues who are intolerant, rude or actively discriminate against you because you've had a baby will just have to be ignored as best you can. The most important thing is to make sure that whatever you do you are doing it with the approval of your immediate manager. A stiff upper lip, as hard as it is to manage sometimes, can come in handy. In extreme circumstances talking to your employer or taking action via the anti-discrimination legislation will be warranted. There is more detail on this in Chapter 9.

Managing the expectations of work colleagues

So, we've already established that you're not taking it easy—in fact, you probably end up working more hours and more efficiently than many of your colleagues with no children (not that we're biased). You'll constantly amaze yourself just how efficiently you manage your tasks when you return to work after children. That's partly because your time is not open ended and partly because you're looking forward to seeing your child at the end of the day.

It is unlawful to be discriminated against because you have children or to be singled out for different treatment. Both these things are against the law. As long as you are working your required hours each week then you don't *have to* stay at the office later than you need to.

While this legal situation exists, this doesn't stop some work colleagues deliberately making you feel uncomfortable about leaving each day shortly after 5.00 p.m. to collect your child, or about needing to take days off to look after a sick child. Sometimes this resentment is unspoken, sometimes it's hearsay from others, and sometimes it is direct. A fact to remember is that you are allowed by the *Workplace Relations Act* to have ten days' paid personal leave each year to look after a sick child or if you are sick in addition to annual leave. You are also entitled to unpaid carer's leave in some circumstances if you have exhausted your paid leave entitlements.

Your contribution at work is valid, just remember that, and you don't have to be in the office extended hours in order to make that contribution. You don't cease to have a brain because you've had a child.

The best solution to this dilemma is to continue to make an effort, be positive to everyone at the office—even to those who may be less than gracious about your hours or perceived lack of commitment. See Chapter 9 for more information about your legal rights at work.

Working smarter not longer

It's true—all women can do more than one thing at once. In fact, once you've had your baby multi-tasking will be a way of life.

And that's the trick. As so many employers will tell you, they love to employ working mothers because they are so efficient. They don't spend idle hours surfing the Internet or gossiping, because they are acutely aware that they are on a deadline to pick up their child from childcare—or get home to help with the bedtime routine.

So the key is to work smarter—not longer. Be more efficient in what you do at work, make lists of things you need to prioritise, people you need to see, what you need to remember. By all means take a break—that's important—but be organized if you have to pop out at lunchtime. Use your work time effectively and aim to get everything done you need to and then you can hopefully switch off when you get home. Or at the very worst not log on until your baby is tucked up in bed.

Managing parenthood and your status at work

Now we all think our baby is the most gorgeous one ever born and most of us are pretty quick to whip out a photo and regale our friends and colleagues with cute little stories about how they smiled or ate banana for the first time. Just remember not everyone is as enamoured with your new little bundle as you are.

In some offices you need to be mindful that the anecdotes that fill your heart with joy may bore the hell out of the bloke at the next desk. Try to keep the stories in check and the photos to a minimum unless you have an appreciative audience. Nor do some bosses want to hear about how tired you are and constant excuses as to why you can't get things done or deadlines can't be met.

While we can only hope most employers have a heart, it is worth remembering that they see your new baby as your responsibility. It's up to you to manage your family and job if that's what you have chosen to do, as hard as that can often be.

Working from home

It sounds like the ideal world. Work from home—either for your own business or for someone else—have your baby with you, breastfeed whenever you need to, *and* save on childcare costs.

There are a few things to consider before you commit to working like this. If your work is people focussed—if you spend a lot of time on the phone or with people who come over to meet you—then you need to think about how you will juggle the baby and work. Who will look after the baby when you are meeting with someone? Are your clients the sort of people who will be fine with a baby being around occasionally? Can you afford to have a nanny there for a few hours each week and arrange to do all your meetings at that time?

" Fiona Ogston, beauty therapist, mother of one

At six-and-a-half-months pregnant I decided to work from home because I worked on my feet and my clients were keen. After the birth of my baby I started seeing clients just five weeks later, but wished I had waited eight. I thought I'd be capable of seeing people two weeks later—how wrong I was. I have a carer here when I'm working. Sometimes it's tricky when the baby wakes up early and I'm with a client, but mostly it works. Now after having done it—and making it work—I'd hate to leave her in childcare. Work was important to me—not so much for the money but for my sense of identity, and human contact. I'm proud of my decision and I wouldn't change for a minute how I've managed my return to work.

If your work is creative or something you do by yourself such as writing—or requires very little contact with other people—then that may be an ideal environment to work from home while the baby is very little.

At least give it a go, trial different schedules, get someone in to give you a hand occasionally with the baby, and more likely than not it'll work really well. Good luck!

Travelling for work with a baby

This is easier said than done. As often is the way, travelling for work usually entails a plane or lengthy car trip, meetings and long days. Taking your baby away on a work trip is possible, it just needs a reasonable amount of planning.

Looking at other options might work best for you and your baby—even if you are still breastfeeding—like expressing throughout the day to keep up your supply and leaving a supply of frozen breast milk behind for your carer/partner if your baby takes a bottle.

Some women with small babies or children, such as politicians for example, who have to travel back and forth to Canberra when Parliament is sitting, often go back to work after only a few months' maternity leave, and arrive with a husband, mother or nanny in tow for the first few months. This isn't possible or necessary for us all, so there are a few things to think about before you venture away on a business trip with your baby.

Things to consider are:

- Who will be looking after your baby while you are at meetings, site visits or meals with clients on the trip away?

- Can I travel at times that will fit in around the baby's sleep times, such as early in the day rather than late at night?

- If you are driving you'll need to stop for feeds and nappy changes—you need to factor this time in.

> **Sometimes you've got to think** through whether it will ever work—particularly if your baby is very little. When my second child, Frida, was just two weeks old I flew to Melbourne to speak (this I could barely manage) to a local government conference—an invitation I'd accepted months before. In support, my husband and son accompanied me as I was breastfeeding six times a day. I was exhausted, my son went feral in front of two hundred conference delegates and we spent most of the time attempting to sterilize bottles in the small kettle in the hotel room! In hindsight I probably should've stayed at home! – **Jo**

When Talia was just six months old we took Sunrise to Hawaii for a week. As I was still feeding her and I didn't want this to be the reason to stop, the family came with me. The packing alone took almost as long as the trip—small babies and their three-year-old brothers don't travel light.

I boarded the plane tentatively—a tiny sleeping baby in my arms, and sat down in my seat next to a lovely lady. I smiled and was about to say hello when, in a loud American drawl, she announced to the whole plane 'Oh god, I hate babies. I am not travelling next to one. I hate them. Oh god who put me near a baby. Hostess? HOSTESS!'

After much hoo haa and shuffling she managed to swap seats with one of my work colleagues—but by then the damage was done. I was embarrassed, stressed and nervous. Talia was screaming. She then proceeded to scream during the entire takeoff. Suddenly I was one of those women I had always dreaded. No one wants to be near a crying baby on a plane, but its even worse when it's your own. I felt anguish, guilt and embarrassment.

Once we were in the air, she fell asleep in the cot and slept the entire six-hour flight.

But the week away wasn't easy. She was still sleeping twice a day and I was feeding between interviews. I know many people travel with their kids and do it effortlessly. But it wasn't for me. It was hard work and it was difficult combining work and family commitments. I was distracted, tired, my poor husband ended up doing most of the parenting—and I didn't really do either of my roles, mum or news presenter—to the best of my ability. – **Mel**

Eating out with your baby

We've all been there. You arrive at a local café for a tranquil Saturday morning breakfast, hoping to catch a quick sneak at the papers. You pop your child into the stroller or the restaurant's highchair and order a coffee and them some toast and bingo—it's on—big tantrum, food throwing, spitting. Do you stay or do you go?

In our view, educating your kids early on about the fun of eating out is good for you and them—budget permitting. Some families decide to eat out regularly, say once a month or so, and pop in to local coffee shops occasionally as well. And some find the whole thing very stressful and a waste of money. The decision is ultimately yours and you'll make it through trial and a whole lot of errors.

Eating out with baby top tips

- Get *recommendations* from women in your mothers' group or from friends on child-friendly restaurants and cafés. It makes all the difference if the staff is welcoming, provide your child with toys or crayons and paper the moment you arrive and have a child menu available. Your child will pick up on the vibe and have more fun too—we assure you. These sorts of places expect that you'll make a mess (to a certain degree), so don't worry about it!

- Check out the variety of *online resources and websites* in your area that recommend restaurants and tell you if they are child friendly, or not. Try an internet search first up.

- Make sure to *check that the restaurant has a highchair*. It will make all the difference to your enjoyment if you don't have your child crawling over the table or the floor—and it will contain the mess! You can book a highchair in advance at some places when you reserve a table. Or take a portable one.

- *If your child has any allergies call ahead* to ensure that they can cater for them—such as gluten or peanut allergies.

- *Book a table if you are arriving at a busy time.* Six p.m. sittings can be booked out for family sittings, so always call ahead.

- Some types of restaurants are generally more tolerant toward babies and young children than others, such as Italian or Chinese. They also cater for them better as well. Yum Cha at Chinese restaurants is a great thing for little children—lots of movement, small plates of different things to try, fun, fast and cheap.

Travelling with your baby

It's easy to put off travel when you have a little baby, but these days it's really become inevitable at least every once in a while— even if it's only the occasional long weekend on the coast. Some of us are more adventurous and pack the kids up overseas as soon as it's safe to do so. Whatever you do you need to plan way ahead, get organized and get the art of packing down to a fine art before you venture out the door.

Here are some simple suggestions and travel tips to make your travels easier, calmer and fun.

Passport

If you intend to travel overseas fairly often or at least once a year, it's a good idea to organize your new baby's passport soon after they are born. That way there won't be a mad rush a week or so before you depart when you remember that you don't have one.

Inoculations and medications

Planning ahead for these is really important. You will need to arrange to have all necessary inoculations well in advance of your departure date. And if your children take any medication ensure that you have enough for the whole time that you will be away. Make sure that you take all medications with you on the plane—and for peace of mind, carry a letter from your doctor verifying the need for the medication as some countries have restrictions on certain medications. Check with the relevant consulate or airline to find out more about any restrictions.

Travel insurance

Even if it's a week in Queensland or a nearby Pacific island you'll be really pleased that you spent the small amount on travel insurance if something does go wrong. Travel insurance will cover you for medical bills, if your baggage gets lost, flights are delayed or for theft. You can buy this from your travel agent or airline—some credit cards offer free travel insurance and very competitive prices are also available online. If you are going overseas it's a must, because of the high cost of emergency medical attention. Don't leave home without it.

Flying with babies

When you book your flight check to see that you will get a seat with a bassinet—there are only a few of these on each plane so be sure to insist that you will get one, and book it early.

Make sure you order the right food if your baby eats solids. Baby *or* child meals are available. Babies get baby food in jars and children get a child-size portion of more solid food. The best bet is to fully explore the options when you book with the travel agent or airline and don't accept a fob off. Airlines do not carry baby formula and can't guarantee that your preferred brand of food will be on board—if your baby prefers a certain brand then make sure you have it with you when you fly.

Resist bringing loads of toys with you, particularly on board, as they get lost under seats or down aisles. The stewards will give your child a child's bag (unless they are very tiny) and you can always improvise with what's available on board. Remember it's all new to your baby so they'll be fascinated by what's around them.

If flying with a little baby make sure to breastfeed or bottle feed them, or give them a dummy if you use one, on takeoff and arrival—it reduces the pressure on their eardrums.

Availability of baby products

Make sure you research what will be available at the other end when you arrive. If you have a fussy eater who will eat only a few types of bottled baby food, be sure to bring enough with you unless you can guarantee you can obtain it at your destination. On the other hand, if your baby eats anything it should be easy to get a range of food wherever you are.

Stock up on nappies and wipes. If you like a particular brand then bring what you need for the entire trip. This will leave stacks of room in your bag for any tourist shopping items you may buy.

First aid kit

Wherever you go this is a really important item to pack as well, as your baby could suddenly get a temperature or cut itself.

You should include the following items:

- A thermometer that works

- Pain relief such as Baby Panadol or Baby Nurofen, and an eyedropper to dispense it

- Band-Aids and sterilizing lotion or powder

- Mosquito repellant (some brands make a slightly less potent variety for young children) and anti-itch cream. Particularly if you are going somewhere tropical or hot.

- Make sure you bring any special medications that your baby may need—such as Ventolin and a spacer for asthma, or for any allergies—even if they haven't had an attack for some time. You may not be able to get them at your destination and it's better for peace of mind.

Accommodation

There are lots of ways to book—via a travel agent, a reputable website that provides assistance for families, via travel guides or online. Word of mouth and recommendation is always better, but remember a place that a friend thinks is 'fantastic and tranquil' may not be your perfect holiday destination or accommodation.

The Internet is a great tool to find accommodation, make bookings and even secure the services of a babysitter. Trouble is, how do you know you can trust the promises on a website or if the photos are accurate? Well, if you rely on the Internet it may be a bit of a gamble, but you also stand to get somewhere a lot cheaper and minus the overheads that a travel agent, tour operator or website adds on.

Things to consider when booking:

- Is the room near water or a pool and, if it is, is it safe to be so close with a little baby? Are there rooms further away?

- What bedding is provided? Check to make sure there will be a cot, sheets and blankets all ready on arrival. Do they have mosquito nets?

- What options are there for booking a babysitter and are they trained and reputable? Can you get a police check for peace of mind?

Travel top tips

- Once you get off that plane, it's highly unlikely you'll ever see any of those passengers again—so don't worry. When they leave the terminal they will get over it and hopefully you will too.
- When travelling, always cater for the smallest child.
- Turn up to the airport *very* early. They might give you a good spot.

Resources list

- *Travel with Children*, Cathy Lanigan and Maureen Wheeler, Lonely Planet
- Australian travel website www.byokids.com.au contains great practical travel hints as well as loads of websites and destinations that are child friendly.

Baby etiquette—handy hints

- Remember it's you that makes the rules on who gets to ogle and cuddle your baby. And as long as you handle the interest and grapples of your family, neighbours and strangers politely, you're completely within your rights.

- Your new family is really precious—and because of life's pressures time together can be a rarity. Socialize with friends and family when you want to, on your terms. You'll be happier and ultimately your family will understand and fit in around you.
- Once you've headed back to work balancing work with your baby can be tricky. Be honest with your employer about what you're hoping to do—whether that's a more flexible work schedule, breastfeeding in the office on occasion or popping out to see your baby at childcare if they are nearby.
- Be firm and polite to cynical work colleagues who don't fully understand your situation as a new mother. If they don't eventually come around then don't despair, there will be plenty of allies at your workplace who will understand.
- Plan a work trip thoroughly if you find you need to bring your baby along—food, bedding, and childcare needs.
- You can enjoy eating out with your baby—you just need to reduce your expectations and pre-plan.
- Travel with a baby is entirely possible—the secret is to be organized, research your destination and what you may need well in advance and think ahead about all the particular things you'll need for your baby, and bring them with you.

chapter 11
budgets and the future

In this chapter:

- How to financially prepare and plan for a family.

- Places to go for help.

- The cost of education.

- Preparing for the unexpected.

The set-up costs for a new baby can be pretty pricey by the time you buy a cot, pram, car seat, clothes and all the other things that are needed. The more you can plan for all this well before your baby is born the better. Once you have a newborn, a few extra hormones and no sleep, finances are the last things you want to be worried about.

Financial counselling services say that money problems are the most common cause of relationship breakdowns, so let's not make things any harder than they will already be.

Some of the things you will want to plan ahead for include medical bills, surviving without your income while you are on maternity leave, and the cost of childcare for when you return to work. Let's take them one at a time.

Medical bills

This cost will depend on whether you choose public or private health care and your level of health insurance. But you can at least plan ahead for this by doing all your research up front— what your doctor will charge, what tests you may be advised to have and what they will cost.

Medical costs are covered in more detail in Chapter 1, but we suggest you put together a quick list and at least tally up a ballpark figure of what you may be up for. It will take some of the sting out of the tail when the baby comes if you can plan ahead and have some money earmarked for these costs as they arrive. And factor in a little extra if you can to cover any unforeseen medical expenses for either yourself or your baby.

It's also worth asking your private health insurer, if you have one, what they cover in the way of neonatal intensive care. We hope you will never need it, but it's worth knowing what is covered should it be required.

Maternity leave

It's a good idea before you become pregnant to get used to living on the wages you will have available during maternity leave. You may be lucky enough to have maternity leave provisions which will ease a lot of the burden. You may have stored up enough annual leave to allow you to take some paid time off while maintaining your income.

Worst case scenario is you may have no paid maternity leave income or you may have quit your job, in which case you will need to adjust to living off your partner's income alone.

Whatever your situation, we suggest sitting down, together with your partner, and working out what money you will have and ways you can trim your non-essential expenditure while your income is reduced.

Childcare costs

For many families this can become one of the most expensive, if not the most expensive, parts of raising children. Once you have explored your options for childcare, as explained in more detail in Chapter 7, it's worth doing some sums. This is vital before you make the final decision to return to work—or whether to return full- or part-time. Many women have found it financially unviable to return to their full-time position when the cost of childcare will just outweigh or almost negate what they bring home each week.

Childcare expenses could have a lot to do with your decision about when to return, for how many days and how many hours. Find out the rates at the childcare centre you like, or the carer you are interested in, and do your sums now. Also start thinking about the sort of education you are planning for your baby, and if private schooling is on your radar, start planning today.

How to financially prepare for a family

Most people plan when to have a baby, so it only adds up that we should plan how we are going to afford one. The most important part of this equation is managing without your wage. The other part is covering all the associated costs of your baby.

Apart from what we call set-up costs, that is buying a cot, pram etcetera, the first twelve months are the cheapest. Your baby will cost about two and a half thousand dollars—but it only goes up from there.

Money planning

> ❝ **David Koch, financial guru and father of four**
>
> About a year before you plan to become pregnant start pretending you're already on one wage. Many couples may already do this—using the second wage as a saving or maybe an investment builder—but still many, many more don't. The lure of the good life is too strong. Yet this is the absolute best time to make the most of your financial couple power. I can't stress this point strongly enough. You must start planning for your financial future, and anything it may bring, as soon as possible. It doesn't need to be just a year before you intend to get pregnant, in fact the earlier you start the better. The important thing is to start.
>
> You'd need to start with a budget and like all budgets it means some deep soul searching. Be open and frank with each other. This is the time to discuss whether that weekly half carton of beer will still fit into the equation, not when baby has arrived and one party may be feeling pushed out or put upon. Prepare for what may happen. Talk to each other and crunch those numbers.
>
> If you're surprised at how tough it is at first to live on one wage that will give you an idea of just how much tougher it will be when there is a third little person to consider. If you keep practising this for that year and then maybe through the nine months of your pregnancy—then two things will happen. You'll be ready to tackle parenthood on a single wage and you'll have saved a nice little nest egg that can be your emergency or contingency fund or maybe the beginning of your future.

Depending on your current lifestyle and how much time you intend to have off work, this could be as painful as the labour itself. Think of forward planning as a little pain relief.

Budget

This brings us to that great monetary juggling act, the budget.

You need to sit down with paper and pen and discuss how much you spend on eating out or buying shoes, and do it now. Not when you are at home nursing a newborn feeling tired, bloated, emotional and in need of some retail therapy. Everything needs to go on the list from weekly treats, clothes, food, entertainment, holidays, wine and beer, medical costs and childcare.

There are stacks of books and websites out there to get you started, written by people with far more knowledge than we have in this area (we are good spenders though!). But Mel has picked up a few key tips after sitting next to Kochie each morning for so many years. He often talks about the Great Koch Family Summit. With a family of six to feed he says they needed some organizing, so in his best 'dad' voice, he gave the 'money doesn't grow on trees' lecture and finally got around to doing a family budget.

We'd never tell him, but he makes so much sense—so here is Guru Kochie's survival plan.

Getting to grips with your finances

1. *Turn the TV off*

Put aside a night and, with no distractions, start to look at where your money is going. Clear the dining table and grab all your credit card and bank statements, used cheque books and pay slips.

2. *List your income*

This is usually the quick and easy bit. On a blank piece of paper make a column for each month. List all your income, from wages to interest, dividends and government payments.

3. *List your expenses*

This can be scary! Just promise each other up front there will no recriminations for past spending splurges. List your essentials, such as rent or mortgage, utilities, car rego, fuel, food, and so on. Don't forget occasional payments like shoe repairs, haircuts and DVD rentals. But be ruthless. Spend a couple of weeks writing down everything you spend.

If you spend more than you earn, then you need to cut back.

4. *Cut down on luxuries*

This could be tricky as everyone's idea of a luxury is different. But you have to be tough as this is where you can really save some money.

5. *Cut up your credit cards*

Like most of us, you can probably do a little trimming here. Keep the card with the interest-free period, pay it off on time and cancel the rest.

6. *Pay off your debts*

Do your best to pay off that personal loan with the massive interest, and stop using your credit cards until any unpaid balances have been paid off.

7. *Review your insurances*

A bit of shopping around could wield some serious savings.

8. *Set a savings budget*

Don't rely on what's left at the end of the month. Put some of your income away before you spend it.

Government assistance

It's worth remembering that you are eligible for some federal government assistance.

Regardless of your income or assets, you are entitled to the 'baby bonus' (per baby, ie, triple it for triplets). Other payments are income tested, but you may be entitled to the Child Care Benefit and the Family Tax Benefit. There are also parenting payments and Carer Allowances depending on your circumstances and a Medicare Newborn Allowance which provides free or low cost subsidised medical care for low income earners.

For all the details contact your local Centrelink office or go to their website at www.centrelink.gov.au.

Getting the family finances in order

Okay, this might be a 'perfect world scenario', but if you have some time at home on maternity leave and you happen to have given birth to a good sleeper, now could be a good time to get the family finances in order.

There is always the good old fashioned manual filing system—but today there are so many other options. Your bank will probably have some sort of budget software you can use, or you can buy programs, by Microsoft, Apple and Quicken.

You might want to sort your documents. Income tax returns, group certificates and receipts for claims need to be kept for at least five years. Bank and credit card statements only need to be kept until the next one comes and online banking makes it even easier as all transactions are recorded automatically and summarized.

Take a good look at your credit cards. Ausralians owe about thirty-four billion dollars on credit cards and most people get into trouble because they don't understand how their cards work.

According to the Australian Securities and Investments Commission, if you simply paid the minimum monthly balance on a two-thousand-dollar credit card balance, it would take twenty-five years and nine months to pay off the debt and you would have paid 3,671 dollars in interest. But pay an extra one hundred dollars a month on top of the minimum monthly balance and the debt would be cleared in just over two years with interest of 355 dollars.

Take the time to look into your card and its conditions. You probably use it one of two ways—either to pay all the bills and you then settle your account at the end of the month, or you fund bigger purchases and pay the interest. Either way, make sure it's working for you and not just your bank.

The cost of education

This will be one of the biggest costs you will face in raising your children, regardless of whether you choose the private or public system. At the moment it seems a long way away—but the more you plan now, the easier it will be in the future.

Enrolment

Your baby probably hasn't even graduated to solid food yet, but if you harbour ambitions that one day they will graduate from a private school, book in now.

It almost seems beyond comprehension, but a lot of Australia's elite private schools take bookings when you are still pregnant. To secure a place in many of these in-demand schools, you will need to put your child's name down as soon as they are born and often, even then, you only make it onto a waiting list.

Where you want your child educated can depend on a lot of factors—from where you live, to where you went to school and your experiences in the education system.

If you want your child to have a private education do your research before they are born and choose the school or schools and get their name down quick smart. You will most probably have to pay a booking fee and once they are offered a position, a placement fee which in some cases can be up to a few thousand dollars. This is usually non-refundable.

The public education system is a lot easier, with enrolment only required the year before attending. This goes for both primary and high school education. Preschools are another matter though and in high demand—and it's certainly worth doing some very early research while you are on maternity leave if you are considering preschool. Some are attached to government primary schools, and many more are privately or council run, often with long waiting lists.

Selective schools

These operate in some states and are government run so shouldn't cost any more than a normal public education will cost. Positions in these schools are highly sought after and are offered in the last year of primary school on the basis of a selection test—and some parents elect to send their child to selective school coaching, which can cost many thousands of dollars. This is something to keep at the back of your mind.

Private and religious schools

Religious schools can be a mix of both. Some in-demand GPS schools in some capital cities need enrolment from birth.

Costs

Education certainly isn't free anymore and that cost is not only climbing, but also extending. Private school fees run into thousands each year and the Higher Education Contribution Scheme (HECS) now means young university graduates start their working life in debt unless they (or you) can pay up-front.

It all seems a world away now, but you can start planning and saving to relieve some of that stress down the track.

Education savings tips

- Start an automatic debit on pay day that transfers some of your salary in to an investment account.
- Drop your change at the end of the day into a (well hidden) jar.
- Open a bank account in your child's name or in trust for them. Children under eighteen are exempt from fees.
- Talk to your adviser or bank manager about putting that money into bank shares or managed funds.
- Investigate some of the education and scholarship programs such as the Australian Scholarship Group.

Preschool

Preschool will come around a lot quicker than school and it's also worth looking into now. Fees can vary between private and council, but primarily it's enrolments you need to think about at this stage. Once you have found one you like, find out their enrolment policy. Some require you to book in immediately, others will only take your child's name when they turn two or three.

Make a note of when to book and put your child's name down now if you can. You can always knock back the offer down the track if you move or change your mind.

Returning to work costs

If you are heading back to the office, don't forget to factor into your budget some money for a bit of a wardrobe overhaul. You may still be carrying some baby weight, or you may find you haven't updated your wardrobe for over a year, as last season you were pregnant.

If you intend to do some work from home you may need to factor in some set-up costs, such as computing or filing equipment. If you are starting your own business from home there will obviously be costs involved here as well.

Prepare for unexpected contingencies

Always expect the unexpected with parenthood from the moment your little bundle of joy is born. From when they vomit on Aunty Mavis to when they first roll over and no one is looking. You can't do much about controlling those events, but you can put a few plans in place to prepare for factors that may change in your life.

There are three ways to protect your family's income should something happen to one of you: *income protection insurance* which looks after your salary if you can't work. This protects up to seventy-five per cent of your gross salary for whatever reason you are unable to continue working due to sickness, disablement or accident; *life insurance* where the money provides an income for your partner to ensure their lifestyle; and *trauma insurance*, which is paid as a lump sum.

Now that you have a new family member and you and your partner are facing a few extra financial responsibilities, it may be worth looking into insurance. A chat to a financial adviser will steer you in the right direction.

How to find a financial adviser

Treat this project the way you did when looking for a doctor or midwife. Ask friends or colleagues for any recommendations. Ring the Financial Planning Association or ask your accountant, solicitor or bank manager. Have a look at websites, such as www. selectadviser.com.au and don't forget the good old telephone directory.

You'll want to interview a couple of potential advisers before you decide. Ask them about their background, what types of clients they have, and what ongoing services they provide. What commissions do they receive, who owns their company and pays their bills? Make sure you find out as much information as possible and ensure that everything is fully disclosed.

They must also be licensed and be a member of the Financial Planning Association.

At the end of the day, you and your family are the most important thing. Sure, we need money to pay the bill and keep the roof over our head, but don't lose sight of what really is priceless. Work hard, spend wisely—but your most important investment is you and your partner.

Resources list

Books:

- *Kochie's Guide: How Smart Couples can Start with Nothing and Create Real Wealth,* David and Libby Koch
- *Kochie's Guide to Keeping it Real,* David Koch
- *Smart Investing,* Noel Whittaker
- *Debt Free, Cashed Up and Laughing,* Cath Armstrong and Lea-Anne Brighton

Websites:

- www.selectadviser.com.au
- www.centrelink.gov.au
- www.cheapskates.com.au for simple ways to save money
- www.simplesavings.com.au to help you budget by buying cheap alternatives

✳ Financial planning—handy hints

- Plan as much as possible. The more you know what else the stork has in its bill, the better.
- Do a family budget. Now is as good a time as any to consolidate the family finances, particularly if you will be living on one wage for some time.
- Don't forget your baby bonus, and to check with Centrelink if you are entitled to any other payments.
- Start giving some thought to education. If you want a private school, book in now and start saving.
- Tally up what sort of return to work costs you may be up for, such as some new clothes or tools of trade.

where to from here?

There is no doubt having a baby will change your life—but it will be overwhelmingly for the better.

Sure, you will be tired, you will have times when you struggle to manage it all and days when you can't get out of the house. Parts of your life will be forced to take a back seat for a while and some days you will wonder if you'll ever get your old self back. You will question yourself endlessly: Did I really pick the best time to have a baby? Will I ever get out the door again in under an hour and not smelling of milk? Have I ruined my chances of promotion? Will I ever wear delicate lingerie again?

Yes, Yes, No and Yes!

You won't ever get your old life back but what you have now is so much more wonderful and fulfilling.

You *will* be able to manage your new life and work. Just take it slowly, one day at a time, don't expect too much of yourself and you'll do it.

Remember, in the eyes of your gorgeous baby, you are now *the most important person* in the whole world! A mother's love can move mountains, its strength will both overwhelm and humble you. Just when you think they can't get any sweeter, your little baby will smile. Just wait for the moment they throw those tiny arms around your neck and tell you they love you.

Your relationship with your partner will change, but hopefully for the better. You and your partner are now a formidable team, with the responsibility of caring for another life—your child's. Take strength from your new family unit—you are now the mother lion.

You'll probably look at your own parents a little differently—appreciate in a whole new way what your mum did for you. Your girlfriends are now your very own support crew. Where you used to cry over broken hearts together, you will now agonise over broken sleep. Other mums will understand better than anyone what you're going through and just how tough it really can be. So look out for each other. We're now in a pretty special club that requires honesty and no judgement. So on those days when it turns a little messy, when you're exhausted, wrung out and struggling, remember it will get easier.

One day your baby will be out of nappies, off the breast and able to eat in a restaurant with you. One day they will be able to walk on their own, then run, then drive, then move out of home. Its true—time really does fly.

It's those special moments you will most remember. The sunny afternoons spent at the park, the mornings cuddling in bed, their first ice-cream cone, the stories before bedtime.

So don't think about the chores that await, or the mess, or all the other things you should be doing. Enjoy those most precious moments with your new baby.

resources and references

Chapter 1   Preconception

Books and magazines:
Fertility and Conception by Zita West.
Fit Pregnancy (US).
Natural Pregnancy by Zita West.
Pregnancy & Birth, Practical Parenting or Mother & Baby
Up The Duff by Kaz Cooke.

Websites:
A Little Pregnant: www.www.alittlepregnant.com.
Australia's national infertility network: www.access.org.au.
The Family Planning Association or FPA Health (formerly Family Planning NSW) www.fpahealth.org.au or phone 1300 658 886.
For information on foods to avoid: www.foodstandards.gov.au/ foodmatters/pregnancyandfood.cfm   or   www.rhw.org.au

(the Royal Hospital for Women).

Information on genetic risk factors: www.genetics.com.au/.

Information on the safety of medications: www.motherisk.org/index.jsp.

Life in the Stirrups: http://layout-lady.livejournal.com/.

The Royal Australian and New Zealand College of Obstetricians and Gynaecologists: www.ranzcog.edu.au.

The Waiting Womb: www.waitingwomb.blogspot.com.

The Queensland Government's free preconception and pregnancy support advice line: 1800 777 690.

Each state government or state health centres provides an Internet portal as a gateway to a range of services and information about having a baby. Do an Internet search to find yours.

Ovulation calendar: there are lots of these on the Internet.

Chapter 2   So, you're pregnant

Look at your state's website such as in NSW Department of Health: www.mhcs.health.nsw.gov.au or in Victoria: www.health.vic.govau.

Australian College of Midwives in Canberra: www.acmi.org.au

Australian Council of Trade Unions: www.actu.asn.au

Birth Central: www.birthcentral.com.au.

Home Birth Australia: www.homebirthaustralia.org

My Child magazine: www.mychildmagazine.com.au.

Relationships Australia: www.relationships.com.au.

Chapter 3   Pregnancy and preparing for your baby

Books and magazines:
The CHOICE Guide to Baby Products produced by CHOICE magazine
    and available through their website: www.choice.com.au.
The Nappy Bag Book.
Sydney's Child magazine, also available in city-specific versions in
    Adelaide, Brisbane, Canberra, Melbourne and Perth.

Websites:
www.babygap.com
www.baybeecino.com.au
www.butterflykiss.com.au
The Global Shopper: www.theglobalshopper.com.au.
www.kidscentral.com.au
www.lillylolly.com.au
www.pumpkinpatch.com.au
Australian Breastfeeding Association: www.breastfeeding.asn.au
Sudden Infant Death Association: www.sidsandkids.org
Safety: www.babysafety.com.au or www.kidsafe.com.au.

Chapter 4   Maternity leave

Books:
Baby Love by Robin Barker, Pan Macmillan.
How to Stay Sane in your Baby's First Year by Tresillian.

Website:
Mothers' and parents' groups: www.mothersgroup.com.au/

Chapter 5   How to cope

www.findababysitter.com.au

www.kidspot.com.au

Parents Without Partners: www.pwp.org.au.

Relationships Australia: www.relationships.com.au.

Single parents: www.singleparentbible.com.au and
    www.singlewithchildren.com.au

Chapter 6   Health—you and your baby

Books:

The Baby Book by Karitane.

Baby Love by Robyn Barker.

Sheyne Rowley's Dream Baby Guide by Sheyne Rowley (to be
    published in 2008).

Touchpoints by American paediatrician T. Berry Brazelton.

Websites:

www.australianbabywhisperer.com.au run by Sheyne Rowley

www.beyondblue.org.au

www.breastfeeding.asn.au

www.charlotteswebdirectory.com.au

www.cs.nsw.gov.au/Tresillian

www.karitane.com.au

For further information or pre- and post-pregnancy exercise
    classes: www.lizmillardphysio.com.au.

www.mumknowsbest.mumspace.net

Chapter 7   Childcare

www.CareforKids.com.au
www.findababysitter.com.au
www.kidspot.com.au
Police checks: www.aifs.gov.au
Tax advice: www.ato.gov.au

Chapter 8   Returning to work

www.motherinc.com.au
www.mumsinbusiness.net offers seminars and training for mums
    so they too can have their own business.
www.workingmother.com

Chapter 9   The law and working mothers

Human Rights and Equal Opportunity Commission (HREOC)
    Phone: (02) 9284 9600
    Complaint info-line: 1300 656 419
    General enquiries and publications: 1300 369 711
    Website: www.hreoc.gov.au

ACT Human Rights Office
    Phone: (02) 6205 2222
    Website: www.hro.act.gov.au

Anti-Discrimination Board New South Wales
    Phone: (02) 9268 5544 (general enquiry service)
    Toll free: 1800 670 812 (for rural and regional NSW only)
    Website: www.lawlink.nsw.gov.au/adb

Anti-Discrimination Commission Queensland
    Phone: 1300 130 670
    Website: www.adcq.qld.gov.au

Office of the Anti-Discrimination Commissioner—Tasmania
    Toll free: 1300 305 062 (statewide)
    Website: www.antidiscrimination.tas.gov.au

Victorian Equal Opportunity & Human Rights Commission
    Phone: (03) 9281 7100
    Website: www.humanrightscommission.vic.gov.au

Northern Territory of Australia Anti-Discrimination Commission
    Toll free: 1800 813 846
    Website: www.nt.gov.au/justice/adc/index800.html

Equal Opportunity Commission of South Australia
    Toll free: 1800 188 163 (statewide)
    Website: www.eoc.sa.gov.au

Equal Opportunity Commission of Western Australia
    Toll free: 1800 198 149 (statewide)
    Website: www.equalopportunity.wa.gov.au

Office of Workplace Services
    Phone: (02) 8293 4683 or 1300 724 200
    WorkChoices Infoline: 1300 363 264
    www.ows.gov.au

Community Legal Centres—see your phone book for listings

ACTU

>   Toll free: 1300 362 223
>   Workers' Hotline: 1300 362 223 (for help with a workplace
>   issue)
>   www.actu.asn.au

Australian Industrial Relations Commission

>   Phone: (02) 8374 6666
>   Website: www.airc.gov.au

Chapter 10   Baby etiquette

Book:

Travel with Children, Cathy Lanigan and Maureen Wheeler, Lonely
>   Planet.

Website:

www.byokids.com.au

Chapter 11   Budgets and the future

Books:

Debt Free, Cashed Up and Laughing, Cath Armstrong and Leanne
>   Brighton.
*Kochie's Guide: How Smart Couples can Start with Nothing and Create
>   Real Wealth*, David and Libby Koch.
Kochie's Guide to Keeping it Real, David Koch.
Smart Investing, Noel Whittaker.

Websites:

www.centrelink.gov.au

www.cheapskates.com.au

www.selectadviser.com.au

www.simplesavings.com.au

acknowledgements

As working mothers we largely constructed and organized this book in the way a lot of women communicate to each other these days—via email or text message—quick and efficient. Our communication was meaningful—and at times just a few lines of text, punctuated with a lot of 'xxx's or 'hello lovely's. Melissa would email Jo on her arrival at work, hours before the dawn broke. Jo would email Melissa her latest thoughts close to midnight— just a few hours before Melissa was to rise for work.

Our husbands stepped in and took over for much of the year we were writing this book. They bought the groceries, entertained, cajoled, bathed and soothed our children as we meet on weekends or after hours to talk, write, work on words and ideas—drink coffee and gossip—with the occasional moment of shopping to ensure balance.

First our gratitude to our editors Jo Paul and Catherine Milne who believed in the project and had the foresight to see that thousands of Australian working mums needed some practical help to manage work and motherhood. Jo and Catherine pacified us as they helped us develop our ideas and managed our trepidation and concerns with perfect calmness. And our deepest thanks to Belinda, Kelly, Lauren and Karen and all the great people at Allen & Unwin who have helped us along the way.

We're not experts on anything other than stemming the madness and juggling the craziness of being a working mother. Thousands of other women do just that each and every day— dozens of them shared their stories with us and we thank them all (with one or two dads thrown in) for their honesty and for their wonderful survival tips: Feyi Akindoyeni, Emma Angel, Natalie Barr, Suzie Cameron, Kalinda Cobby, Kath Cummins, Kate Deverall, Catriona Dixon, Melissa Donnelly, Kaylene Ferguson, Regina Fikkers, Jacki Frank, Justine Kelman, Donna Kennedy, Susan Larson, Anne Laurie, Kate McCabe, Clare McHugh, Lois Oakey, Fiona Ogston, Sharine Ruppert, Donna Saltram, Voula Serbos, Jacki Stevens, Abbi Stove, Robyn Thornton, Monique Tompson, Angus Trigg, Sue Vercoe, Carmel Wall, Mandi Wicks and Nareen Young.

For expertise we needed the help of people who know stuff—and our gratitude goes to all of them who spent hours and sometimes days of their precious time providing expert advice on health, medical, legal and financial content, reviewing drafts, giving expert feedback and guidance: Renee Adair, Birth Central; Professor Michael J. Bennett, Royal Hospital for Women; Andrea Billcliff, midwife; Sharan Burrow, ACTU; Leslie Cannold; Shea Caplice, Kogarah Home Birth Program; Peter English, Surry Partners; Kerrie Goodwin, Clinical Nurse Specialist; Cerentha Harris; Anne Hollonds, NSW CEO, Relationships Australia; Rebecca Huntley; Angie Kelso, Nannies and Helpers; Dr Debra Kennedy, Royal Hospital for Women; David Koch, finance guru; Jo Lamble, psychologist; Claudia Keech, motherinc.com.au; Dr Devora Lieberman, Sydney IVF; Dr Ronald McCoy, Royal

Australian College of General Practioners; Pat McDermott, Royal North Shore Hospital; Liz Millard, physiotherapist; Susan Price and Christine Mena, Bartier Perry; Geoff Morgan, Director, Morgan Investments Pty Ltd and Talent2 Recruitment; Sheyne Rowley, The Australian Baby Whisperer; Nicole Sheffield, Pacific Magazines; Dr David Smith, Obstetrician and Gynaecologist; Mercedes Soldo, Thomas Carlyle Children's Centre; Delia Timms, findababysitter. com.au; Dr Christine Tippet, President, Royal Australian & New Zealand College of Obstetricians and Gynaecologists; Dr Barbara Vernon, Australian College of Midwives; Tim Wain, The Infant and Nursery Products Association; and Cathy Wilcox.

And our thanks to a team of people that helped with all the pre-production work for our book cover including Anthony Denman, Brett Allatt and Holly Blake from Challis Studios in Sydney and hair and makeup artists Liz Tagla, Sonya Downie and Fi Havilland who primped and preened us for our photo shoots.

And to our wonderful families for their support: our patient husbands Andrew and John for their love, understanding, extra child-minding duties and helping us find balance and, of course, our beautiful happy children, Nicholas, Marlow, Talia and Frida for inspiring us to write this book and giving us a reason to try and do it all.